JOSEPH HISLOP: GRAN TENORE

For Emma

Joseph Hislop: Gran Tenore

MICHAEL T. R. B. TURNBULL

Scolar Press

Published by
SCOLAR PRESS
Gower House
Croft Road
Aldershot
Hants GU11 3HR
England

Ashgate Publishing Company
Old Post Road
Brookfield
Vermont 05036
USA

British Library Cataloguing in Publication Data is available

ISBN 0 85967 893 8

Printed in Great Britain at the University Press, Cambridge

Contents

Foreword by John Steane   vii

Acknowledgements   xi

  I THE RISING STAR (1884–1920)
    1 Starting to Sing (1884–1911)   3
    2 With the Swedish Royal Opera (1913–1919)   17
    3 Italian and British Debuts (1919–1920)   38

  II GRAN TENORE (1920–1934)
    4 Opera (1920–1921): London, Chicago, New York   49
    5 Opera (1922–1925): Winning Golden Opinions   61
    6 Opera (1925–1937): 'You Sang like a God Yesterday'   80
    7 Opera Tours (1921–1933)   99
    8 Individual Recitals (1921–1941)   111
    9 Concert Tours (1920–1923)   127
    10 Recital Tours (1924–1930)   136
    11 Recital Tours (1931–1934)   148

  III NEW DIRECTIONS (1929–1977)
    12 Film and Light Opera (1929–1934)   165
    13 Teaching in Sweden (1934–1947)   180
    14 Teaching in the UK and Retirement (1947–1977)   190

Appendix 1   Stage Roles (1914–1937)   208
Appendix 2   Opera House Debuts   210
Appendix 3   Concert Repertoire   211
Appendix 4   Discography   220

Select Bibliography   234

Sources   236

Index   242

Foreword

To the biographer fall many privileges, for a whole life opens before him, or as nearly open as it will probably ever be to human eyes. He also has his share of restraints and restrictions, most of them self-imposed.

Self is, indeed, to be largely extinguished. The biographer searches for facts and objectivity out of which he hopes will come understanding. Paradoxically, to take full possession of his subject he often has to keep it at arm's length. To see the person, he will have to abandon his own little observation-post. The preoccupations and prejudices which sparked his interest in the first place will also have to be stamped out before they create a smoke-screen between him and the truth.

Happily the writer of a foreword is under no such obligations. I can tell you straight what Joseph Hislop means to me and why, if I saw a book about him on the shelves, I would have to have it.

It *is* personal after all. Hislop was the first 'real' singer whose recorded voice I ever knew, and that was at a very tender age. Most of the records in the little pile to which I was allowed access were of military bands, comedians and massed choirs. There were three records of 'real' singers. One had a bright red label and the name of Amelita Galli-Curci upon it. It was said to be precious and that alone was forbidden me. Another had a purple label and was of Dame Clara Butt, which I was allowed to play but didn't want to. And then there were two songs from Lehár's *Frederica* sung by Joseph Hislop, tenor.

These gave me my first experience of the thrill of the singing voice. When 'O maiden, my maiden' came to an end, with that passionate expenditure of high notes, there was nothing to do but wind up the gramophone, put in a new needle and hear it all over again. On the other side, 'A heart as pure as gold' exercised a more subdued attraction. But there was one phrase in it, the words trite enough, 'O listen to that song', yet as a child of (what would it be?) six or seven, I knew the appeal of the singer's voice in those six notes as well and as personally as I knew any of the living voices, or indeed the faces, around me.

That was the Joseph Hislop I came to renew acquaintance with some years later, at about twice that original age, in a number of Scottish songs: 'Turn ye to me', 'Of a' the airts the wind can blaw', 'An Eriskay Love-Lilt' and 'Herding Song'. Now these – it cannot be simply the accident of a childhood memory revived – seemed to me then, and still do, to be the singing of a very special artist.

He could, to be sure, make the tone ring on high and produce the thrill peculiar to a powerful operatic tenor voice. But he could also make it tell of a personal affection, with a gentleness and warmth that evoked the 'sighs and vows among the knowes' and the 'shadows gathering around the ben', so that the songs lived a vivid, intimate life of their own which passed from the imagination of the singer into that of the listener and bore witness to the great gift of a true artist – the gift of communication.

That, in a sense, is the *soul* of the artist which in turn makes you wonder what manner of man he was. Truth to tell, I don't believe biographies are ever likely to answer such a question where an artist is concerned. The soul is there in the singing. With Joseph Hislop we shall never come closer to it than when we hear him call, 'Come, come hither, darkness is falling' or perhaps sing some phrase of Faust's or Rodolfo's.

Part of the fascination of biography, and sometimes a rather painful fascination, is that it shows a man with no more outward sign of 'soul' about him than anybody else. He writes prosaic, dully informative letters; he cracks his not very good jokes, fixes his mind on his fee, boards a liner, plays a round of golf. The soul of the artist who so hauntingly colours a softened phrase seems nowhere to be found.

Would one even have *liked* him very much, if for instance one had been present at the meeting from which he withdrew saying 'There aren't any' (when English songs were under discussion), or if one were the talented pianist of whom he said (in the man's hearing) 'You've got to get rid of him'? Yet artists in their time have said (and done) much worse things than that, and it is one of the hard features of any honest biography that the life and the art have such different identities.

In this book Michael Turnbull has exercised (it seems to me) remarkable restraint in abstaining from personal judgement or intrusion of any kind. Without so much as a nudge or a wink he gives the reader freedom of the material and, when the facts leave off, the freedom of speculation.

The facts of Hislop's career are eloquent enough. It was a remarkable gift and a remarkable personality, too, that transformed the Edinburgh housepainter's son into the leading tenor of the Stockholm Opera, especially at a time when foreigners were discouraged if not prohibited. It was also something of an achievement to be engaged by Covent Garden to sing with Melba, Selma Kurz, Dinh Gilly and the great Chaliapin. These, mind, were the international seasons from which native talent was so often and so pointedly excluded.Nor were there many British artists of that time who sang abroad at all, or with any regularity, and certainly not with singers as celebrated as Galli-Curci and Ruffo in Chicago, Claudia Muzio in Buenos Aires or Toti dal Monte at La Scala.

His concert tours, followed so closely in this book, extended him further, while his teaching made a vigorous *coda* to a long life, keeping him active and in touch with the world of music right up to the end, at the age of 93.

There was, to be sure, one other internationally famous opera singer who came from Scotland. Mary Garden, having been one of the most talked-about women in Paris, became for some 20 or 30 years famous in the United States. Like Hislop she returned to Scotland in her later years and at her funeral there were (I believe) four people present. It took a lot of persuading before, several years later, a commemorative plaque was placed on the wall of her home.

This, the posthumous story of Mary Garden, was mentioned at a public ceremony in the Usher Hall at Edinburgh on 15 April 1989. The occasion was the presentation and unveiling of a bust of Hislop, given a permanent place in the Hall in recognition of being a distinguished son of the City.

Gaining that recognition had also required some persistence; it needed someone with initiative and conviction to set such a plan in action. It was on this occasion that I met Michael T. Turnbull, without whom it seems highly unlikely that any such event would ever have taken place. A busy man, a lecturer with several other publications to his credit, he has devoted a substantial portion of his middle years to the service of Joseph Hislop's memory.

His book chronicles the life of an eminent fellow-countryman about whom none other has been written. In these pages we read about the man; the *soul* of the man is in his recordings. The happiest outcome would be that this book, which brings the achievements of the man before our eyes, should encourage readers to find the soul of the artist through the evidence of their ears.

John Steane

Acknowledgements

I should like to acknowledge the support and assistance of Joseph Hislop and Agnete Sylvan and George and Isabelle Donald. Also Brian Hunt who helped shape the book.

I am most grateful for financial support from William Grant and Sons in the form of a Glenfiddich Living Scotland Award (without which the book could not have been written) and to the Belmont Trust.

I am indebted to the following for supplying photographs: The Swedish National Archive of Recorded Sound and Moving Images (ALB), George Donald, Joseph Hislop jnr, Catherine McCall, Charles Mackay, John Veale.

I gratefully acknowledge permission to quote from the following: Managing Editor, *The Gramophone*; Victor Gollancz, *Great Singers on Great Singing* by Jerome Hines; *It Don't Seem a Day Too Much* by Claude Kingston (Weldon Publishing); The British Library, *Recorded Sound*, No 38; Sveriges Radio Forlag, 'Från vintergatan mot aftonstjärnan' by Sven-Olof Sandberg; Ian Wallace – *Promise me you'll sing* MUD, John Calder; Bertil Hagman – *Jussi Björling: En Minnesbok* (Bonniers).

I should also like to thank the many correspondents whose contributions have not been acknowledged by name but whose encouragement and enthusiasm were a source of inspiration.

Every effort has been made to trace all copyright holders of photographs reproduced in this book. The publishers will be pleased to hear from any whom they have been unable to locate and undertake to insert any missing acknowledgements in future editions.

Part I
THE RISING STAR
(1884–1920)

1 Starting to sing (1884-1911)

Joseph Dewar Hislop (known to family and friends as 'Joss') was born on 5 April 1884 in a tenement under the green volcanic crags of Holyrood Park, the second son of a housepainter and a housemaid. By the time he was five the family had moved to the west of Edinburgh near Haymarket Station and the Caledonian Distillery. Here the family came under the influence of the Scottish Episcopal Church with its magnificent new Cathedral in Palmerston Place.

The two boys were sent to the Episcopal School only yards away from home and soon found themselves caught up in the ornate liturgies of St Mary's Cathedral, presided over by Bishop John Dowden who had strong views on education. Heaven was for good little boys who were content with the state of life to which they were called. Hell was for bold boys, discontented boys, boys who were disrespectful to the upper classes of society.

Again the family moved, this time only a mile, close to the glistening Water of Leith, to the hooting and puffing of Roseburn Station and the steady rumbling of Arbuckle's flourmill. The two boys were enrolled in Coltbridge Public School where the Inspectors' Report of 1889 commented that their singing was very good, with excellent attainments in the note-tests.

Joseph Hislop later recalled that his voice seems to have aroused some interest at the early age of five or thereabouts but, because of shyness, he could only be induced to sing if a draught screen were placed between him and his audience – the family. There, unseen and unseeing he would warble quite happily to the apparent delight of his parents.[1]

In spite of its advantages, Coltbridge School suffered from overcrowding. Perhaps this explains why on 1 December 1892 a Special Report of the School Board complained about the continued absence from school of the children of Mrs Mary Hislop. The school was closed two years later and the Hislops once again moved back to Parkside Street on the east of the city beside St Leonard's Station and the Coal Depot. After only a few weeks at a recently-opened local school, where he often had to defend his older brother with his fists,[2] Joseph auditioned for the Choir school of St Mary's Episcopal Cathedral. Shortly after, he was enrolled as a probationer.

All members of the regular Choir were full-time day pupils at the Choir school whose aim was to provide a liberal education in the ordinary branches of learning. At school each chorister sported a Glengarry hat with a silver badge. As well as being given free books and education, each boy was paid for singing at services. Joseph received the enormous salary of £2 for the first year, rising by £2 per annum thereafter. He had become a professional singer!

Thomas Collinson, the tetchy choirmaster with a walrus moustache, was a Northumberland man. He was an organist, hornplayer and violinist blessed with perfect pitch. He was also a strict disciplinarian. The choir, in black cassocks and white surplices, was divided into two, half on the north of the chancel (the Cantoris), half on the south (the Decani). The latter was Joseph's place, sitting in the carved dark walnut stalls on a floor of Sicilian marble with wrought iron screens picked out in gold behind.

At morning service the sun poured colour through the stained glass; at evening service beeswax candles flickered over the brass music stands.

One can imagine the impression St Mary's Cathedral might make on a tiny chorister. It was over 260 feet in length, with a spire almost 300 feet high and fitted with an organ boasting four manuals, 59 stops and 2 500 pipes. Joseph later confessed that he used to love to go to the churches in the city and listen to the music. The sound of it stirred great chords in his heart and brain. He never cared for what were called popular songs, as they rarely interested him. It was the great appealing music of fine old church organs that he loved.[3]

The repertoire of the Cathedral Choir included Handel's *Messiah*, Bach's *St Matthew Passion* and Mozart's *Requiem*. Outside church duties, choristers were encouraged by their steely-eyed schoolmaster, John Keith, to take an interest in football, athletics, cricket and boxing. At one annual choir outing Joseph won a high jump competition. Although slightly-built, every inch was strength, with biceps and shoulders like a boxer. In his young days he was a cricketer, once scoring a top score of five! He was also a footballer, and, had he only persevered might have qualified as a successful fifth-class junior. From the days he swam in the Infirmary Street Baths in Edinburgh as a youth, he was always able to lift his own weight above his head.[4]

Early in 1899 Joseph left the Cathedral school and the choir. His voice had broken. He was nearly 15 and it was time for him to make his own way in life. Internationally, the 'Jameson Raid' had sparked off the Boer War and in due course recruiting began in Edinburgh. In a surge of patriotism and as a healthy and active young man, Joseph presented himself to the medical examiners at the recruiting-office in the Lawnmarket. However, he was not able to satisfy their stringent requirements.

In looking for a civilian job Joseph had to take into account his education and training. From an early age he had a talent for drawing and painting. The fact that his father was a housepainter disposed his children to enjoy colour, design and the excitement of splashing and experimenting with paint. Perhaps it was his uncle Stephen, a travelling salesman in the stationery trade, who steered him into an apprenticeship at Messrs Hislop & Day, Stamp Cutters and Photo Engravers in Edinburgh's New Town.[5]

The camera was to be the tool of Joseph's trade, a large heavy wooden box fitted with bellows for focusing. Light for exposure came from an open arc flame, its ultraviolet radiation and tendency to produce smoke harmful to eyesight and lungs. Into the camera Joseph fitted glass plates which he had coated with photo-emulsion mixed from white of egg, liquid gun-cotton (collodion) and silver nitrate. Almost ten other chemicals would have to be used to process the glass plate into a negative. Some of these were highly poisonous (potassium cyanide, for example). Others, like the foul-smelling sodium sulphide, were unpleasant to work with, to say the least.

Once the image was exposed onto the metal plates Joseph made it acid-resistant and then etched it in baths of nitric acid and ferric chloride, both hazardous to clothes, skin and lungs. Then the artistic work followed, for he would have to paint the tones onto the plate with a fine brush, etching and re-etching, scrutinizing his handiwork with an eye-glass.

It was the reproduction of works of art that interested Joseph most. He spent many hours examining, copying and photographing the paintings of old masters in Edinburgh's galleries. He was sent to classes at the elegant Greek temple of the Royal Institution at the foot of the Mound. An eager student, his secret ambition in life was to be a professional portrait-painter.[6]

He still had a love of music but, at the turn of the century, singing of international quality was seldom heard in Edinburgh, while sound recording was still in its infancy. Living there, a young man could have little idea of how beautiful a well-trained and cultivated voice could be. Moreover, being rather shy, he was a little afraid of his mature voice. Except at 'Free and Easies' among his friends, he only sang when everybody had left the house and he was alone with his tuning fork.[7]

In 1905 Joseph Hislop completed his apprenticeship and moved to another firm to broaden his experience. He joined the Dux Engraving Company in Glasgow where he worked for a year, saving and studying. He rose at one o'clock in the morning and trudged six miles to his work in the centre of town.[8] Having a sister firm in London at Brixton Hill, the Dux Engraving Company sent Joseph south early in 1907. There he went to classes in three-colour reproduction at the famous Bolt Court School in Fleet Street.

Joseph as a young man, c. 1907

London in April 1907 was a world rich in music and art. Joseph believed that here he would have a better chance of becoming a portrait-painter and took a course of art lessons. He haunted the picture galleries and lost himself in wonder at the masterpieces he saw. If only he could paint like that!

There were summer art exhibitions and a thrilling season of Wagner at the Royal Opera House, Covent Garden. In the London Ballad Concerts at the Queen's Hall, he could have heard Clara Butt or the young John McCormack. In May there were exhibitions of French and Spanish painting. At the Royal Opera House the unparalleled team of Melba, Caruso and Scotti (all three destined to cross Joseph's path in the years to come) sang a series of Verdi and Puccini operas. While he may have visited the exhibitions, Joseph could not afford seats at the Opera. It would be seven long years before he heard Caruso for the first time in a live performance.

The principal at Bolt Court was A J Newton who had previously held several advisory positions in Scandinavia. One of his contacts was with Waldemar Zachrisson, the dynamic owner of one of the most modern printing firms in Sweden. Zachrisson had travelled widely in search of new technical methods. His firm was in a fine six-storey building in the commercial area of Gothenburg close to the docks where he employed a staff of over 100. The Swede asked Newton if he knew of a young man who would like to come over to Gothenburg. He would pay him £2 per week. If he was capable, he would take him on for a year to begin with.

At this point fate appeared to beckon in a different direction. Joseph's elder brother Willie, a baker and confectioner, wrote out of the blue saying that Joseph was wasting his time in photoprocess engraving. He urged him to give it all up and devote himself to singing. Willie even offered to pay for a course of singing lessons.

Before accepting this unexpected and generous offer Joseph felt that in all honesty he should have the opinion and advice of a musician of standing. He therefore applied to his former choirmaster, Mr Collinson, organist of the Cathedral and of the University and conductor of the Royal Choral Union.[9] Joseph went up to Edinburgh and sang a Scots song to him. After a moment's thought Mr Collinson said 'My dear boy, you sing with fine expression but I am afraid your voice will never take you into the professional ranks'.[10] This was a tremendous blow to Joseph's hopes and ambition, but he accepted Mr Collinson's judgement and regretfully declined his brother's offer.

Looking back, he tried to find a reason for Mr Collinson's quick decision. Although untrained and uncultivated, his voice must even then have shown some fundamental *quality* or timbre that deserved a wiser judgement. In fact, Mr Collinson's opinion was probably based on one single criterion – vibrato or tremolo. He preferred voices that were hooty and lacking in vitality, probably because a vibrating voice would suffer considerable distortion in the generous acoustics of a large Cathedral. The choirmaster held out one crumb of comfort. He gave Joseph a letter of recommendation to a baritone from Newcastle, Frederick Hosking, a professor of music who taught at his home in Haverstock Hill, London.

Mr Hosking accepted him as a pupil, charging him 12 guineas for 12 half-hour lessons (paid in advance); in the year 1907 this was a great deal of money and the price a shock to Joseph's Scottish upbringing. All he could remember of those three expensive lessons was 'Do you smoke cigarettes?' 'Yes, a few.' 'Then don't – smoke a pipe, much better for the voice.'[11]

After only three lessons from Mr Hosking the Gothenburg engagement with Waldemar Zachrissons AB was finalized, whereupon Mr Hosking told him he could have the remaining nine lessons on his return. He never saw Mr Hosking again. On reflection, he believed he had the better part of the bargain.

Sweden was a land of opportunity. Joseph had nothing to lose and everything to gain. The journey across the North Sea in June, however, was hectic, damp and uncomfortable.[12] Meeting Joseph in Gothenburg harbour was Mr Möller, a former student at Bolt Court who had arranged for his food and lodging. Joseph later called round to Zachrissons AB. He found Herr Zachrisson very welcoming and friendly, with reasonably good English. He showed Joseph over the splendid premises which were equipped with all the latest machinery. Besides photoprocess engraving Zachrissons were involved in all branches of the printing trade.

In spite of a few teething-problems at his roof-top studio in Zachrissons, Joseph was immediately taken by his new home. Gothenburg appeared to be a very fine town with a climate just like that of Scotland. He thought he could like it if he could manage the language. As June turned to July his appreciation increased. Gothenburg in the summertime with its archipelago and wonderful fishing, sailing and bathing facilities seemed a marvellous place for a young man accustomed to the smoke and noise of London.

One early friend Joseph made was Harold Baxter, a young Edinburgh man. Sailing back to Gothenburg from Leith after the Christmas holidays, Baxter and Joseph found themselves sharing a cabin. From that time they shared digs in Gothenburg, two 'brither Scots' abroad.

In the run-up to Christmas Joseph had been busy at Zachrissons reproducing the most striking modern paintings from the Gothenburg art galleries for *Julstämning (Christmas Spirit)*, a publication brought out for the festive season by Erik Åkerlund (later head of Ahlén & Åkerlund, one of the leading Swedish publishers of magazines and weeklies). He also began to do photoprocess work on a freelance basis.

Early in February 1908, Joseph was at Gothenburg's Konserthuset (Concert House) to hear the great Vilhelm Herold[13] whom Joseph considered the finest tenor he had heard. In a letter home Joseph wondered what his father had thought of the Welsh tenor Ben Davies[14] then appearing in Edinburgh.[15]

By this time Joseph had returned to music lessons. He practised as often as he could, although he was often too tired. His singing teacher, Ragnar Grevillius, who was music critic of the Gothenburg *Morning Post*, arranged a concert every year. He asked Joseph to sing at the next one which was due to take place in May. Joseph felt this would give him time to improve. There was also the problem of acquiring a dress suit. Because clothes were dearer in Gothenburg he asked his parents to buy one for him.

The long Gothenburg winter and the lack of ventilation indoors exasperated Joseph and possibly accounted for his poor health that winter. His daily routine was also quite vigorous and unvaried. Every morning he started work at 8 o'clock for a weary hour before breakfast on the premises. He then worked till 1 o'clock when he stopped for half an hour to eat a sandwich. He finished at 5 o'clock and dined soon after with Baxter. He sang at about 7 o'clock and then read and talked or wrote till supper time which was taken with the other people in the house. He then killed time in the salon or in his room for an hour, occasionally going out with Baxter to play bridge.

On 16 February, one of the best local male voice choirs, the 'Till Sång' (The Love of Singing) gave a concert of folk music in Gothenburg. Grevillius encouraged Joseph to attend; he himself was closely involved with the 'TS', valuing the dedication and style which it brought to unaccompanied four-part harmony. In fact, for its size, Gothenburg was extremely fortunate in the class of concerts it hosted. Joseph attended one nearly every week, sometimes more often.

There were other things weighing on Joseph's mind by April 1908. He was expecting his new camera within a week. He was also making progress with what he thought would be a revolutionary colour process. At that very moment Zachrissons' manager was in Munich consulting its inventor, Dr Albert. Apparently Zachrisson intended to go in for colour work in a large way and was sparing no expense. Although, as a foreigner, Joseph did not feel totally confident about the future of his job, he knew his own worth. Also Zachrisson himself was always very friendly towards him, coming up every day and discussing things enthusiastically.

With spring in the air, Joseph set his mind towards a more relaxed lifestyle. Following Swedish custom he was poised to move out into the country. One outdoor activity Joseph enjoyed tremendously was golf. He had just been beaten by one stroke to second place on the first class list at the Easter Meeting of the local golf club. He felt his play had improved a good deal; he was now a backmarker.

The day of Grevillius' concert arrived, having been postponed from 8 to 14 May. The Handelsinstitute was crowded. The audience showed its appreciation vociferously, first to violinist Julius Ruthström, then for the singing of Ragnar Grevillius himself. The composer Ruben Liljefors accompanied the singing throughout the programme which ended with 'en musikälskare' (a music-lover) Joseph Dewar Hislop, no less, wearing his new shirt from Edinburgh and his smart new dress-suit. This was his debut, albeit incognito, as a singer on the concert platform.

Some days later Joseph set out by train with Harold Baxter for the seaside resort of Särö, about an hour's journey south. Deciding on an excursion, they got out of the train at Brottkärr near the Hovås golf course they often played on, about 12 kilometres from central Gothenburg. Strolling along the rocky shore in the sun the two Scots came upon a large house with a big garden full of people. They walked up the drive and were met by a cheerful girl with blonde curly hair.

'Hello there. We'd like to book into the hotel, please,' said Joseph with a winning smile. The girl burst into laughter. 'This isn't a hotel, it's a private house! You'd better try at Billdall, just down the coast. It's got plenty of holiday accommodation.' So, a little sheepishly, the two young men made their way back to the train and on to Billdall.

Two days later Joseph found an excuse to return. He met the blonde girl again whose name was Karin Asklund. He invited her out for a walk on the golf course and, after some time wandering in the sunshine among the sea-breezes they sat down on the grass. Joseph took her hand and softly sang her a Burns song, 'My love she's but a lassie yet'.[16]

And then another link in the chain of fate was forged. Near Karin's home at Brottkärr was a wooden two-storey house facing the sea, basking in the shelter of the black rocks. Here four young men who worked in Gothenburg and were all members of the male voice choir 'Till Sång' came to stay the summer. One of the Swedes, Hans Sjöblom, invited the two Edinburgh lads to join them in their country house, *Hjertvillan*. So began the first of three summers of swimming, fun, sun and vocal harmony, with games of golf and glasses of Swedish *punsch* (nectar made from arrak and drunk ice-cold with coffee) and golden mornings woken by the cry of sea-birds.

When food was in short supply the six young men would walk 500 yards to Karin Asklund's house, *Matildehem*, and serenade Mrs Asklund. She would see that the merry band was supplied with fruit from the garden and warm bread (her husband employing 180 workers in a bakery business whose turnover was one million Swedish kronor).

Joseph had first been formally enrolled into the 40-strong TS by a colleague at Zachrissons who was an excellent baritone. He then began rehearsing in the ranks of the tenor section. By November 1908 both Joseph and Baxter were fully-fledged members of the *Sångsällskapet* (singing society) TS. Joseph was at this time in fine fettle, busy both with work and choir practice.

In 1909 a new choirmaster, Tage Bilde, arranged a June tour of towns in the vicinity of Gothenburg: Marstrand (a yachting and fishing centre on the west coast), Lysekil (a holiday resort surrounded by whale-backed rocks sloping down to the sea), Uddevalla (a harbour town, one of Sweden's oldest seaside resorts) and Trollhättan, at the head of the canal leading to Lake Vänern. At Trollhättan Joseph was first entrusted with performing a solo in Swedish – a folk song, 'Alls ingen flicka lästar ja'.

An important date for the now 60-strong choir came on 30 November 1909 when it gave a charity concert in Gothenburg's Nya Teatern. The concert realised Kr. 1 323, a welcome sum donated to Gothenburg hospitals for needy children and for those suffering from tuberculosis. However, the music critics were not impressed. The acoustics of the New Theatre were difficult for vocalists, especially so for an uneven mix of amateur voices. One critic complained that the choir contained no really youthful or exciting timbre; with the exception of the baritone, the soloists had an impenetrable cloud smothering the tone of their carefully-drilled performances.[17] Little daunted, the choir presented a concert of Christmas music in the Betlehemskyrkan three weeks later.

May 1910 marked a dramatic turning-point in Joseph's life. After the final rehearsal for a TS concert in the Konserthuset, a professional singer by the name of Magnus Lindström, who had been engaged for the concert, came from Stockholm to go over his solos. After the serious rehearsal was over, the whole choir as usual returned to the Phoenix Restaurant where they gathered around a long table loaded with food and drink. They laughed and joked and vigorously rendered many well-known quartets and folk songs.

During this pleasant evening Lindström asked Tage Bilde if there was any new talent in the choir. He was advised of a young Scot with a good voice. Joseph was persuaded to sing and, his shyness allayed by the good cheer of coffee and punsch, burst into 'Oh my Dolores, Queen of the Eastern Sea' from *Floradora*. With increasing self-confidence, he put the last few bars up an octave. When he'd finished Lindström exclaimed, 'Good voice! That's more than a good voice! With real training you might even become an international opera singer!'[18]

Lindström took Joseph aside, advising him to audition for his teacher in Stockholm, the famous Dr Gillis Bratt.[19] Dr Bratt was not only a celebrated teacher (who was to number among his pupils the Swedish soprano Göta Ljungberg as well as the Norwegians Kirsten Flagstad and Ivar Andrésen), but was also a Doctor of Medicine, a throat specialist and an amateur light baritone.

Lindström himself was a young blonde giant, over 6 feet 6 inches in height. He often came to Gothenburg as his father's house was also at Brottkärr, close to *Matildehem* and *Hjertvillan*. With a magnificent heroic tenor voice, Lindström's promise was great but he sadly died all too young.

Magnus Lindström, the tenor who discovered Hislop in 1910

After days of thought, seeking advice and planning, Joseph met Lindström one Sunday at his father's home and sang a few songs. Magnus assured him that he should grasp the nettle. After two years' training he would be ready to sing anywhere. But how to finance those two years of study? Joseph's friend Baxter had very generously offered him Kr 100 a month to exist on in Stockholm. Lindström also believed that Dr Bratt might be prepared to waive his normal tuition fee (Kr 10 an hour). Also Lindström thought that, after a few months' study under Dr Bratt, Joseph might find some rich patron. He had already arranged for Joseph to sing at The Valand, a restaurant in Gothenburg, for Kr 40 a night in order to finance his trial trip to Stockholm. Even so, Joseph dared not accept. He felt he should wait until he could sing properly and then make a bigger impact.

The moment of truth came at the end of 1910 when Joseph took the biggest decision of his life. With the encouragement of the Asklunds and of his friends in the TS, he left Gothenburg for Stockholm and made his way to Dr Bratt's apartment with Magnus Lindström. His accompanist was to be Erik Lemming,[20] another very tall man and the then Olympic gold medallist in the javelin. Imagine Joseph's feelings walking between these two giants! Nevertheless, Joseph sang his audition piece with as much feeling and style as he could. When he had finished singing Dr Bratt looked him in the eye and said unhesitatingly, 'God has given you a very fine voice. In a few years I shall make you one of the best tenors in the world'.[21]

Thus, early in 1911, Joseph moved permanently to Stockholm, having made his farewells to Waldemar Zachrisson (with whom he remained on good terms for the rest of his life), to his friends in the Sångsällskapet TS and to the Asklunds. Joseph found the scale of the capital city overpowering – with its massively solid stone walls, the epic grandeur of its gilded roofs and the sweep of the sea right into its heart. Nor were finances easy, especially considering Stockholm's high rents. However, he soon found a good room with a piano at a very reasonable price at Upplandsgatan, on the North edge of the city, the drawback being that he now had a good bit farther to travel into town every day.

That Dr Bratt believed in his ultimate success was beyond doubt. He did not request payment and even gave Joseph Kr 50 from time to time. Fru Lublin, Dr Bratt's best accompanist, had also begun to play for him gratis. When Dr Bratt explained that with hard work he would make his debut at the Opera the following spring, Joseph's hopes soared. He now wrote to Edinburgh and asked his younger brother Stephen to go to a secondhand bookstall and buy French and Italian dictionaries to enable him to translate French and Italian songs and arias into English. Joseph knew he had an enormous task ahead of him.

The vocal method used by Dr Bratt was based on that of Francesco Lamperti.[22] It was the method of classical Italian *bel canto* in which the importance of the diaphragm took second place to the correct formation of tone in the vocal chords and a 'sweet' attack. This was a method diametrically opposed to the school of 'forward placement' of the voice in the 'mask' around the nose and one which abhored any violent glottal attack on the note. Singing 'on the breath' and ease of production were paramount. Because of his intimate medical knowledge of the larynx Dr Bratt was a leading authority on vocal training; inevitably his methods were considered by some to be controversial.

Early in December Joseph was back in Gothenburg appearing with the TS in front of a large audience. He sang 'Drömmen' by Hallén and

Dr Gillis Bratt, Hislop's teacher (1922)

'Trollsjön' by Söderman, ending with 'Lensky's Aria' from *Eugene Onegin* as an encore. The critics noted that he had an unusually clear and tuneful voice, strong and promising that, after further training, would surely enable him to enter the ranks of Sweden's professional singers.[23]

After spending Christmas in Gothenburg Joseph organized and appeared in a soirée in the Intima Teatern in April 1912 accompanied by Fru Lublin and Fru Dahlström. (The latter also played for him the following October in the Grand Hotel during a meeting of the English Society choir). Strange to say Joseph was hardly nervous at all and never performed better. He apparently received hearty applause after singing many songs in which the richness of his voice was impressive. Dr Bratt was also very pleased, stating that Joseph's singing had exceeded his expectations. In a letter home, Joseph confirmed that his soirée had been a success, both artistically and financially. All the tickets had been sold out a week in advance, mainly because the tenor Dr Hybbinette[24] – who would not accept any payment – was on the programme. All in all, Joseph cleared about £50. This only increased Joseph's delight.

By now Joseph had made many friends at Uppsala University. One of the students' clubs there offered him their hall at an exceptionally low price if he could give a concert. His close friends would sell the tickets privately since Dr Bratt did not yet want Joseph exposed to official press criticism. This concert was subsequently postponed to the first week in April.

On 16 January 1913 Joseph sang in one of a series of music history concerts in an evening devoted to Richard Wagner. The piano accompaniment was by the composer W Peterson-Berger,[25] who also chose the programme. Joseph sang three times: 'The Prize Song' from *Die Meistersinger*, Siegmund's 'Spring Song' from *Die Walküre* and Lohengrin's 'Narration'. Between these a soprano, Valentine Schwartz, delivered Senta's 'Ballad' from *The Flying Dutchman*.

In an effort to keep body and soul together by what he earned privately, Joseph went in March 1913 to Uppsala for a weekend. He sang at Professor Josephson's[26] on the Saturday, and on Sunday at a charity concert for the nominal fee of Kr 20 and expenses. On Monday a splendid notice appeared in the principal newspaper: Joseph had an unusually beautiful and well-cultivated voice which (especially in the higher register) had a most brilliant ring. Besides revealing his excellent vocal resources, Joseph was said to have shown sound musical taste.[27]

That same month the Ladies' Fencing Club in Stockholm held an international competition at the Grand Hotel. In the evening various forms of entertainment were offered; the musical interlude featured Joseph. Singing 'O paradiso' from *L'africana*, his sensitive delivery apparently produced enthusiastic applause.

Bookings were becoming more frequent. The famous Uppsala Students Select Choir was going to Germany that year and asked Joseph to join them, offering him all expenses and Kr 300. If this did not clash with his engagements as soloist for Stockholm's Students Choir (which was to tour southeast Sweden from 5 to 10 June), then he intended to accept.

He was now in very strict training for his big Uppsala concert the following week. His health was now reasonably good and he had made astonishing progress in singing during the past six months.

References

The principal research material for the biography of Joseph Hislop is located at the National Library of Scotland (Acc 10304 and 7080) (NLS)

1. MS notebook in private possession.
2. Anecdote told to author by the late Mrs Nancy Hislop.

3. The People's Journal, 13 August 1921.
4. The Dundee Evening Telegraph, 31 October 1923.
5. Hislop & Day, 9 Albany St, Edinburgh.
6. The People's Journal, 13 August 1921.
7. The Dundee Evening Telegraph, 31 October 1923.
8. ibid.
9. Dr Thomas Collinson (1858–1928).
10. Hislop, J. (1969) 'Some Reminiscences of my life.' *78 rpm*, No 4.
11. ibid.
12. Letter to parents, 1 June 1907, NLS.
13. Vilhelm Herold (1865–1937) Danish tenor. Member of Stockholm Opera 1901–03 and 1907–09. Opera Director at Theatre Royal, Copenhagen 1922–24.
14. Ben Davies (1858-1943) Welsh tenor. Principal in Carl Rosa Company.
15. Letter to parents, February 1908, NLS.
16. Anecdote told to author by Joseph Hislop jnr.
17. Unidentified Gothenburg newspaper, 1 December 1909, NLS.
18. Eves, G. (1970) *Recorded Sound*, No 38, April.
19. Dr Gillis Bratt (1870–1925) MD. Nose and throat specialist; distinguished teacher of voice for singers and actors. Amateur baritone. Studied (1897–98) with French-trained bass baritone Algot Lange and also with Agnar Strandberg. Had a considerable reputation in Germany (where a number of his pupils were successful) as well as in Scandinavia. His teaching method was disapproved of, notably by John Forsell, Director of the Swedish Royal Opera (1923–39) and teacher of many well known Scandinavian singers, notably Jussi Björling.
20. Erik Lemming (1880–1930) won both the javelin (54.83 m) and freestyle javelin (54.44 m) in the 1908 London Olympics and in 1912 retained his title with a throw of 60.64 m.
21. MS notebook in private possession and Fife Herald, 24 January 1973.
22. Francesco Lamperti (1811–92) Italian singing teacher and professor of singing at the Milan Conservatory from 1850.
23. Unidentified Gothenburg newspaper, 5 December 1911, NLS.
24. Dr Samuel Hybbinette (1876–1939), surgeon and amateur tenor.
25. Wilhelm Peterson-Berger (1867–1942), composer who also translated Wagner's libretti into Swedish.
26. Professor Carl David Josephson (1858–1939), obstetrician, gynaecologist and patron of the arts.
27. Letter to parents, 11 March 1913, NLS.

2   With the Swedish Royal Opera (1913-19)

Joseph's first widely-advertised public concert, at Uppsala in the North Sweden students' union on 17 April was a great success. The reviews next day remarked that Joseph had a beautiful high tenor voice and an effortless production. After more study, his fine voice and cultivated musicianship would prove a valuable asset to Swedish musical life.[1]

The more intimately lyrical pieces seemed to suit him best. Songs full of dramatic expression, like Melartin's 'Morning Song', were at this stage still beyond him. In the more tender atmosphere of Peterson-Berger's 'The Maiden under the Lime Tree'(*Jungfrun under lind*), his musical qualities were displayed to better advantage. Joseph responded to the hearty applause by singing an encore, 'For You Alone'.[2]

The Uppsala Students Choir, *Orphei Drängar* (The Sons of Orpheus – OD for short), met in the Grand Hotel in Stockholm on Saturday, 31 May 1913, for one of their final rehearsals before their German tour. That evening they performed outdoors at the pleasure-garden of Skansen (with its open-air museum and zoo), and again three times on the Sunday. Then they returned to Uppsala for another concert half an hour before midnight.

On Monday, 2 June, Joseph had a hectic programme. After a 1.30 pm rehearsal with the choir at Uppsala he travelled to Stockholm where he sang the solo in Olsson's 'Hymn' with the 50-strong Stockholm Students Choir in the Östermalmskyra before rushing back to Uppsala for another rehearsal at 6.30 pm! On the whole the next reception given the choir – in Västerås cathedral – was good. Considering the difficulties of the composition (increased by the acoustics of the church) the young soloist was thought to have performed very satisfactorily and proved to have 'a fine tenor voice and good musical sensibility'.[3]

On 3 June the OD rehearsed one final time before setting off on its trip to the Swedish Music Festival in Stuttgart. The tour began 90 km west of Stockholm at Västerås on the north shore of Lake Mälaren, continued south-west to Eskilstuna and then to the iron mining town of Örebro with its island castle surrounded by weirs of gleaming water. Next to Kristinehamn on the cold shores of Lake Vänern. Then round the north side of the lake to Vänersborg and Gothenburg where Joseph and his friend the bass Åke Wallgren were the soloists in two concerts, one in the Betlehemskyrkan, the other in the Konserthuset, both conducted by the composer Hugo Alfvén. In Helsingborg the beauty and strength of Joseph's voice was remarked on in his 'Värmlandsvisan' solo during which the rest of the choir hummed an accompaniment.[4]

Another concert in Malmö was followed by a glorious Baltic crossing from Trälleborg to Sassnitz and then through North Germany to Hamburg, which seemed livelier than usual as the birthday of the Kaiser was being celebrated with great festivity. That night a huge firework display took place over the Alster, and, with his gigantic airship, Count von Zeppelin roared over the town.

Listening to the OD's concert at the Convent Garden, the small Hamburg audience was struck by the many very beautiful folksongs sung by the Swedes. The power and brilliance of their voices were impressive. They had a strong, almost unbridled, vitality best heard in humorous or war-like material. From time to time, however, they tended to force the tone. The two soloists were praised for singing with 'warm voices and genuine artistry.'[5]

Next day they set out for Dortmund which had been the main venue of the 1912 festival. Many of their former hosts welcomed them either at the station or at the concert itself. As well as being assigned to the smaller Kronenburg Hall, their regular conductor, the composer Hugo Alfvén, was called away to Stuttgart, his place being taken by G Limberg. Reaction to their concert from the local press was good, although it was noted that the small audience and the tremendous heat unsettled the choir, as did the change in conductor. One critic's verdict was that the OD had 'great vocal technique combined with complete spontaneity in performance.'[6] The two soloists, the baritone Frederick Jansson (Åke Wallgren had gone ahead to perform in opera at Stuttgart) and Joseph, received very warm applause.

Another feature of the OD which was unusual for the German audience was the position of the tenors who were placed in the middle between the basses. The tenors sang without any falsetto, everything was produced with a chest-voice. Frequently this made for a sharp, apparently unsophisticated yet always manly and fresh sound, even in soft passages. The singers held their white caps in their hands for they sang everything from memory. They were full of sonority and spirit.

The choir's schedule was not an easy one. Next morning they rose early to travel to Cologne where they hurriedly organized an hour's break in the timetable to admire the world-famous cathedral. On the following day the students arrived in Coblenz where they boarded the paddle-steamer *Loreley* for an exhilarating six-hour journey down the Rhine. Having been unable to arrange a concert in Wiesbaden, they continued on to Stuttgart.

In their Stuttgart concert the OD's technique and programme were certainly admired. The quality of their voices, clear and strong in the tenors – vigorous and powerful in the basses – testified to the unaffected freshness of the North.[7] Surprise was expressed at Hugo Alfvén conducting without a baton but his compositions, together with those of Liljefors, Wennerberg, Söderman and Berg were warmly clapped by the large audience who had assembled in spite of the rival attractions of the Midsummer Festival taking place in another part of town. There was nothing soft or effeminate in their performance. When the OD ended their concert with 'Die Wacht am Rhein', a German patriotic song, there was such cheering as was rarely heard in that part of the world.

While in Stuttgart, Joseph and the singers of the OD shared the stage with the finest musicians in Sweden. Wilhelm Stenhammar performed his own works on the piano. The baritone John Forsell, (later to be director of the Swedish Royal Opera) and Julia Claussen impressed with their singing. Hugo Alfvén conducted his compositions for male voice choir and orchestra.

After almost a week of music-making in the festival atmosphere of Stuttgart, the OD moved on to Berlin where they sang in the largest concert hall in the capital, the Philharmonie, to a packed audience. This was a triumph, with many of the critics expressing delight at the Swedish singers. Powerful, deep voices mixed with light, trumpet-bright tenors formed an unusual ensemble whose virile freshness was a special joy. Once again 'Die Wacht am Rhein' brought the audience to its feet. Then, regretfully it was time to go home.[8]

Summer passed and Joseph returned to the hard grind of cheap living and singing lessons from the meticulous Dr Bratt. In mid-November he joined a number of well-known names from the Royal Opera (including Nanny Larsén-Todsen, Karin Branzell and Conny Molin) at an early afternoon concert in the fashionable Berns Salon. A week later Joseph was back in Gothenburg to celebrate the tenth anniversary of the Sångsällskapet Till Sång. A grand public concert was held at the Konserthuset under Sven Körling's baton. Joseph was cheered and presented with bouquets of flowers. After the concert the whole choir sat down to supper, entertainment and dancing in an open-air restaurant. Then Joseph again joined his friend Åke Wallgren to appear in a church concert 70 km north of Stockholm at Norrtälje, singing solos (including the 'Flower Song' from *Carmen*) and the duet 'Crucifix' by the French baritone Jean-Baptiste Faure.

Joseph knew that the time had now come to break into the professional operatic world, the essential first step being to gain entrance to the opera class at the Conservatoire of Music. But, on returning to Stockholm he learned that the opera class had just been taken over by the Royal Opera House. Unfortunately the auditions had unexpectedly taken place and the course had started some weeks before.

Joseph called on the director of the Royal Opera, Count Hans von Stedingk, First Gentleman-in-Waiting to the King of Sweden, Gustav V. He told him he would be grateful if he could become a student. The Count regretfully informed Joseph that the opera class could not admit foreign nationals. So Joseph then asked permission to call again when he had a major role ready for performance. With regret the Count informed him that he was unable to grant him rehearsal facilities. The young Scot felt totally dismayed. When just about to leave, von Stedingk, for some reason, called Joseph back, relented and informed him that there was a meeting of the Music Committee the following morning. 'If you would care to audition on stage at 12.45 tomorrow, I will call the Committee to hear you.'[9]

Joseph spoke to Dr Bratt about von Stedingk's offer. He advised him 'Don't sing. They are only curious about you. When you are an even better singer perhaps they will treat you differently.' Joseph then told Åke Wallgren the story. He advised him 'Sing for goodness sake, sing! The Committee won't stop you.' Wallgren promised he also would be present in the auditorium to give moral support.

Next morning Joseph walked onto the darkened stage of the Royal Opera House with butterflies in his stomach, feeling very small and ill at ease. He was brought up with a start by a bald-headed, elderly man sitting at the piano, who ordered him to hand over his music and start singing. Joseph turned on him and said, 'With or without your permission, I shall sing when I feel ready.' After great efforts to steady his nerves he went over and, like Walter von Stolzing in *Die Meistersinger*, said to the pianist 'Now begin'.

Joseph sang the 'Flower Song' from *Carmen* in Swedish. The following day he was accepted for the Opera School.

In the Opera School, Joseph's teacher in score-reading was a harpist in the Royal Orchestra, Josef Lang from Bohemia. The initial lesson was comical in some ways because, rubbing his hands together as harpists do, his first advice was 'Now Mr Hislop, you must be very careful about pronunciation.' He said this in a strong *German* accent![10]

The grounding Joseph was given at the Opera School was thorough, especially in stage technique – something often neglected by the operatic artist. Every role was analysed and the students encouraged to think themselves into the characters in addition to absorbing their musical identities.

The students were instructed not only about costumes and weapons from different centuries, but the accompanying manners and actions. Every movement and pose in a role had to be carefully thought out beforehand.

Many singers annotated their scores with little marks showing preferred positions of the arms and body throughout the opera.[11] These elements were thoroughly studied until they became instinctive and would not intrude when the time came to concentrate totally on singing.

December soon came with St Lucy's Day, a magical celebration in Sweden with young people carrying stars and candles. Then Christmas, when Joseph and Karin received some fine presents. Joseph longed to spend Hogmanay with his mother and father and friends in Edinburgh. He was able to send them a postcard with the good news that he had been awarded a bursary at the Opera School. The welcome bursary turned out to be Kr 100 a month for each year with no conditions attached.

In the middle of January 1914 Joseph cut his first test recording, 'For You Alone'. Made for The Gramophone Company in Stockholm, the test was sent over to Fred Gaisberg at Hayes, for his verdict. Joseph kept his fingers crossed.

For the young apprentice singer money was very short, especially to one previously used to earning a reasonable living as a technician. To eke out a little extra cash Joseph accepted engagements from time to time, although negotiating them often needed bare-faced cheek! A variety of concerts came Joseph's way over the next few months. A church concert, an appearance at the Ragtime Club in the prestigious Strand Hotel with the cabaret singer Jean Claeson, and another church concert around Easter. Finally there were guest appearances at the glitzy Phoenix Palace restaurant and concert hall in April where he would bowl the audience over.

He had been sent for by the management of the Phoenix Palace to speak to the conductor of the orchestra, Mr Trobeck. Joseph dismissed the idea of a formal audition: 'That won't be necessary. I think the orchestra is excellent and the way you conduct, Mr Trobeck . . . . There's really no need for any audition.' Trobeck accepted Joseph's pointed hint but explained that he would still have to speak to the manager himself. Next day, instead of going to the manager's office, Joseph sauntered into the restaurant in his smartest suit, sat down and, with his last krona, ordered a cocktail. Then he called for the manager. After some polite negotiations Joseph was given a contract for ten nights at Kr 100. There would also be a 25 per cent reduction on the food and drink he and his friends ordered. Even then Joseph had some talent as a salesman! He also sang for six extra nights.[12]

At the beginning of May, Joseph and his fellow opera students had their first taste of professional opera. He played the walk-on part of a servant in an opera by the Swedish composer Wilhelm Stenhammar, *Gillet På Solhaug*, (*The Banquet at Solhaug*), the story taken from an Ibsen play set in Viking times. The critics observed that, with his exceptionally beautiful voice, Joseph was wasted in a role where all he had to do was declaim.[13] However, the Stenhammar production was instructive in a number of ways. How to control nerves, for example; how to listen for cues; what could be learned from rehearsals and the mistakes which other singers made.

Joseph seems to have learned his lessons well for at the end of the spring term of 1914 he was offered a student contract with the Opera. He examined it in detail, found some of the clauses too restrictive and reluctantly refused. Then in May he was called up and asked about his plans. This time Joseph told Count von Stedingk that he had been invited to go to London to make his first records for The Gramophone Company. His plans would thus depend on the success of the records. Apparently afraid of losing Joseph, von Stedingk offered him a five-year contract which he accepted.

A pleasant event in the middle of May was a concert given at the Physicians' Society premises in Stockholm by Joseph along with other pupils of Dr Bratt. This was by way of paying tribute to an inspired teacher. Then came a Baltic tour with Joseph's friends in the TS.

The Gramophone Company recordings Joseph was to make were scheduled for 17 June 1914. Along with his friend the young conductor Nils Grevillius and the actress Harriet Bosse, who had been the last wife of the playwright August Strindberg, Joseph arrived in London for a short working holiday.

Caruso was then singing at Covent Garden. Joseph was determined to hear and, indeed, meet the great man. Some days before the recording was to take place, the three visitors from Sweden went to Pagani's restaurant in

With the Swedish conductor Nils Grevillius, early 1920s

Great Portland Street which they had heard was always frequented by Caruso and other famous musicians and theatrical figures such as the composer Paolo Tosti, Paderewski and Sarah Bernhardt. Arriving in the crowded restaurant at lunchtime, they found a table, sat down and waited for Caruso to come from his suite in the Savoy. Pagani's was full of animated chatter and noise. It was the height of the London season. Suddenly there was silence. Joseph and his friends turned to look towards the door where the imposing figure of Enrico Caruso, his doctor and his manager, was making an entrance, smiling and acknowledging the excitement of the diners.

Never before had Joseph asked anyone for an autograph, but being the only English-speaking member of the party, he was urged to go over to Caruso's table and ask for his. Joseph was answered by a frown of irritation. After explaining he was a tenor from the Royal Opera House in Stockholm, Caruso's attitude immediately became friendly. He spoke to Joseph as if to a colleague. Caruso confided that he had once been attracted to a soprano in the Stockholm Opera whose name he could not recall. He said she was blonde and had a turned-up nose.

Later, Joseph left Pagani's and took up a position outside the entrance. In due course Caruso emerged into the sun. Joseph snapped him posed at the door wearing a smart grey suit with a soft hat, swaggering nonchalantly with his cane. His associates, like Joseph, wore black bowler hats. Then the young Scots tenor had his photograph taken talking to his idol. They chatted amiably and parted in good fettle, with a friendly Italian farewell. (The photograph of Caruso and his friends has fortunately survived, though the original print of Joseph and Caruso has been lost).

The day before the Hayes recording session Joseph accepted an invitation to look over The Gramophone Company's factory. This took an exhausting two hours. Returning to London feeling worn out, he went for a very heavy meal of hot pea soup and roast beef. He had paid a boy to keep his place in the Covent Garden queue and eventually managed to get a hard wooden seat in the gallery. Though almost delirious with heat and fatigue, Joseph managed to keep awake to hear the magnificent voice of Caruso filling the house. Such were the uncomfortable circumstances under which, for the first time, he was to hear that great Singer of Singers whose voice he adored.

On a sweltering afternoon the next day Joseph arrived at Hayes, Middlesex to make his recordings. Possibly accompanied by Grevillius, he made six rather jerky and nervous records which were to be released on the budget Zonophone label. In later years Fred Gaisberg, the Gramophone Company's pioneer recording engineer, used to play these early Hislop Zonophones to visiting artists and then follow them with some of his Red Label recordings from the early 1920s. Few could believe they were by the same singer.

June 1914: Enrico Caruso, his doctor and manager, outside Pagani's restaurant, photographed by Hislop. (Courtesy Hislop & Day, photo-engravers)

Gaisberg's motive was to show just how much a voice could improve with further study and experience.[14]

When Nils Grevillius got back to Stockholm the photograph of Joseph and Caruso was published in the press. So was the story of the Swedish soprano with the turned up nose. 'Who is Caruso's blonde girlfriend?' trumpeted the newspapers.[15] In due course the story filtered back to Caruso. Grevillius received a furious letter from him, written in French, upbraiding him for his ungentlemanly behaviour in disclosing a confidence about a lady.

Joseph meantime had left London for Edinburgh. There he spent a fortnight with a repetiteur, the teacher and conductor Reginald de la Haye, in preparation for his forthcoming debut at the Royal Swedish Opera as Faust as well as for subsequent performances as Lieutenant Pinkerton.

On 28 June the Austrian Archduke Ferdinand was assassinated in Sarajevo by Bosnian Serb conspirators, so setting in motion events which would lead to the declaration of the First World War. Britain declared war on Germany on 4 August 1914 and Austria on Russia a day later. Joseph, aged 30 and on the brink of a promising new career, must have had mixed feelings about remaining in Sweden. His brother Stephen, now a doctor, was to join up and serve in France.

His new career spurred him into activity however. On Saturday, 12 September, Joseph appeared as Faust in Gounod's opera, singing his first performance as a soloist on the operatic stage. Playing opposite him were Åke Wallgren as Mephistofeles and Magna Skogman as Margaretha, under the baton of Adolf Wiklund.

The press reports spoke of his beautiful voice, warm in timbre, skilfully used. They noted that his pronunciation of Swedish was first-class. Joseph was enthusiastically applauded and, at the end of the opera, presented with bouquets of flowers. 'Everything shows promise, especially the melting and beautifully resonant voice whose brilliant high C produced a sigh of enchantment through the house.'[16] However first-night nerves had led to some excessive vibrato. His lack of acting experience could be seen in his awkwardness on stage. After several performances of *Faust*, Joseph asked his teacher Sven Nyblom what he had to learn next. 'Faust in Gounod's opera,' he replied coldly.[17]

Tullio Voghera, an assistant conductor at the Metropolitan in New York for five years and a one-time accompanist of Caruso, was looking for a young tenor to play Pinkerton in *Madama Butterfly*. He asked Armas Järnefelt, the chief conductor, if he knew one. 'Yes, certainly,' replied Järnefelt. 'There's a young Scot who naturally knows exactly how to pronounce "whisky"!'

Joseph prepared very hard for the role of Pinkerton, practising every moment of the day. He was to appear with Marguerite Gauntier-Wennegren as Butterfly and Karin Branzell as Suzuki. However, on the first night as the American naval officer Joseph was good only in parts. He wore a 'mournful expression' for much of the opera, a few detached brilliant high notes failing to compensate for his exceptionally awkward appearance. He looked unmanly and slightly ridiculous. Moreover, on several occasions, his voice was drowned by the rich sound of the excellent orchestra.[18]

Life was not easy financially for a young tenor. Joseph's two debuts had cost him a lot of money in extra lessons. However, it was money well spent since he had to build up a repertoire. September cost him £24, only a small amount of which went on entertainment: a supper he stood for Karin and Mrs Asklund and two friends after his Faust debut, and a smaller supper for Dr Bratt and Sven Nyblom after *Madama Butterfly*.[19]

As Faust in Gounod's *Faust*, Stockholm 1919

Physically Joseph was not yet strong enough and he still had much to learn. How different were the tactics of a singer on the operatic stage in front of a huge orchestra to those of one on the concert platform. His lower notes, especially in quick passages, did not yet carry well enough. Over the next months Joseph continued to appear three or four times a month, by the end of the year giving nine performances of *Faust* and four of *Madama Butterfly*.

November saw him make four recordings in Swedish ('Because', translated by Dr Bratt, 'I wonder who's kissing her now?', 'Serenad' by Widéen and Sir Edward Elgar's 'Salut d'Amour').

'Salut d'Amour' was a very appropriate title, for in Gothenburg on Christmas Day 1914 Joseph became formally engaged to Karin. This called for a double celebration in the Asklund family and much flowing of song and Swedish *punsch*! They planned to get married at the end of the Opera season after Joseph had finished a short concert tour about the end of June. Joseph wrote to his brother Willie that Karin was a knockout.[20] Since her brother had been called up for six weeks military training, Karin was in full charge of the office and cashier. She was thus extremely busy, running 40 shops, various agencies in different towns and a huge bakery.

In January and February, Joseph gave only one performance each of *Faust* and *Madama Butterfly*. In any case he was having to cope with physical problems. Having always been rather thin, he found he did not have the strength to sustain a big opera part to the end. The doctor he consulted found him quite sound but told him to eat twice as much as usual, including as much porridge, cream and butter as possible, and return in a week. Joseph did so and to his great astonishment had gained six pounds in seven days. Then he put on another six pounds. He was determined to persevere until he had gained 20 pounds or more. Though always subject to chilblains during the trying Swedish winters, since putting on weight he had no trouble on that score.[21]

The Zonophone recordings Joseph had made at Hayes the previous June were suddenly issued in Britain. Writing to his brother, Joseph complained that he considered his English records a failure. He tried to stop their publication but was too late. The London office appeared to be managed by 'a lot of damned fools.'[22]

Ironically, a number of wax masters he had made were smashed in an accident on their way to the pressing plant in Hanover and only two survived. Among the losses were 'Celeste Aida' from *Aida* in English (for the British market) which would have to be recorded again. He was determined that next time it should be first class to make up for the poor quality of the Zonophones. The two songs which escaped damage had been issued the previous month but were completely sold out.

Politically life had become difficult for British subjects since the Swedes' fear of Russia made them more sympathetic to German policy. Joseph was constantly getting into heated debates. His more intimate friends avoided any mention of politics in his presence. If any dared say a critical word about Britain, he threatened to 'knock their damned heads off'.[23] There was also a special tax on foreign artists in Sweden which amounted to 10 per cent of their income. Joseph felt intensely British. He had no intention of changing his nationality, even if offered a pension.

During the following month Karin came up to Stockholm to hunt for a flat. Joseph took a small part in four performances of Henri Rabaud's comic opera *Marouf*, based on *The Arabian Nights* and translated into Swedish by Joseph's teacher at the Opera School, Sven Nyblom. In defiance of the winter and the war, the opera was set variously in Cairo, in a sultan's palace, in a harem and an oasis. Neutral Sweden was trying hard to be an oasis of quiet amidst the tumult of war.

After another *Faust* early in April with the Russian-trained soprano Maj Schultz-Lindberg as Marguerite, Joseph made his debut at the end of the month as Faust in Boito's *Mefistofele*, the name part being taken by Åke Wallgren. The aria 'Dai campi, dai prati' ('över skog, över äng' in Swedish) from Act I of *Mefistofele* was one of a number of Swedish Pathé recordings Joseph later made.

The conditions under which acoustic recordings were made were primitive. When Joseph recorded for Pathé Frères in Stockholm he did so in a high-roofed hotel room squashed between the crates which had transported the recording equipment.

The wax recording cylinder revolved on top of a waist-high wooden frame to which it was securely clamped. From the cylinder a slender seven-sided horn stretched up to within one foot of the singer's mouth with an aperture roughly the size of his face, the end of the horn being suspended from an overhead boom. At the side of the room on a raised platform sat the pianist. The recording engineer with his pince-nez stood beside Joseph, one hand on his shoulder as he sang, signalling for variation in loudness or softness by the pressure of his fingers. The operator of the equipment watched the needle closely as the cylinder turned. In this makeshift fashion the recording was made.

On 26 May 1915, Joseph and Karin were married at the Asklund residence in Brottkärr. A large and happy throng gathered around the newly-weds in the warm summer sunshine. Most of the young men from the carefree days at *Hjertvillan* were there, including Joseph's best friends Hans Sjöblom and Willie Baxter and their wives.

There was a comical side to the occasion. Joseph's father-in-law was deeply religious and a strict teetotaller. Only lemonade was served to the guests and Karin's mother could not understand why the young people were getting merrier and merrier. The answer was quite simple – someone had hidden a hoard of schnapps and punsch in the little house at the other end of the lawn!

The honeymoon over, Joseph returned to the usual round of open-air concerts in Stockholm such as the Hasselbacksfesten given in June to raise funds for artists in war-torn Paris. Here Joseph and his operatic colleagues sang in dinner suits, wing-collars and black bow ties while in the vicinity were tombola and the ladies with extravagantly-feathered hats.

In September came news of a personal tragedy. Joseph's father died in Edinburgh after a difficult illness, never having seen his son sing in public. Joseph felt the loss greatly.

At the end of October Joseph appeared in Boito's *Mefistofele* again with his friend the buffo bass, Emile Stiebel. Joseph's voice was admired but his lack

Karin Hislop, Edinburgh, *c.*1920

of satisfactory acting and vocal execution was noted. Some critics feared that Joseph's clumsiness on stage might threaten to become permanent.[24]

Christmas 1915 stuck in Joseph's memory because of a bizarre concert given in the forbidding old-fashioned Långholmen prison in Stockholm. Various factors contributed to Joseph's shock and distress: the bitter cold of the day, the threatening attitudes of the guards, the ghastly exhibits displayed in the prison museum and the sight of two prisoners wearing masks in order not to be identified by their fellow inmates. Joseph had to put an iron grip on his nerves in order to be able to sing at all.[25]

On 1 January 1916 Joseph appeared in a small role in Meyerbeer's *Les Huguenots* and on 23 February he made his debut as a British Army officer,

Gerald, in a new production of *Lakmé* by Delibes with Andrejewa von Skilondz. During the second act of the opera, Karin and Joseph's first child was born. She was christened Geraldine after the role Joseph was singing.

Surprising improvements were at last to be seen in Joseph's acting; vocally, too, he was making great progress. Among signs of his developing dramatic confidence was the fact that, on his first entry onto the stage, Joseph stood with his back to the audience until the time came for him to sing. Nevertheless, he still had problems with his Swedish accent, the double consonants in particular.[26]

A new production of Massenet's *Manon* was then being prepared, with David Stockman playing the Chevalier des Grieux. However Tullio Voghera,

As Gerald in *Lakmé*, Stockholm, 23 February 1916

who was to conduct, advised Joseph to understudy the role. Joseph attended many rehearsals, including the final one. The following morning the producer Harald André phoned him with the news that Stockman had bronchitis and would be off for three weeks. André asked Joseph how many rehearsals he would need to be able to sing it. After some thought Joseph asked André to assemble the whole cast for a run-through to check whether or not he knew the part. He did. As David Stockman was a much heavier man the costume department had to work overnight to make five completely new costumes.

The result, on 29 March, was a complete triumph, Joseph's acting in the duel scene being particularly striking. Also especially remarked upon was his singing in the St Sulpice scene of Act III. In effect he seemed to have been brought to life, dramatically as well as musically.[27]

Massenet's *Manon* brought Joseph to the attention of the public for the first time and established him in the front rank of Swedish singers. Des Grieux was an ideal role for him both vocally and visually. Voghera, an outstanding conductor, was deeply impressed by the Scot's achievement. 'I have heard Caruso in this part 12 times but tonight Hislop sang his "Fly, oh fly" aria with greater brilliance and vocal expansion than Caruso himself.'[28]

A month later Joseph made his debut in a new production of Gounod's *Roméo et Juliette* mounted for the Shakespeare Festival with Ingeborg Suneson as Juliette. Joseph's old clumsiness on stage was almost gone. Instead there was a more purposeful body posture, a more expressive face, a more personal touch in his singing. At long last he had broken out of his Anglo-Saxon reserve.

During the long hot summer which followed Joseph invited Voghera to spend four weeks with him at Brottkärr to study the role of Radames in *Aida*. (In the mid-1930s Voghera would perform a similar service for Jussi Björling over a number of summers, thus providing a link between Caruso and two of the finest tenors in Sweden). Being Italian, Voghera had a fiery temperament; because of his stern approach and his iron discipline, he was not particularly popular with Joseph's Swedish colleagues. Nevertheless Joseph said to himself that a man who had been Toscanini's assistant at the Metropolitan Opera and Caruso's accompanist could be as difficult as he liked. Without doubt he could learn a lot from him.[29]

Mrs Hislop, Joseph's mother, came over from Edinburgh in the first week of August and was present on the 16th when, under the baton of Tullio Voghera, he sang Radames, his first role from an opera by Verdi with the American contralto Mme Charles Cahier (Sarah Jane Layton-Walker) who had just completed two seasons at the Metropolitan Opera. The presence of his mother was a terrific morale-booster for Joseph. It was a wonderful feeling knowing that, somewhere in that packed house, his mother was waiting to hear him sing opera for the very first time. Critically, his performance as Radames was considered his best so far. Joseph showed poise and balance and was very effective in the duet with Aida in the third act and in the moving finale.[30]

Another debut came the following year when in March Joseph sang the Duke of Mantua in *Rigoletto*, an opera which had never been a particular favourite in Sweden. The hunchback jester was played by John Forsell, Maddalena by Karin Branzell and Gilda by Andrejewa Skilondz. Joseph's foreign accent still grated on Swedish ears and he did not play the Duke with the frivolous elegance the part required.[31]

June saw Joseph play Turridu in *Cavalleria Rusticana* as a smouldering Rudolph Valentino figure, smoking a cigarette, knife stuck in his belt, full of menace. Opposite the Santuzza of Mme Cahier he showed great improvement in every aspect of vocal and dramatic technique. His higher notes were now much stronger and of better quality; his stiffness on stage was gone.[32]

The end of August witnessed the first of many Hislop Rodolfo's with broadbrimmed felt hat, a cloak, loud checked trousers, waistcoat and flowing cravat. Vocally, he was magnificent, with real Italian *brio*.[33]

His first Cavaradossi was seen in late September, a role particularly appropriate as Joseph was still a keen amateur artist himself. Again, improvement was noted in every aspect. His singing was excellent and by now his acting technique compensated for any lack of innate dramatic talent.[34] He also had enough taste and culture to make up for 'the failings of his vocal temperament and deeper musical intelligence'. Joseph was now a singer of real class, with heroic high notes who would no doubt be well received on the Continent.

As 1918 opened Joseph was studying Bizet's Singalese opera, *The Pearl Fishers*. He made his debut in February as Nadir opposite Mme Skilondz as Leila. His voice – wonderfully warm and beautiful – never failed to make an impression on the audience, while his improved control of *legato* was also very evident.[35]

Before the 1918 season began again in August, Joseph took some time off to be with his wife Karin who had just presented him with a second daughter, Elsa. Then he set about his work with great energy.

Besides his opera commitments he was arranging several big concerts for the forthcoming season. He was also in touch with the authorities in London and intended doing propaganda work for English music.

He wrote home asking for a few pounds of tea, first class tea which cost about £8 a pound in Sweden. The cost of living had gone up at a ridiculous rate. He also pleaded for some socks for himself, fairly heavy woollen socks.

On 19 September, the 20th anniversary of the Swedish Royal Opera in its present home, two new operas by the Austrian boy composer Korngold were presented. The first was *Polykrates' Ring* with David Stockman and Greta Söderman. The second, *Violanta*, set in 15th century Venice, starred

As Turiddu in Mascagni's *Cavalleria rusticana*, Stockholm, 1917

As Rodolfo *La Bohème*, Stockholm, 1917

Nanny Larsén-Todsen with Joseph as the Don Juan figure of Alfonso, illegitimate son of the King of Naples. Although Joseph captivated the audience with his magnificent tenor voice, his interpretation could have conveyed more of the libertine.[36]

After the performance was over the whole Royal Opera company (the front-of-house personnel, soloists, conductors, chorus members, dancers and back-stage staff) gathered in the Operakällaren, the exclusive restaurant built onto the back of the opera house, for a grand celebration, ending in a ball.

November was chosen for another Hislop debut, as Canio in *Pagliacci*, while on 27 December he sang his first *La traviata*. On a chill winter's evening he managed to inject a romantic aura into both voice and acting as the devoted suitor, Alfredo.[37]

On 30 December, Georges Pozemkowsky, a young tenor from the Imperial Opera in Petrograd, sang in *Roméo et Juliette* with Maria Kuznetsova who had recently escaped from Russia in a trunk on a Swedish ship disguised as a boy. During the following January, Joseph partnered her in *La bohème* and *Madama Butterfly*.

About this time a new face entered Joseph's career, that of the American pianist Spencer Clay. Clay had spent five years before the War as a vocal

As Alfredo in Verdi's *La traviata*, Stockholm, 1917

coach at the Chicago Opera and had since built up a reputation as an accompanist in England.

Joseph spent the second half of March in Oslo where Spencer Clay accompanied him in three concerts at the University Hall. Joseph also found time for a single performance of *Tosca* in the Norwegian capital.

Back in Stockholm another significant event occurred on 15 April when he sang Cavaradossi at the Royal Opera House. Unknown to him until the second act, Albert Coates, the well-known conductor, sat in the audience. Joseph made a good impression on Coates who hoped he could arrange for him to appear at the end of Covent Garden's Grand Season in Italian Opera in late June. However, this would be difficult since a full complement of singers had already been engaged. Coates decided that on his arrival in London he would confer with the directors at Covent Garden and telegraph their decision. A positive result would necessitate a substantial rescheduling of Joseph's forthcoming engagements.

His five-year contract now over, the Hislops were preparing to leave Sweden. Besides the bronchitis which was worrying him at times, Joseph had some bank debts caused by the high cost of living during the last three years of the war. However, he would be able to pay them off and have a good bit over from the £700 he and Karin had made on the sale of their furniture. He also had an old friend from Gothenburg, Gösta Dalman, now a millionaire shipping magnate, who financed him to almost any extent when necessary. Joseph gave a concert in Kristiania (Oslo) on 26 April. He had also arranged to sing in Copenhagen from 10 to 30 June, for which he would be paid £450.

Joseph made a final, painful farewell to Stockholm and Sweden by giving an enormously well-patronized concert in the Auditorium on 23 April with the composer Ragnar Althén as accompanist. 'Hislop's departure from the Royal Opera House is a great loss' complained the press sadly.[38] Flowers began to arrive after the first song and, by the end of the evening, the tributes had grown almost to a mountain. On leaving the theatre, Joseph was ambushed by his fans and tossed into the air in triumph.

References

Note: 'Unidentified newspaper' refers to cuttings filed with no record made of their provenance. In all cases they are located in the National Library of Scotland (NLS). ALB = Swedish National Archive of Recorded Sound and the Moving Image.

1.   Upsala Nya Tidning, 18 April 1913.
2.   ibid.
3.   Westhalands Allehanda, 6 June 1913.
4.   Unidentified Gothenburg newspaper, 11 June 1913, NLS.

5. Unidentified Hamburg newspaper, 17 June 1913, NLS.
6. Dortmunder Zeitung, 18 June 1913.
7. Schwäbische Kronik, 23 June 1913.
8. Unidentified Stockholm newspaper, 29 October 1914, NLS.
9. Berg, Ulf Börge (1972), *Carusos Kronprins* ALB.
10. Anecdote told to author by Joseph Hislop jnr.
11. *Opera* Vol 1, No 11 (1923).
12. Lindfors, Per (1960). *Joseph Hislop* ALB.
13. Svenska Dagbladet, 3 May 1914.
14. Eves, G (1970), 'Joseph Hislop', *Recorded Sound*, April, No 38.
15. ibid.
16. Dagens Nyheter, 13 September 1914.
17. Anecdote told to author by Joseph Hislop jnr.
18. 'A.E.' Unidentified Stockholm newspaper, 30 September 1914, NLS.
19. Letter to mother, 2 October 1914, NLS.
20. Letter to brother, 18 February 1915, NLS.
21. ibid.
22. ibid.
23. ibid.
24. Unidentified Stockholm newspaper, 1 November 1915, NLS.
25. Eves op. cit.
26. Svenska Dagbladet, 17 August 1916.
27. Svenska Dagbladet, 30 March 1916.
28. Scenen, 15 April 1933.
29. Berg op. cit.
30. Svenska Dagbladet, 17 August 1916.
31. Unidentified Stockholm newspaper, 14 March 1917, NLS.
32. Unidentified Stockholm newspaper, 5 June 1917, NLS.
33. Svenska Scenen, 15 September 1917.
34. Svenska Dagbladet, 22 September 1917.
35. Svenska Dagbladet, 13 February 1918.
36. Svenska Dagbladet, 22 September 1918.
37. Svenska Dagbladet, 28 December 1918.
38. Unidentified Stockholm newspaper, 24 April 1919, NLS.

3   Italian and British debuts (1919-1920)

In London Albert Coates' discussions with the Covent Garden management proved fruitless; there was no room that year for another tenor,
however gifted. Since Joseph would have to wait until the following season,
he set off on a concert tour to Norway.

Billed as the *primo tenore* of the Stockholm Opera and the most popular of
all singers in Sweden, Joseph, accompanied by Piero Coppola, appeared at a
series of concerts in Oslo at the University Hall during late April 1919. The
local press published a caricature of Joseph with the bald-headed Coppola
flourishing his arms over a Bechstein grand. One critic observed that Joseph
didn't look like an opera singer at all. More like a football player![1]

A day after the second concert, Coppola also conducted Joseph over two
nights as the Duke of Mantua in *Rigoletto* at the Opéra Comique, an annual
event organized and funded by a consortium of businessmen. Singing the
name part was the American William Beck, with Maria Javór as Gilda. The
critic Jens Arbo was impressed by Joseph's performance, admiring in particular his skill in modulation, shading and dynamic colour, as well as his
convincing, sensitive phrasing – not just forte-fortissimo, but crescendo,
diminuendo, smorzando! Needless to say, Joseph was rewarded with storms
of applause.[2]

At the end of May Joseph again sailed to Oslo to sing Pinkerton at the
Nationalteater with Anna Edström as *Madama Butterfly*. His portrayal of
the raffish, cigarette-smoking, irresponsible young American was much
admired, as was as his brilliant ringing tenor voice.[3]

Then to the Apolloteater at the Tivoli Gardens in Copenhagen early in
June. There he took part in a guest season presented by the Swedish Ballet
under the direction of Mikail Fokine. Joseph appeared in the interval
between *Les Sylphides* and *Scheherazade* under the baton of his friend Nils
Grevillius. Although engaged for 30 days, the ballet was enjoying only
moderate success, so Joseph was invited to sing extra arias every night to

keep the audience from leaving. In this emergency he gave duets from *La bohème* in costume with the ballerina and soprano Ebon Strandin, a colleague from Stockholm where she was regularly called upon to dance. Although his enormous volume of voice was noted, Joseph was criticized for having apparently copied his style from Caruso (which may partly have been due to Tullio Voghera's coaching).[4] In spite of such critical carping the audience applauded enthusiastically. This was the beginning of a long love affair between Joseph and the Tivoli audience where he was to become a regular attraction during the summer season year after year.

The remainder of June was spent in Britain. Joseph and his mother went to see *La bohème* at Covent Garden starring Melba and Giovanni Martinelli. The opera was conducted by Leopoldo Mugnone, who was to play a key role in Joseph's career in Italy some months later.

Returning to Sweden he made final preparations to leave for his debut in Italy. In November, Joseph sent his wife and children to Scotland while he himself took the train through Germany to Milan to meet Tullio Voghera. There he lodged at the world famous Pensione Bonini, in the Piazza del Duomo, the boarding-house for talented, struggling operatic hopefuls, managed with an understanding eye by Signora Bonini. Within a week Karin was on her way to meet him.

Signora Bonini, meanwhile, had arranged for Paolo Longone, a dapper, pencil-moustached violinist-turned-agent, to meet and audition Joseph. Longone acted for the great baritone Titta Ruffo among others with whom Joseph was to sing in Chicago the following year. Longone also had some influence in America where he had access to Caruso's intimate circle of friends. Longone called for an accompanist and listened to Joseph's voice. He liked what he heard.

In the mornings Joseph crammed the Italian language with a teacher from the Berlitz School force-feeding him. In the afternoons he studied his roles in Italian with Voghera. After learning Montemezzi's *L'amore dei tre re* Joseph was taken by Voghera to audition for the conductor Tullio Serafin.

In the meantime a telegram arrived from Longone telling Joseph to go immediately to Naples for an audition at the renowned San Carlo Opera. There he sang 'Celeste Aida' and 'E lucevan le stelle' in Italian, projecting as much as he could into the vast auditorium. The auditioning panel was impressed. Half an hour later he signed a four-month contract starting from 16 December. He was to keep himself available to sing in Naples, Rome and Palermo – the three greatest houses in Italy at the time (La Scala, Milan, being closed). Joseph was well satisfied with this outcome. Plans to appear in the United States would have to be postponed. Instead he would sing at Covent Garden the following May if offered the right financial incentives.

In Italy Joseph was on stand-by. A full complement of seven first-class tenors, amongst them the finest in Italy – Beniamino Gigli – had already been engaged and their names published, along with the operas to be performed. Joseph was simply to cover for the other tenors during the coming season. For these reasons and because he was unknown in Italy, Joseph was content to accept a modest salary. Simply taking what was offered him also helped put him on good terms with the director. Now he faced four months of very hard work. In fact, Joseph was horrified whenever reminded of the list of operas he had contracted to sing: *Mefistofele*, *Iris*, *Aida*, *Tosca*, *Rigoletto*, *La traviata*, *Loreley*, *Lucia di Lammermoor* and *Il Trittico*. The last three Puccini's one-night operas he had never seen or heard. But he would do what he could and did not regret taking this momentous step. If he did well it would mean very much for his career in England and America the following year.

Joseph had now had other offers too. Both Trieste and Florence had asked him to sing *Lohengrin* under Tullio Serafin at higher salaries than he was receiving from the San Carlo. However, working in Trieste or Florence would not match the prestige of his present contract; nor did he want to make his Italian debut singing in a German opera.

Joseph and Karin moved to Naples in December by which time he was suffering from a severe cold. The rooms Longone had found for them in a private house had marble floors and no heating, so they changed to a modest but warmer hotel. Naples, with its long operatic history and the tangy nostalgia of its folk-songs, its connection with Caruso and its enjoyment of good Mediterranean food, was a revelation to Joseph. Traditional folklore was part of the culture, including a form of pastoral play at Christmas. A curious custom, too, was that for a few weeks before Christmas the shepherds came down from the hills with their bagpipes and oboes. Like the minstrels of old they would play and sing before each wayside shrine on the highway.

Joseph's agent Longone had already provided the chief conductor Leopoldo Mugnone with a list of the roles which Joseph knew intimately. By mistake he had added the role of Edgardo in Donizetti's *Lucia di Lammermoor*. Mugnone sent for Joseph to run quickly through the part. Then Mugnone congratulated him. 'You're singing this very well. Could you play Edgardo next Sunday if I can manage to put your name on the bills and programmes in time?' He rushed off to the office and returned rubbing his hands. 'E fatto' (it's done)'. Later he had Joseph sing through the part twice more.[5]

Joseph must have wondered whether he was being stupid, irresponsible or foolhardy. What he was attempting was not really to be recommended. He had had no movement rehearsals at all, although he had studied and planned it all out during his convalescence. Naturally he had learnt the role musically. He had also had a lot of stage experience, but he could have been badly caught out.

Mugnone had been so impressed that he wanted Joseph's debut on a gala evening in order to make a big impression. But after due consideration and in order to save time, Joseph sang without previous advertisement and without any rehearsals whatever with the other artists and without stage or orchestra rehearsals at all. He was only introduced to the other principals behind the curtain minutes before the performance![6]

Joseph thus made his Italian debut on 15 January 1920 as Edgardo, having only just recovered from a very bad attack of bronchitis. Miraculously, it was fantastic.

Singing opposite Joseph was Ayres Borghi-Zerni as Lucia with Benvenuto Franci as Lord Ashton. The whole opera company together with the

As Edgardo in *Lucia di Lammermoor*, 1917 (debut 1920)

Neapolitan press were enthusiastic, congratulating Joseph for showing his worth as a singer and actor in such spectacular fashion. The public thought that his acting and singing were sensational. In the days that followed, he appeared in *Tosca* equally successfully, sharing the role of Mario Cavaradossi with Gigli.

Joseph's wife Karin recalled the tension of those first nights in Naples.

> The time I was really most frightened was at the San Carlo Opera. The Italian people are so critical in opera, and they had begun to like an Italian tenor Gigli very much. After him my husband was to sing and we were very eager to know how they would take his rendering. He sang thirteen times after Gigli, and every night had to sing the last aria 'E lucevan le stelle' twice, sometimes even three times. Every night too the house was so packed that the director of the opera had to give me his chair to sit on.[7]

Hislop reading the reviews, Naples 1920

There were amusing as well as hair-raising moments in Naples. At least one night at the opera turned into farce. Joseph was in the audience when *La traviata* was being played and the tenor, a young Neapolitan of good family, was making his debut as Alfredo.

He was scared stiff, but faced his audience bravely, so that few guessed how his knees were shaking. After the famous scene when he sings to Violetta, 'Violetta lives only for me', there was a cut and the debutant had to get off as elegantly as possible.

Everything went well until he reached the last step of the stairs, when his foot slipped and he fell through the window. He went through it head first with his feet to the audience, and there he stuck as the curtain went down, with the nethermost portion of his anatomy wedged firmly in the scenery amid shrieks of mirth![8]

There were times when Joseph was so tired that he forgot his words. During one Sunday matinée of *Rigoletto* he actually forgot the words of the second verse of 'La donna è mobile' and was probably the only one in the opera house who didn't know the words. He sang 'La-di-da-di-da-di' for a few bars before recovering.[9]

Joseph's contract in Naples expired at the end of April 1920. He returned regretfully to Stockholm, giving a farewell concert at the Auditorium there before going on to Oslo where he sang in front of the King and Queen of Norway. His agent Longone had meanwhile secured an engagement for Joseph for the following season at the Chicago Opera under Mary Garden. Arriving in London at the end of April, Joseph rented comfortable rooms in Montague Street, Russell Square, and prepared to audition for the Covent Garden Grand Opera Syndicate. With May Day celebrations in progress, London seemed tumultuous, full of the joys of spring. In the Albert Hall 5 000 people heard the massed cooperative choirs sing 'England Arise' and 'The International'. They were addressed by Sylvia Pankhurst speaking in support of the Bolsheviks of Russia.

Joseph met the heads of the Grand Opera Syndicate on 3 May and, after a trying audition, was informed that his debut would take place on Saturday week, 16 May, in *La bohème*. He would sing with Maria Kuznetsova as Mimi and the fine French/Algerian baritone Dinh Gilly as Marcello. Troubles ensued, however. A programme note on 13 May informed the public that, owing to a delay in the arrival of some of the principal artists, it had been necessary to rearrange the repertoire. In consequence *La bohème* would be given the following evening.

Imagine the young Scot's nervousness at having his debut suddenly brought forward by two days. Then more upheaval. Five minutes before curtain-up on 14 May, Sir Thomas Beecham (who with the Sir Thomas Beecham Opera Company was the lessee of the Royal Opera House) appeared backstage and announced to the conductor Albert Coates that he had decided to take over for the evening at the request of some American friends of his who had just arrived in London and wanted to hear him conduct. To increase Joseph's apprehension he had just heard that Giacomo Puccini himself would be in the audience, having come to London to supervise the première of his *Il Trittico* at Covent Garden.

'Is there any part of the opera that you would like to discuss before we begin?' Sir Thomas asked Joseph. 'Excuse me, sir. Three minutes to discuss the whole of *La bohème*. Impossible! However, when I enter with Maria Kuznetsova as Mimi in Act II there is such a commotion on stage that it is almost impossible to hear the orchestra. Could you please give me a clear lead at that point?' Sir Thomas complied. At the end Joseph sensed that his first British appearance in opera had been a resounding success.[10]

The morning after the performance Puccini came round to the opera house and met Joseph, showing him the manuscript score of *Il Trittico*. He congratulated him warmly on his British debut and gave him a signed photograph of himself with the inscription: 'A mio Rodolfo ideale, Giuseppe Hislop'. Some weeks later a very tempting offer of an engagement in South America arrived for which Joseph strongly suspected Puccini was responsible. Unfortunately he was unable to accept it.

The press spoke admiringly of Joseph's debut, with the exception of *The Times* (15 May 1920) which refused to be carried away.

> His is a voice of good quality, though not of exceptional power, and it has the advantage, which not all bigger tenors have, of keeping its quality on the middle notes. His singing, too, was musical, showing a feeling for the melodic outline which suggested that he will be a valuable addition to the company.

The Morning Post (15 May 1920) allowed itself a little more enthusiasm.

> His deportment was easy and natural, and he was able to enforce his personality without any obvious effort. He produces a sweet-toned voice with ease throughout its compass, and with his command of sympathetic expression claims a high place among operatic tenors.

Both *The Morning Post* and *The Daily Mail* (15 May 1920) seized on one important aspect of the Scotsman's performance.

> Foreign singers may charm us and then are gone, but the successful appearance of another British opera singer [Eva Turner was then singing with the Carl Rosa Opera at the Lyceum] may mean a useful recruit for the national company from which, as time goes on, we hope to get most of our operatic fare.

The Daily Telegraph (15 May 1920) continued in the same vein:

> Mr Hislop is an outstanding example of the cases I am constantly referring to, the cases of British singers who, finding no outlet at home, have gone abroad.

Some weeks later in *The Musician* (June 1920), F E Barrett was to comment that 'a Scot from Stockholm has turned up in Mr Joseph Hislop, who has a good voice for a Briton. It is of a quality that does something to remove the famous reproach that there are three kinds of tenors. Good, bad, and English!'

It was not only Joseph's voice that impressed. 'Mr Hislop was the most convincing Rodolfo one has ever seen. Caruso, for instance, in this part never made the least impression of a struggling and penurious poet. Mr Hislop had "composed" his part. He is a slightish young man, with sharp-cut features. He looked "pale and interesting". There really for once was verisimilitude in the figure cut by this poet.'

A note of caution came from Ernest Newman in *The Sunday Times* (16 May 1920) .

> His first appearance in this country was a decided success. His voice could do with more body in it in its *mezzo forte* moments: it is a matter not so much of lack of carrying power as of a !ack of those broader and deeper resonances that save the tenor voice at its best from even the suspicion of effeminacy even at its softest. But in the main Mr Hislop's is an excellent voice with quite enough power for all ordinary purposes, especially in its highest register. He phrases well, and his Rodolfo suggests that he is an actor.

'No Rodolfo in recent years has walked the Covent Garden stage for the first time so well,' wrote *The Daily Telegraph* (17 May 1920), 'so to the manner born as Mr Hislop, and no tenor in that period has come within measureable distance of Mr Hislop in sheer inevitableness. To a voice of lovely, smooth quality, and of abundant range and power he adds an ease and an address that are a sheer delight from first to last. He is one of the born stage kind. He sings his role as convincingly as he would talk it, and he sings it because it must be sung, not talked.'

One Scottish observer gave a moving personal view: 'It was a never-to-be-forgotten occasion. I was high up amid the red-plush seats of the vast auditorium; below in the boxes and, still further below in the stalls, were the leaders of London's musical world, and its highest society. Holding the attention of that great audience was the slightly-built but robust tenor'.[11]

It was perhaps *The Westminster Gazette* (15 May 1920) which wrote with greatest abandon. 'NEW SCOTTISH TENOR'S REMARKABLE SUCCESS' ran the caption 'It was a case of "Hats off!" at Covent Garden last night. What is certain is that a new tenor of exceptional promise presented himself for the first time before the London public in the person of Mr Joseph Hislop. Now he may be said to have acquired a world-wide reputation at a bound by his extraordinarily successful debut at Covent Garden last night. It was emphatically Mr Hislop's night and it will not be forgotten soon by those who were present.'

References

1.   Unidentified Oslo newspaper, April 1919 Musikmuseet, Stockholm.

2. Unidentified Oslo newspaper, May 1919 Musiksmuseet, Stockholm.
3. Arne van Erpekum Sem, unidentified Oslo newspaper, May 1919, NLS.
4. V.C., Berlingske Tidende, 10 June 1919, NLS.
5. Eves, op. cit.
6. Letter to mother, 16 January 1920. Reproduced on sleeve notes to Rubini GV 43 (by M.F. Bott).
7. The Sunday Post, 23 October 1921.
8. ibid.
9. Eves, op. cit.
10. ibid.
11. Unidentified Dundee newspaper, 17 November 1923, NLS.

Part II
GRAN TENORE
(1920–1934)

4 Opera (1920-1921): London, Chicago and New York

Beginning to make his mark on the stage of Covent Garden, Joseph looked about him in 1920 and saw a capital city restored in spirit. London had a spring in its step after the austerity of the war years. 'BACK TO THE MAY-TIME INVASION' sang the newspapers. More than one well-to-do lady agreed that May was an excellent time for a holiday in town. The dressmakers furiously sewed Epsom and Ascot frocks. Then there was the opera, which fashionable ladies loved as it was unavailable at home in the provinces. One woman visitor was asked what changes she noticed in post-war London. The answer was simple: more hustle, more brusqueness, more foreigners, more colour, brightness and gaiety, more enthusiasm, more activity, more inspiration. Joseph Hislop had become the talk of the *cognoscenti*. In the record shops there was a rush to buy his five green and gold Zonophone label recordings made six years previously.

In those days opera productions at Covent Garden were almost literally thrown together at the last moment. Singers were given little opportunity to rehearse with each other and had to rely on their own stock interpretations both musically and dramatically. Artistic direction was very much a DIY affair; the conductor was left to hold together what happened in the pit with what took place on stage. Often the results were disastrous.

After a weekend basking in his success as Rodolfo, Joseph was thrown in at the deep end yet again on the following Monday, 17 May. Caruso's protégé, the Metropolitan tenor Riccardo Martin, who had been engaged to sing Lieutenant Pinkerton in *Madama Butterfly*, was suddenly taken ill. Sir Thomas Beecham asked Joseph if he could sing the part. Since he had not quite finished learning it in Italian, Sir Thomas suggested he sing it in *Swedish*. Having last sung Pinkerton 11 months previously in Oslo, Joseph asked for a few hours to sit down with his piano score. He wanted to see if he could refresh his memory of the Swedish libretto by writing out the words.[1]

After due consideration Joseph agreed to sing the part. The next problem was the prompter. Joseph suggested that Karin, his wife, might be suitable. Sir Thomas agreed. During the performance when Joseph stood beside the prompt box, Karin smiled up at him and whispered an affectionate 'Hello'. The rest of the cast sang in Italian. Butterfly was Gilda Dalla Rizza, the Suzuki was Louise Bérat. Dinh Gilly appeared as Sharpless and Luigi Cilla as Goro; Gaetano Bavagnoli conducted. Joseph was justifiably proud of being the only singer at Covent Garden ever to have sung *Madama Butterfly*, or any other Italian opera, in Swedish.

However, the newspapers were not entirely sympathetic. 'Misfortunes of that kind,' wrote *The Times* (18 May 1920), 'must happen from time to time, and they are more complicated by our modern internationalism than they would be in either a national opera company or in a foreign company when the language is always that of the opera. At Covent Garden, however, the question of language is rendered comparatively unimportant by the difficulty of hearing any words at all!'

Of Joseph's performance, *The Times* declared that 'considering the short notice and the lack of rehearsal, he filled the place very creditably'. For *The Morning Post*(18 May 1920) 'he was well able to display the good points of his voice, of which the sweetness is an outstanding feature'. *The Westminster Gazette*(19 May 1920) noted that 'he interpreted the role with beauty of voice and general finish of style'.

A second *La bohème* followed on Saturday, 22 May, with Gilda Dalla Rizza as Mimi and Désirée Ellinger as Musetta. Albert Coates was given his chance to conduct the opera without the intervention of Sir Thomas Beecham. 'Mr Albert Coates brought freshness and energy into the orchestral playing and showed that energy does not imply noisiness' observed *The Times*(24 May 1920). 'Mr Hislop as Rodolfo improved considerably on his first appearance, singing with greater ease and confidence'. Considering the circumstances of Joseph's first Rodolfo that was hardly surprising.

By 26 May the announced production of *Manon Lescaut* was cancelled because of the continuing illness of both Riccardo Martin and Gilda Dalla Rizza. Instead Rosina Buckman stepped into the role of Butterfly for a performance that drew condemnation from *The Times*(27 May 1920)

> Evidently *polyglot* performances are to be a feature of the season, and Covent Garden is to become an operatic Tower of Babel. But this is merely a symptom of a more serious defect: singers who are got together on the spur of the moment, who are quite unused to singing together or to the methods of the conductor cannot be expected to blend well or to achieve a satisfactory ensemble.

One performer who on this occasion could count himself lucky to survive the ordeal was Joseph; he had taken only eight days to finish learning the part of Pinkerton in Italian. (The chorus sang in English!)

A third *La bohème* was presented on 29 May (largely with the same cast), a matinée performance conducted by Percy Pitt. On 3 June came another Hislop Rodolfo, this time with the delightful Miriam Licette as Mimi.

A matinée was announced for 4 June at the Oxford Theatre in aid of the French Hospital Dispensary. The swashbuckling actor Sacha Guitry and his fascinating wife, the singer Yvonne Printemps, appeared in a new playlet. Others taking part were the ballerina Anna Pavlova, and the two sensations of the 1920 Covent Garden season, the soprano Graziella Pareto and Mr Joseph Hislop (both appearing by kind permission of Sir Thomas Beecham, as the posters announced).

Joseph's final Covent Garden Rodolfo was on 15 June (again with Gilda Dalla Rizza, now recovered from illness). Elsewhere on the same day there was an historic technical development in the history of music when Nellie Melba gave a radio concert which reached the greater part of Europe. It was held at the invitation of *The Daily Mail* at the Marconi Company's station in Chelmsford.

His contractual obligations now over, Joseph was able to relax from the other side of the footlights. He was in the audience at Covent Garden which heard the Lancashire tenor Tom Burke on the first night of Puccini's *Il Trittico* on June 18 at Covent Garden in the presence of the composer. In the orchestra was a future great British conductor, John Barbirolli, with whom Joseph was later to make some important recordings.

London was now Joseph's oyster. 'There are only two places I like to live in, London and Stockholm', Joseph told a Swedish journalist.[2] 'I have just come back from Paris where I've been discussing some plans for engagements. For the next season I have a contract for 25 performances. Without boasting I can tell you that engagements have been showering down on me, but I had to say no to most because I need to conserve my strength.' The contract he was referring to was with the Chicago Opera starting in November. Joseph knew he must restrain his appetite for work which, together with the bronchitis which afflicted him from time to time, meant that he was often too tired to perform as well as he might.

Leaving London behind, the Hislop family spent a long lazy summer in Gothenburg. At Brottkärr there was the sparkling sea to swim or sail in, golf, tennis, family fun and visits from friends who would share the abundant seafood and Swedish punsch into the warm summer nights, making music and arguing about the meaning of life.

Autumn came and then winter. Joseph left Europe in the first week of November on his way to join the Chicago Opera Company, autocratically administered by the ravishing and legendary Scottish soprano Mary Garden. She had been chosen by Debussy to sing in the première of his

Pelléas et Mélisande in 1902 and had a very distinguished international reputation. In later years Joseph would recount with awed amusement his first meeting with Mary Garden. She sent for him to her suite at the Blackstone Hotel, still in bed, sitting propped up and pillowed like an Empress at a levée.[3] The Aberdeen lassie was curious to see the Edinburgh-born 'Swedish Caruso' (as the local papers were already calling him).

Joseph made his debut in a Saturday matinée on 20 November as Cavaradossi in *Tosca* opposite the tempestuous Polish soprano Rosa Raisa as Floria Tosca and the Russian Georges Baklanoff as Baron Scarpia under the ruthless baton of Gino Marinuzzi.

According to one critic,

> This heralded tenor was the personification of the lithe, romantically youthful masculine, but this is not the most grateful role in the world to make a debut. Mr Hislop did his best singing in the first act. Therein he disclosed a voice swiftly certain in attack, without stain of lyric forcing or affectation in its clarity. He is more than a charming personality and skilful singer, he is a thinking musician.[4]

For a tenor the vocal competition in the Chicago Opera Company was intimidating. Eleven élite tenors had been engaged. Two of the finest, Tito Schipa and Alessandro Bonci, had not yet made their appearance while another, the American Riccardo Martin (for whom Joseph had substituted at Covent Garden), would not have sung at all but for the sudden illness of Edward Johnson.

Five days later in the holiday atmosphere of Thanksgiving, Joseph was in one of his most telling roles, Rodolfo in *La bohème*. 'His is a voice with splendid power, touched with a poignant lyric charm and richness,' wrote the local press:[5]

> There is a fine sensitiveness about his clean-cut phrasing, and his interpretations are dominated by the innately poetical. Lean and thin-featured, he looked more like a poet than any other singer previously heard here in the role. Also he broke with the tradition that requires Rodolfo to be dressed like a tramp. He wore a frock coat with a nondescript vest to give the effect of poverty.[6]

Throughout what was to be a long career as singer and teacher Joseph Hislop was only ever in awe of two singers: Enrico Caruso and the baritone Titta Ruffo. It was a revelation to rehearse with the magnificent baritone voice of Ruffo (managed, like Joseph, by Paolo Longone) in preparation for an extra performance of *Rigoletto* on Sunday afternoon (28 November), out of the subscription series. The size of Titta Ruffo's voice was unbelievable. 'When Ruffo opened up to full volume it was like a goods train going over the points' Joseph remembered.[7] Years later Joseph was to write:

> I shall never forget when singing the part of the Duke in our first performance together in Chicago. You'll recall that the Duke is seated on his throne when

Rigoletto makes his entrance from up stage. The impact on me of his voice pouring over my head to the audience was immediate and thrilling. In my opinion Ruffo's voice for sheer beauty, power and brilliancy was the greatest of his time.[8]

'Joseph Hislop,' noted *Musical America* (11 December 1920), 'as the Duke of Mantua, found a role that exactly suited his rich, pure tenor voice. He sang with a careless abandon and joyous vocal beauty that marked him as a truly great singer of the operatic stage.'

On stage there had been heightened drama not intended by the composer. During the performance Joseph was singing with the mezzo Carmen Pascova as Maddalena; Pascova insisted on deliberately upstaging him. Joseph was a good actor and his stagecraft was above reproach, but he had a furious temper when crossed. He got so angry that all through the scene he sang each short phrase to the audience and then, turning to her during the rests, let fly an Anglo-Saxon curse.[9]

There was drama too *after* the performance. Ruffo and Joseph had gone for a meal in an Italian restaurant. Stepping back into the street they were immediately aware of a violent commotion. Suddenly shots rang out and a bullet smashed into the wall very close to Joseph. A gunbattle had just started between mobsters and the police. Quickly the two singers stepped back into the restaurant and opened another bottle of Chianti till the shooting stopped.[10]

Joseph appeared in another performance of *Tosca* the following day. Then a week later came a change of period and style in the Sunday 5 December matinée performance of Verdi's *Aida*. There were some fireworks from Rosa Raisa singing the name part; one critic remarked that she 'attempted to remove the Auditorium roof with her voluminous vocalisation'.[11]

> Rosa Raisa was chock-full of temperament when she came from the wings to take a bow after the first act of *Aida*. The applause was so tremendous that a stagehand was sent to call Joseph Hislop from his dressing-room to take a bow with her. Hislop assumed that the tenor and soprano bow together. Raisa (the fiery Pole) was burning with rage when the curtain finally descended. A clash was averted by stagehands. Raisa accused Hislop of stealing her applause. In vain Hislop tried to explain. The tilt lasted throughout the performance. In the second act Hislop was without a partner when he made his entrance to sing to the noted soprano. Raisa was found hiding behind the wings. She charged Hislop had violated stage etiquette.[12]

The misunderstanding was patched up after the show, with Hislop's manager Paolo Longone explaining to the press what had happened. Both singers were now said to be the best of friends!

In many ways however the most thrilling performances were Joseph's two appearances in *Roméo et Juliette*, the first on 12 December. Unlike his other appearances in Chicago (which had been in Italian) Joseph sang Gounod's

Roméo in French. Playing Juliette was the extraordinary half-Spanish, half-Italian coloratura soprano, Amelita Galli-Curci. The *Chicago Daily Tribune* (13 December 1920) music critic commented in particular on 'the blending of the miracle of Galli-Curci's voice with the fine timbre of Hislop's in the love music of the balcony scene'.

After repeats of *Tosca*, *Aida* and *Rigoletto*, *Roméo et Juliette* was presented again on 22 December. It was declared to be over-long but nevertheless delightful under the baton of the French conductor, Henri Morin. 'Mr Hislop is the product of a perfect art', noted one critic.[13] 'Joseph Hislop shared honors with the soprano, although he faced the difficult task of singing before an audience which had known Lucien Muratore [the French actor/tenor] in the role. His cantilena was at its best, and his singing of the cavatina "Ah lève-toi, soleil" was a beautiful example of rich tenor tone and expressive interpretation.'[14]

Three days later, on Christmas Day, Enrico Caruso was taken ill after his final appearance at the Met the evening before as Eléazar in Halévy's *La Juive*. In fact, he had been in considerable pain throughout the performance. Now the prospect of his long illness cast a shadow over the festive season and beyond.

On the first day of 1921, Joseph sang Lieutenant Pinkerton to the Butterfly of Rosina Storchio (who had premiered the role), making her Chicago debut. A second performance given ten days later was a personal triumph for Joseph who 'never sang with more admirable art.'[15] Joseph's final appearance at the Auditorium was in *Tosca* on the evening of Saturday 15 January. By this time the Company was gearing itself up to transfer to the Mrs Oscar Hammerstein's Manhattan Opera House in New York.

New York was bursting with musical life. Luisa Tetrazzini, the 'Tuscan Thrush', appeared at the Hippodrome on 24 January; the master pianist Cortot the same night at Carnegie Hall; Arturo Toscanini gave his final concert on 25 January and the violinist Fritz Kreisler three days later. Joseph was to work with all four at various times in his career.

At the Metropolitan Opera House were the sopranos Claudia Muzio and Frances Alda and the baritone Giuseppe De Luca (all of whom were to sing with Joseph four years later in Buenos Aires). The tenors at the Met were Giovanni Martinelli, Beniamino Gigli, Orville Harrold, Mario Chamlee, Giulio Crimi, Johannes Sembach and the Englishman Morgan Kingston.

A long bitter feud was underway between the Manhattan and the Met as each house tried to outdo the other. The opening of the season at the Manhattan on 24 January 1921 was suitably imposing. The work given was Bellini's *Norma* with Rosa Raisa. Two days later it was Joseph's turn to

Joseph Hislop as Roméo and Amelita Galli-Curci as Juliette in Gounod's
Roméo et Juliette at the Auditorium, Chicago, December 1920

appear in *Tosca* with Yvonne Gall and Georges Baklanoff.'*Tosca* Given in
Listless Manner. Hislop the Star!' was the verdict of *The New York Tribune*
(27 January 1921).

> The event of the evening was Mr Hislop's first appearance in New York. He
> has a fine, full-bodied voice, impressive in quality and well trained. Tall and
> lithe, he was prepossessing in appearance, a personable Mario. His acting left
> little to desire. Unlike one or two Italian tenors he was not consumed with
> passion, frenzied in his return of Tosca's caresses.

Joseph's agent, Paolo Longone, was a member of Caruso's privileged inner
circle. Apparently Caruso had promised some time before to be present at
Joseph's New York debut but his sudden illness had prevented him. Joseph
always recalled that apparently Caruso's first words on waking up the
following day were 'How did young Hislop do?' The effect of knowing that
Caruso had thought of him on his sick-bed gave Joseph renewed confidence
and strength to do his best. 'Have you ever lived alone in a big, strange city?'
Joseph confided many years later. 'Have you stood at the crossroads of your
life without support, without friends and without encouragement? If you
have, then you know what Caruso's interest meant to me.'[16]

After a fortnight's break Joseph was on the boards again on 7 February
with Rosina Storchio, whose first appearance in New York as Butterfly was
eagerly awaited. The critics were unanimous as to her ability as an actress
but her vocal powers were clearly diminished.

Joseph acquitted himself well in the eyes of the critics. 'The fine voice
and engaging presence of Mr Hislop did what could be done for the
distasteful part of Lieutenant Benjamin Franklin Pinkerton.'[17] 'Mr Hislop
was a politely passionate Pinkerton,' was another judgement.[18] Two days
later the papers were full of rumours about who would take over Caruso's
roles. 'Report Mentions Joseph Hislop and Tito Schipa for Some of the
Lighter Caruso Roles,' wrote *The New York Times* (9 February 1921).

During the intervening two weeks before his last New York role Joseph
was able to see more of the city, to visit the Met and to join in the general
speculation as to the size of Galli-Curci's fees, whether she would sing the
following season with the Chicago Opera or the Met (or both), the ru-
moured resignation of Mary Garden as manager at Chicago and the very
uncertain future of the Manhattan Opera House where Mrs Oscar
Hammerstein was facing great financial difficulties.

Joseph's last appearance was in a repeat of *Tosca* on 22 February,
Washington's birthday, with Raisa and Baklanoff conducted by Gino
Marinuzzi. Summing up the Chicago Opera Company's season *The New
York Times* (6 March 1921) commented, 'Of the new artists presented, Mr
Hislop made a favorable impression by his excellent lyric tenor voice, his
youthful and sympathetic presence, his skill in acting.'

The end of the Chicago Opera Company's residency at the Manhattan
came on 5 March. An announcement was made of a 20 to 50 per cent cut in
salary for all the artists except those stars who had been re-engaged (Garden, Galli-Curci and Lucien Muratore). Almost immediately the Company

left New York for a long transcontinental tour of the USA. Joseph, who had not yet signed a contract, found himself out in the cold. His existing contract was $700 a week, with an option for $1 200 and then $1 500. Had he closed with the option in Chicago, Joseph would have been with the Company on tour, but his agent Longone had waited until they got to New York and then run up against the cutbacks. For the time being then, Joseph had to return to Europe.[19]

Caruso had by this time also returned to Italy. On 26 July a highly significant letter winged its way from the influential Assistant Manager of the Metropolitan Opera, Edward Ziegler, to the General Manager, Giulio Gatti-Casazza in Milan, where he had gone when Caruso's health deteriorated.

The Met authorities were still greatly perturbed over Gigli's cancellation of his last performances with them the previous season. Gigli was about to appear in Buenos Aires, but Ziegler was unsure whether pique, physical or temperamental disorder might prevent Gigli from continuing his career in the New World. In light of this uncertainty Gatti instructed Ziegler to engage another lyric tenor for at least the first part of the season, possibly the American Charles Hackett, who had made his Met debut the previous season. Then perhaps Alfred Piccaver would be available for the winter.

Ziegler replied that Hackett was already heavily committed in concert work. Joseph Hislop, on the other hand, was in London and had been engaged by the baritone Antonio Scotti for his Second Transcontinental Tour at $300 a performance. Hackett (who was in fact engaged by Scotti along with Joseph) would have been offered $800 by the Met; Piccaver $750.[20] 'Regarding Hislop,' wrote Ziegler,

> I heard him once last year, and it is not a bad voice. It is a voice probably a little bit freer and clearer than Hackett's, but as an artist he has not the refinement that Hackett has on the stage, and makes an impression of great arrogance. All told, he did not impress me favorably, but he got quite good press notices for his voice and singing. Higgins[21] told me in London last year that as far as the voice was concerned, it was very good, but that the man did not take good care of himself and he did not think he would ever develop into a very fine artist. I am told that Hislop is not engaged by the Chicago people for next season but can get no more information regarding this at present.[22]

As it turned out, Gigli's appearance in Buenos Aires was an enormous success, thus relieving Gatti of the need to engage another tenor.

Ziegler's disparaging remarks about Joseph's lack of refinement and 'great arrogance' were probably based on his heartless, brusque and condescending portrayal of Pinkerton during the 7 February performance when Rosina Storchio made her New York debut. Ziegler's reference to Hislop's not taking care of himself was occasioned by Joseph's slight physique, his bronchial attacks and his punishing zest for work. There is no evidence that in later years Joseph ever had to withdraw from his commitments through exhaustion any more often than did his colleagues. Nor was his professionalism on stage ever affected by drink! It may be that Joseph was a victim of Higgins' differences with Sir Thomas Beecham (who actively supported Hislop). In any event Joseph was to sing 16 more times at Covent Garden in spite of Higgins' predictions.

What cannot be disputed is that Ziegler's assessment effectively closed the doors of the Metropolitan Opera House to Joseph for the remainder of his career. Neither was Piccaver ever to sing there and, in spite of the rumours which suggested that Tito Schipa was under consideration along with Joseph, the former did not make his Met debut until 1932.

Just over a fortnight after Ziegler's letter came the shattering news that Caruso had died early in the morning of 2 August at the Hotel Vesuvius in Naples with Joseph's agent, Paolo Longone, at his bedside. From the time of his first illness in December 1920 the question of Caruso's 'successor' had been a topic of much debate. Now it intensified. 'Hislop a likely British Candidate for World's Supremacy,' wrote the *London Evening News*, (3 August 1921). 'Three at least of the "possibles" are of British nationality: Joseph Hislop, John McCormack and Tom Burke. A fourth, Orville Harrold, is an Irish-American. Add to these Martinelli (Italian), Ansseau, a young Belgian and a Canadian singer named Johnson, and the list is complete. I shall be surprised if Joseph Hislop is not universally recognised as Caruso's successor. He has everything in his favour, youth, enthusiasm and stability of character.' Clearly he had not heard of Beniamino Gigli or even of Aureliano Pertile or Tito Schipa!

When he returned to America in October, Gigli was disgusted by this debate which he described as irreverent, macabre and unnecessary. He spoke for every other operatic tenor when he told reporters who badgered him in New York. 'I don't want to be another Caruso; I just want to be Gigli!'[23]

At the time of Caruso's death Joseph was in Edinburgh saying goodbye to his family before sailing back to America to join the Scotti's Grand Opera Company on its Second Transcontinental Tour (for details, see Chapter 7). Before his departure, Joseph and his accompanist Spencer Clay (who before the war had been a coach at the Chicago Opera for five seasons) went to The Gramophone Company's studios at Hayes to record the 'Addio alla madre' from *Cavalleria rusticana* by Mascagni (DB 522). In this first recording since his Swedish Pathé discs of 1916, Joseph sang with virile youthfulness, half-sobbing with emotion in the Italian manner. This was a good recording but without the swelling marriage of voice and orchestra which he was to achieve in 1928 under John Barbirolli.

In the winter of 1921, Joseph again tried desperately to get a permanent contract. Salt was rubbed into his wounded pride with the unimpressive debut of Aureliano Pertile on 1 December as Mario Cavaradossi to the tempestuous Czech soprano Maria Jeritza's Tosca.

Although by 27 December four of the tenors at the Met – Sembach, Chamlee, Crimi and Martinelli – had been struck down with colds, a restored Gigli was able to cover for them.

By the turn of the year it was plain that Joseph was not going to be offered a contract. On 1 January he watched one new tenor make his debut and another, the Greek Ulysses Lappas, star in New York with the Chicago Opera in *La Fanciulla del West* by Puccini.

Perhaps Joseph had some reason to be bitter in that several other pupils of Dr Gillis Bratt were later to be welcomed into the ranks of the Met: the Norwegian bass Ivar Andrésen in 1930, Göta Ljungberg in 1932, Gertrud Pålson-Wettergren and Kirsten Flagstad in 1935. However, that master of style, Tito Schipa, a member of the Chicago Opera with Joseph, did not manage to be accepted until 1932. Nor were the other two fine British tenors of the time, Alfred Piccaver (the American-raised 'Lincolnshire Caruso') and Tom Burke (the 'Lancashire Caruso'), who had appeared in concert at the New York Hippodrome a year before Joseph, ever invited to join. Only the English tenor, Morgan Kingston, was so engaged.

In conclusion it is worth noting that events could be equally unjust on the other side of the Atlantic. Tito Schipa, Amelita Galli-Curci and the fine baritone Carlo Galeffi (all of them colleagues of Joseph's in America), never appeared at Covent Garden. Artistic ability, unhappily, is not always the deciding criterion for work in opera.

The late David Bicknell, formerly manager of the international artistes department at The Gramophone Company, once stated that Joseph had acquired all the necessary technical equipment to a high degree, (voice, acting ability, musicianship and application), which made him the equal of the best lyric tenors of his day.[24] Sadly he was at the right place at the wrong time; the Metropolitan Opera House quite simply had a glut of tenors.[25]

References

1.   Berg, op. cit.
2.   Svenska Dagbladet, 28 June 1920.
3.   Anecdote told to author by George Donald.
4.   The Chicago Daily Tribune, 22 November 1920.
5.   The Chicago Daily Tribune, 26 November 1920.
6.   The Chicago Herald, 26 November 1920.
7.   BBC Radio Three script, 5 July 1956, NLS.
8.   ibid.
9.   Grahame McIntosh – letter to author, 23 June 1986, NLS.
10. ibid.
11. The Chicago Daily Tribune, 22 November 1920.

12.   Unidentified Chicago newspaper, 6 December 1920.
13.   The Musical Leader, 30 December 1920.
14.   ibid.
15.   The Musical America, 22 January 1921.
16.   Nerman, E., *Stjärnor*, Bokförlaget Natur och Kultur. Stockholm 1933, p. 39.
17.   The New York Times, 8 February 1921.
18.   The New York Herald, 8 February 1921.
19.   Letter to Alberto Sciarretti, 2 April 1929 (in private possession).
20.   Letter to Gatti-Cassazza, 26 July 1921, Metropolitan Opera Archives.
21.   Henry Higgins – chairman of The Grand Opera Syndicate, Covent Garden.
22.   Zeigler op. cit.
23.   Gigli, B (1957), *Memoirs*, London, Cassell & Co., pp. 120–1.
24.   Letter to author, 4 June 1988.
25.   These included Giovanni Martinelli, Beniamino Gigli, Orville Harrold, Mario Chamlee, Giulio Crimi, Johannes Sembach and Morgan Kingston.

5 Opera (1922 – 1925): Winning Golden Opinions

His successes in North America riding before him in the Swedish press (see Chapter 9), Joseph stopped off at Gothenburg to see his family before travelling on to Stockholm where he made the first of some 82 guest performances at the Swedish Royal Opera in *La bohème* on 17 February 1922 in front of a glittering audience which included the King of Sweden and the Royal Family.

Stockholmers who remembered him from two years previously could hardly believe this was the same man. Dr Bratt's Italian technique, with its rigorous simplicity, had flowered to embrace what the Swedes perceived to be all the sophisticated pyrotechnics of the full-blown *bel canto* tenor. It was a voice which had within it everything specifically Italian – flattering tone, sensuality, lyrical intensity, first-class phrasing. His characterization was dynamic, and now, in contrast to his previous practice of performing exclusively in Swedish, he astonished his admirers by singing only in the most magnificent Italian.

Already one characteristic aspect of his style was apparent: 'the restraint in his voice, which permitted it to ring out loudly only at moments of high intensity, is a hallmark of Hislop's artistry'.[1] This was the typical style of the *lyrico spinto* tenor, capable of injecting dramatic intensity of tone and volume when the score of an opera specifically called for it. So it was that in *Tosca* on 20 February his voice was 'full of southern passion, warmth and the real joy of singing.'[2]

Formal recognition of Joseph's achievements in the world of opera and of his promotion of Swedish culture at home and abroad came on the following day when he was awarded the Royal medal *Litteris et Artibus* for distinguished service in the arts. A gold medal worn with a dark blue ribbon, he was the first foreign singer to receive this honour since the late 19th century.

During the days that followed, his performance in *Madama Butterfly* revealed not only his astonishing growth in artistry but also the continuing freshness of his voice in an interpretation which almost managed to make the rather negative role of Pinkerton intriguing. Joseph's Canio in *Pagliacci*, performed in front of the Royal Family, was unusual in that he played the part as a volatile and thoughtless young man without the lurking qualities of a beast. His appearances as the Duke in *Rigoletto* and as Radames in *Aida* reinforced these good opinions.[3] Audience reaction in Sweden suggests that Joseph carefully rethought his approach to each role as he developed in experience. He was therefore disposed to depart from the stereotype whether or not this shattered the mould of audience anticipation.

Three performances of *Tosca* at Gothenburg came next. Then Joseph was back at Hayes (Middlesex) to record 'Che gelida manina' from *La bohème* (DB 522) with an orchestra conducted by George Byng. Although this version was to be surpassed by his 1928 recording, his seamless, ardent tone rises nevertheless to thrilling peaks of emotion, all contained within the bounds of artistry by keen intelligence and taste. Discussing the recording in the newly-founded magazine *The Gramophone* (August 1923), James Caskett wrote that 'Mr Hislop's rendering is among the best. He is a delightful singer in the Italian style and his articulation is exceptionally good.' The editor, Compton Mackenzie, added that 'in many ways Hislop is my favourite tenor'.

The long summer was as usual spent at Brottkärr golfing, playing tennis and cricket, swimming, sailing and enjoying the pleasure of a large extended family in idyllic surroundings. Joseph recuperated and refreshed himself after the rigours of the concert circuit.

At the end of August he travelled to Milan to holiday by Lake Como, taking the opportunity to complete negotiations for a season in Italy. He visited La Scala and met its director Arturo Toscanini. Then Joseph travelled west to sign contracts at the Teatro Regio (Turin) and to spend a day or two in Venice where he was shortly to sing at the Il Teatro La Fenice (Phoenix) appropriately named as it had twice been destroyed by fire (in 1773 and 1836) and rebuilt.

He returned in October and again in November to The Gramophone Company's studios at Hayes to cut two of his most admired interpretations, both Wagnerian: 'The Prize Song' from *Die Meistersinger* (DB 681) and the 'Grail Song' from *Lohengrin* (DB 681), both in English and both conducted by Spencer Clay. The two recordings were later issued as two sides of the same record. The 'Grail Song' in particular conveys a spirit of wonder in repose, swelling with vibrant tone on the word 'Grail'. But both recordings lack the luminous vibrancy of Joseph's 1929 version under Barbirolli.

The following weeks were spent working in Gothenburg, Oslo and Stockholm. Then immediately after Christmas it was time to travel to Venice, Queen of the Seas. Joseph and his family settled into their hotel in a room where Wagner is said to have composed Act II of *Tristan und Isolde*.

They had time for rather cold sight-seeing by gondola through the canals, under the bridges to the Piazza San Marco. There were the local delicacies to savour, seafood and dark wine, the strange mixture of beauty and pagan intrigue which haunts the monuments of that miraculous city even in the height of winter. Shortly, however, Joseph was to be brought rudely down to earth by the harsh realities of Italian operatic custom.

He had been contracted to sing three performances of *La bohème* under Giuseppe Baroni, with Zita Fumigalli Riva as Mimi and Madeleine Keltie as Musetta. The first performance was on 30 December 1922. For Joseph there was a hard lesson to be learnt. Before the performance two men of the claque (applause-leaders) visited him at his hotel. Although initially prepared to pay them, they asked for such a large sum of money that Joseph refused and showed them the door. In those days the claqueurs demanded 5 lire for interruptions with a 'bene' or 'bravo'; 15 lire for insistent applause and 50 lire for a 'bis' (encore). Wild enthusiasm would be provided at a sum to be negotiated. The Claque Master would carefully and subtly orchestrate the applause, having planned it with the singer and cleared it with the conductor. Those who did not appease the claque paid the penalty.

Joseph was soon standing on stage before the large and critical Venetian audience. Almost at the beginning of the aria 'Che gelida manina', there is a pause for the singer during which the strings play a very sweet pizzicato passage. During this passage loud shouts of 'Bravo, bravissimo' came from the claque, giving the impression that Joseph had paid them. It completely ruined his rendering of the aria and the whole audience became tense and nervous. This episode was duly reported throughout the musical press.[4] Happily there were no further disturbances at his other two performances, on 1 and 3 January 1923. The Hislop family then returned to Gothenburg.

Towards the end of the month he set out again for Italy, this time to the Teatro Regio (Turin) to sing 13 performances of *Lucia di Lammermoor* and six of Charpentier's *Louise*. In *Lucia di Lammermoor*, Joseph worked with two former colleagues, Gino Marinuzzi (who had conducted him in Chicago) and the Spanish coloratura soprano Angeles Ottein (with whom he had sung on the Scotti Transcontinental Tour of the United States two years before). The audience went into ecstasies over Ottein and Hislop. Both were applauded, particularly after the duet 'Verranno a te sull' aure'. According to the reviewer from *La Gazzetta del Popolo*, (8 February 1923), Hislop was less prominent in the sextet 'Chi mi frena in tal momento' than at other moments, but he rose to greater heights in the final 'Tu che a Dio',

not in the usual style of our Italian tenors but achieving the desired effect all the same. It's difficult to give the exact number of times that Hislop was recalled, 20, 30 times. Who knows! . . . 'He's still a little unsure in his movements; he's a bit too wooden and mechanical, but given his vocal powers and intelligence it will not be long before he gets to the top of the profession.

His voice is very beautiful, strong and free, generous and warm (unusually so in the upper register).

The timbre tends a little towards the baritonal and is therefore not entirely suitable for the role of Edgardo. He does not yet use a *mezza voce* as often as he should. This leads to sometimes displeasing uncertainties and surprises. Overall, however, this young artist deserves to receive much applause from our large circle of opera-goers.

Evidently, although he appeared the personification of the Italian tenor in Stockholm, he did not conform entirely to the style expected in Italy. His uncertainty around the stage was probably due to lack of rehearsal and to the fact that he had not sung the role of Edgardo since the spring of 1920 in Naples.

While at his Covent Garden debut three years earlier Ernest Newman had pointed to the lack of carrying power in Joseph's *mezza voce* (*The Sunday Times* 16 May 1920) and the absence of 'those broader and deeper resonances', opinion in Turin as expressed in *La Gazzetta del Popolo* advised him to use more *mezza voce* and less 'body'.

During his time in Turin Joseph was summoned to Milan to audition for Arturo Toscanini at La Scala. His singing impressed the maestro who showed him ways of improving his interpretation. Following his guest appearances in Turin, Joseph made his debut at the Teatro alla Scala on Wednesday 11 April in Donizetti's *Lucia di Lammermoor*, the first British male singer to sing a leading role in the opera house since its construction in 1778.[5] He took over the role of Edgardo from Aureliano Pertile. Riccardo Stracciari, with whom Joseph had sung on the Scotti tour in 1921, played Lord Henry Ashton. The great Italian bass, Ezio Pinza, a former racing cyclist, was Raimondo, while Lucia herself was in the capable hands of the vivacious Toti Dal Monte, whom Joseph found a delightful partner. It was the eighth performance of *Lucia di Lammermoor* that season. The first seven had been conducted by Toscanini himself. Now Franco Ghione took over the baton.

The reception given the new Scots tenor was enthusiastic. He faced the difficult task of taking over from the darling of the Milanese public, Aureliano Pertile. 'He overcame the arduous test brilliantly,' wrote *Il Corriere della Sera* (12 April 1923). 'Gifted with a fresh, sweet voice of the pure, lyrical type, Hislop knew from the first how to win the audience's sympathy. They applauded him enthusiastically at the end of each act. They repeatedly acknowledged his appearance at the curtain-calls with the other members of the cast and the conductor.'

Then an extraordinary event took place. At the beginning of the third act the President of the Council, Benito Mussolini, arrived unexpectedly at the opera house. On realizing the opera was so far advanced, he hurried to take the seat always reserved for him in Box 13 in the second tier. Toti Dal Monte began to sing the Mad Scene aria. Then someone in the theatre spotted the President of the Council and gave a shout, 'Long live Musso-lini!' However, 'so as not to disturb the performance, Mussolini moved back into the shadows of the box and left the theatre shortly before the curtain came down.'[6]

In the audience there were also many friends from Sweden who had travelled down to support Joseph, among them his old mentor and fellow-pupil of Dr Bratt's, the tenor Dr Sam Hybbinette.

After his very successful first night Joseph was offered some 45 further performances in the autumn. These he immediately agreed to sing but unhappily the subsequent detailed negotiations over fees and conditions broke down and he never performed again at La Scala (or indeed in Italy). It was partly that he did not want to be tied down in one place for six months. He felt, because of his age, that he needed to put himself about as much as possible. Whether through pride, greed, necessity or business incompe-tence, he asked twice the fee that La Scala was prepared to offer.

This was the biggest and most far-reaching error of judgement in Joseph's career, a significant lost opportunity which in later life he would always deeply regret. Had he signed the contract with Toscanini he would prob-ably, with the great conductor's blessing, have been able to bypass the hostility of Edward Ziegler and gain the access that had so far eluded him to the Metropolitan Opera. Then world recognition of his place in the first rank of international tenors would have followed – a place which his hard work, talent and experience certainly merited. Nevertheless, it was not to be.

After a fortnight's rest in Gothenburg Joseph returned to London to begin rehearsals with the 61-year old Australian soprano Nellie Melba for a performance of *La bohème* on 1 June. This was a gala to raise funds for the British National Opera Company. Among other tenors in Sir Thomas Beecham's Opera Company that season were the Britons Tudor Davies and Browning Mummery, the American Charles Hackett and the Canadian Edward Johnson (later to be General Manager of the Metropolitan Opera, New York).

On the night of the performance the theatre was filled from floor to ceiling, with the King and Queen and the three Princesses in the Royal Box. Percy Pitt was the conductor. It was a case of another 'polyglot perform-ance', Melba and Joseph singing in Italian while the rest of the cast sang in English. *The Times* (2 June 1923) observed that only the original language fitted the emotional effect of the music. When Melba and Hislop 'were alone on the stage together, in the last scene of the first act, the farewell of the third act, and the touching little scene of recollection just before Mimi's death, we got nearest to the charm of Puccini'.

After the second act Melba was presented to the King and Queen. There was much appreciation that an artist of her reputation should have supported the British National Opera Company. After the third act there was a flower show on stage in Dame Melba's honour.

It was noted that in spite of her rapturous reception Melba was not in good voice,[7] while the use of two languages often produced comic results.[8] Moreover the rest of the cast was not, on the whole, adequate to support the two principals. The production 'gave a glimpse of the institution known as Grand Opera before the war, when names were everything and dramatic truth was held to be of no account in lyric drama.[9] 'We were taken back to the days of the star system,' noted the press, ' with all its shams, of which the mixture of languages was not the least. "Moi et quelques poupées" is a citation still to be heard in the wings.'[10]

One critic calmly observed that 'Joseph Hislop is probably the finest operatic tenor Great Britain has ever produced. The result is Great Britain cannot afford him, save on these special occasions.'[11] His acting was greatly admired.'Mr Hislop was the most convincing Rodolfo I have ever seen. He gives the impression of a struggling and penurious poet. His voice is of the finest quality, full, rich, resonant'.[12] 'The finest performance of the evening,' added another critic, 'was unquestionably that of Joseph Hislop.'[13] 'His singing revealed an outstanding sense of style. Throughout it was expressive and remarkable for its 'richness and freedom of tone, for its perfection of style'.[14]

Joseph's next appearance at Covent Garden was on 26 June in *Tosca* under the baton of Percy Pitt, with Beatrice Miranda as Tosca, 24 year old Muriel Brunskill playing a shepherd boy. Dinh Gilly as Scarpia and Joseph sang in Italian, the others in English. 'Mr Hislop's voice has gained in volume as well as in quality, and he undoubtedly gave the most full throated version of the music that has been heard this season' said *The Morning Post* (27 June 1923). 'He is certainly an acquisition' admitted *The Times* (27 June 1923). Joseph repeated *La bohème* with Edna de Lima as Mimi, Percy Pitt conducting, on 29 June.

During his summer break in Sweden, Joseph revealed to the press that he had been invited to sing at the Metropolitan, but the terms had been such that he had had to refuse.[15] Whether or not this was a diplomatic glossing over of the realities is uncertain. It seems to suggest that he may again have been pricing himself out of the market.

Later that year the British National Opera Company travelled to Manchester's Opera House where Joseph sang Rodolfo on 12 October opposite Miriam Licette. The mixture of languages was not much appreciated by the Manchester audience. Joseph sang entirely in Italian. Mimi mostly in Italian, but she managed to sandwich in a little English in the third act. The rest sang wholly in English. 'It stands to their credit,' grumbled one critic, ' that some of them did not break out into Hindustani or Arabic by way of variation!'[16] Another member of the audience was heard to remark, 'If they want an Italian night, let them have it. But don't monkey with it and turn it into polyglot opera.'[17]

The performance itself was a success. One member of the audience commented that 'if anyone could have reconciled us to this grievous innovation it would have been the magnificent singing and dramatic power of Mr Joseph Hislop as Rodolfo. The delicious "O soave fanciulla", with Miss Licette as Mimi, was sung with a tenderness and artistry that linger in the memory.'[18]

Joseph sang in *Tosca* with Dinh Gilly as Scarpia on 18 October. *La bohème* was repeated in Manchester on 25 October, conducted by Julius Harrison. After the performance Joseph was being interviewed in his dressing-room when there came a knock at the door. 'A gentleman wants to know your weight, sir,' the attendant told him. 'My weight. Why, does he want to lift me?' Mr Hislop asked, astonished. 'No, sir. He wants to compare your weight with Caruso's'. Hislop laughed. 'Ah, yes, of course. Well, I am 11 stone 10 lbs. The others were all fat,' he said, turning to me again. 'And shall you not get fat?' came the question. 'Fat! Why should I? Fancy me, a fat man, as Roméo! No, it won't do'.[19] (It is interesting to note some of Joseph's vital statistics. He was five feet nine inches tall, took a size seven boot and had hands small enough to fit women's gloves. In 1914 his weight was ten stone ten pounds but by October 1928 had fallen again to ten stone three pounds).

Before the end of 1923 Joseph had made a batch of six fine operatic recordings beginning with two from *Lucia di Lammermoor*: 'Tombe degl'avi miei' (DB 695) and 'Fra poco a me' (DB 695). The first has a prominent accompaniment from horn, tuba and drums and gives Joseph the opportunity to use an aggressive swelling tone on 'ingrata', 'deserto' and 'morte'. In the second the voice is warmer and fuller with gathering resolve and an exemplary *messa di voce* (crescendo–decrescendo–crescendo). Also recorded with an orchestra under Julius Harrison was a venomous 'Ella mi fu rapita' (DA 226) from *Rigoletto*, whereas 'Parmi veder lagrime' (DA 226) was under George Byng. Joseph also recorded 'Tu che a dio' but this was not issued.

In the words of the broadcaster John Steane, these records show Joseph as a singer

> who knows the traditional Italian arts: the smooth, well-bound legato style and the art of portamento (the graceful carry-over of one phrase into the next). He was also a complete operatic artist as the recitative shows very well. At this stage in the opera the womanising Duke of Mantua has been cheated of a love-affair. The bird has flown.
>
> His anger bites hard in this recording and then softens for a phrase or two as he sings of the sincerity of his passion. It's a good example of Hislop's command of both the declamatory style and the lyrical.[20]

A month later, on 20 December, Joseph and Julius Harrison were joined by the baritone Dinh Gilly and the tenor William Parnis for a double-sided recording from *Madama Butterfly*: 'Dovunque al mondo' (DB 743) and 'Amore o grillo' (DB 743). In the former we can catch something of the deliberate arrogance and casual vulgarity of his interpretation with the cry 'America for ever!' which did not endear him to Edward Ziegler two years previously. In the latter, jaunty rhythms give way to the thrilling surge of his top notes and the authentic Scots pronunciation of 'whisky' (which Tullio Voghera jocularly pretended had persuaded him to give Joseph the role of Pinkerton in September 1914).

Between 2 and 17 January 1924 Joseph sang in six performances at the Royal Opera, Stockholm, most of them with Greta Söderman – two of *La traviata*, two of *La bohème* and one each of *Rigoletto* and *Tosca*. During *Tosca* when Joseph as Cavaradossi was about to be taken away and shot, his 8 year old daughter Geraldine, who was in the audience, apparently stood up and shouted 'You are not allowed to shoot my Daddy!'[21]

When the Grand Opera Syndicate's Italian season opened at the Royal Opera House (Covent Garden), the British National Opera Company presented *Rigoletto* on 8 February with Joseph, Elvira de Hidalgo as Gilda and Umberto Urbano (with whom Joseph had sung at La Scala the previous year when he replaced Riccardo Stracciari) as the jester. Muriel Brunskill sang Giovanna and Percy Pitt conducted. This was to be Joseph's busiest Covent Garden season, with 12 appearances in all.

The opera was given completely in Italian; although the critics expressed a preference for this arrangement over a 'polyglot performance', they would have preferred it in English. 'The chorus gave us some Italian that would probably be a roaring success in Soho, while the Orchestra chased the leading singers about untiringly, and more than once caught them,' commented one critic sardonically.[22]

'Mr Joseph Hislop, with his beautiful voice and his easy way of soaring over the long phrases of the famous songs was, one felt, really "Il duca", not, as the programme described him, merely "Duke of Mantua". He showed how a North Briton, given the necessary schooling and experience, may acquire the grand manner of the Italian opera-house.'[23] A second *Rigoletto* followed four days later.

By 16 February, Joseph was back in Stockholm for eight operas. Then he sang in a guest appearance in *La bohème* at a Gala performance in the Stora Teater (Gothenburg) on 31 March. This was notable for an incident which captures the abandon typical of Gala performances of that period. Joseph had taken over from the regular Stora tenor, Carl Martin Öhman. Before the house lights dimmed Joseph's wife Karin made a grand entrance exquisitely dressed and wearing white gloves. She took her place, with the whole Asklund family beside her. When Joseph appeared on stage Karin stood up in her seat and waved to him. Joseph immediately blew her a kiss. The audience, fired with enthusiasm for their local hero, thought it a delightful gesture.[24]

Joseph returned to Stockholm for eight nights and immediately had an encounter with the Opera Director – his former colleague, the baritone John Forsell, who was an authoritarian administrator (later Jussi Björling's teacher). Joseph had been engaged to sing des Grieux in Massenet's *Manon* but for some reason Forsell decided at the last moment to put on Boito's *Mefistofele* instead. At this, Joseph lost his temper. In front of Pippi Pettersson in the office he declared that he would punch on the mouth whoever had cancelled *Manon*, even if it was the Opera Director himself! The result was that *Manon* was given after all.[25]

Joseph returned to the Italian Season at Covent Garden. During this time the Lincolnshire tenor Alfred Piccaver (who had established himself as one of the favourites of the Vienna State Opera) was also in the company. Like Joseph, Piccaver had had to go abroad to find employment and fame as a tenor. His voice was powerful, but not of a very alluring quality, and according to one critic, his singing lacked ease and finish.[26] Ernest Newman added that his voice was robust and generally agreeable, but rather hard in the upper register.[27] In comparison with Hislop, Piccaver's artistry was not as marked, and his resources and style utterly different.[28]

Joseph's first role that season was the Duke of Mantua in *Rigoletto* with Cesare Formichi as the hunchback and Maria Ivogün as Gilda under the baton of the Argentinian-Italian Ettore Panizza. Although *The Times* (5 June 1924) found that Maria Ivogün sang with 'coloratura plus musical personality', her voice was a little too light for the broad tones of Cesare Formichi (who was physically too bulky for the part). It was 'a little difficult to think of Mr Hislop as a wicked amorist, but he is an exceedingly fine tenor whose voice satisfies the ear in one famous song after another.'

La bohème followed on 6 June (again under Ettore Panizza) with Selma Kurz as Mimi and Edna di Lima as Musetta. It was noted that in an uneven production sung in Italian Joseph was completely at home, for Puccini's mellifluous tunes seem 'to belong naturally to the rich and unforced quality of his voice'.[29] Ernest Newman however, sounded his usual cautionary note, observing that Joseph 'turned on at will the standardised formulae of the Italian style, but his voice had not always its old ease and suavity.'[30]

Opera in London was in plentiful supply that year. At His Majesty's Theatre the BNOC had presented Debussy's *Pelléas and Mélisande* with Maggie Teyte (once coached in the part by Debussy), Walter Hyde, Norman Allin and Muriel Brunskill, to be followed by *Faust* and *Tannhäuser* (featuring the tenors Tudor Davies and Walter Widdop).

Madeleine Keltie (who had last sung with Joseph in Venice at the beginning of 1923) appeared as Butterfly with Joseph on 9 June in her first

Covent Garden performance. With her control a little uncertain, Joseph's voice made the major effect in the love duet. He was in good form and found no difficulty in filling the large auditorium with graceful tones.[31]

The next day the British National Opera Company (BNOC) also performed *Madama Butterfly* with Maggie Teyte and Browning Mummery. A day later the Royal Carl Rosa Opera at the Scala duly presented its version of the same opera!

Friday 13 June saw Joseph as Alfredo in *La traviata* (the name-part played by Selma Kurz, with Dinh Gilly as the elder Germont). Joseph's voice was 'clear and free and he always seemed to be singing well within his natural powers'.[32] In a lengthy review in *The Sunday Times* (15 June 1924), Ernest Newman allowed himself to be a little frivolous:

> it is as good as a fairy tale to see the crinolines of the women, and the marvellous waistcoats and white ties of the men. Did people really go about once upon a time looking like that? If so, they must have had a social technique that baffles the imagination of today; even Mme Selma Kurz, accustomed as she must be to the marvellous garment, got into difficulties with her crinoline whenever she tried to sit down, and Mr Hislop had an anxious time of it trying to be passionately lyrical with a glass of champagne in his hand. The performance went with delightful ease and polish.

A week later Joseph sang Canio in *Pagliacci* under Antonino Votto. Jane Laval from Paris was the Nedda and the corpulent Cesare Formichi played Tonio in what *The Times* (21 June 1924) described as 'an unconventional reading' and Joseph 'sang with his wonted fervour, though he was scarcely at his best in the Monologue, which sounded strangely as "Vesti la giubba"!'

Three days later, on Monday 23 June, Joseph returned with the Canadian soprano Louise Edvina in *Tosca*, followed by *Rigoletto* with Cesare Formichi as Rigoletto and the Norwegian Eidé Norena making her Covent Garden debut. Joseph had last sung with her at the Nationaltheatret in Oslo in May 1919 when he was Pinkerton to her Butterfly. He and Karin later entertained Mme Norena and her husband under the pergola of their roof-garden, catching up on old times in Scandinavia.

Another *Pagliacci* came on 28 June and then the last night of the season when Joseph again sang Cavaradossi. Although London had had the luxury of three different opera companies playing at the same time, by the last week in June the Carl Rosa was to shut down. The Italian season also came to an abrupt end on 1 July (having been originally scheduled to run till 26 July). The statistics clearly showed that the public (who had flocked to *The Ring* and *Der Rosenkavalier* at the beginning of the season) had become jaded with the Italian repertoire. Nevertheless, as the contralto Marguerite d'Alvarez observed in a letter to *The Daily Telegraph* (21 June 1924), 'opera can only be given in something near perfection by a company attached to a permanent opera house.'

In December Joseph made two fine operatic recordings under Julius Harrison. From *Un Ballo in Maschera* by Verdi (long omitted from the repertoire in Sweden because it dealt with the assassination in 1792 of the founder of the Royal Swedish Opera, King Gustav III), came 'Ma se m'è forza' (DB 822) with virile, baritonal notes driven from the chest up into a ringing higher register. Then from Ambroise Thomas' *Mignon* (which he would sing in the Opera House only in 1936 in the twilight of his career) a delightful 'Ah, non credevi tu' (DB 822), full of pathos and masterly decrescendo, holding a note like a filament of silk. These were the last acoustic recordings Joseph made before the electric process was introduced around 1925.

Remembering that after his last performances in French with Amelita Galli-Curci at the Chicago Auditorium in 1920 he had decided to work in French-speaking countries one day, Joseph judged it to be the right time to visit Belgium. Arriving in Brussels, he paid a visit to La Monnaie, the great opera house, with his secretary Spencer Clay and the representatives of his agents, the Concerts Ysaye. The managers of La Monnaie were very curious about the Scottish tenor. They knew that he had performed in French, and he knew that, provided he impressed them in the audition, the theatre would open its doors to him. He did and it did.

Joseph's first Brussels appearance was in *La bohème* on 12 February 1925. 'The large audience which crowded the theatre on Thursday evening were delighted by the dramatic singing of the new tenor. . . . Endowed with a well-placed voice with a very big range, Mr Hislop played the leading role with mastery of stage-craft, controlling his dramatic effects as well as his voice, graduating the latter with highly expressive dynamics where his vocal power never showed itself in sudden bursts and where the carefully-etched touches were achieved with charm and delicacy.'[33] Joseph was considered to have acted with a special individuality in some of his scenes, particularly the last scene of the third act which affected the audience deeply.[34]

Early in March he sang Gounod's *Faust* and Massenet's *Manon* at La Monnaie, before giving four performances with the soprano Selma d'Arco at the Théâtre Royal in Liège of *Tosca*, *Manon* and *La bohème* at the beginning of April.

Reaction in the press to his Cavaradossi was uniformly flattering. 'This artist is endowed with a voice that is free and clear, with perfect evenness of quality throughout the range'.[35] 'As an actor he lives the role, with great naturalness and highly refined artistry.'[36] His 'E lucevan le stelle' was particularly admired; his voice reflected the robust solidity of the North while his singing was free from the liberties in rhythm which Italian tenors so often took.[37]

While *Tosca* had been sung by Mme Martha Horwa, Selma d'Arco joined him in *La bohème*. If houses for the former had been less than full, the reputation of the new Scottish tenor drew enormous crowds for the latter, producing a 'deafening success' in the auditorium.[38] Joseph's elegance of style and real sincerity, together with the fact that he never forced his voice in a demanding role, drew favourable comparisons with the Russian tenor from the Bolshoi, Dimitry Smirnoff, who had sung in Liège the previous season.[39] It was obvious that Joseph Hislop 'had the soul of a poet and that he had studied in depth the psychology of the role'.[40]

Selma d'Arco was a delicious Mimi. She and Joseph sang in Italian while the rest of the cast used a French translation. The overwhelming impression left by Joseph's Rodolfo was 'soberness of action, simplicity of gesture and depth of understanding'.[41]

His first appearance as the Chevalier des Grieux (singing in French) in Massenet's *Manon* was postponed through illness. When it came, the general opinion was that Joseph was not entirely at ease in the French language (as he had been in Italian, with its open vowels). Perhaps the effects of his indisposition were still evident. In 'Le Rêve' he was less mellifluous than the tenors Léon David or Edmond Clément, yet in the St Sulpice scene he showed a rare vocal heroism .[42]

The opera was given before an audience wild with enthusiasm. The French General Moisson was in the auditorium, as was the well-known violinist, Eugène Ysaye. From the balcony a large notice printed in English was lowered, reading 'Hurrah for Hislop! When shall we see you again?' The correspondent of *La Wallonie* (31 March 1925) was astonished to hear Joseph sing 'Le Rêve' in 'chest-voice at half volume without losing resonance, a rare tour de force.' Particularly remarkable was the richness of Joseph's costumes, his elegance and distinction. Again, it was noticed that he *lived* the role of des Grieux.[43]

On 4 April he made his debut at the Théâtre Royale, Antwerp as Rodolfo, opposite the Mimi of Selma d'Arco. The Saturday Gala was to raise funds for the Belgian war-wounded. In spite of the frenetic acclaim of the large audience Joseph gave no encores. His droll Anglo-Saxon humour in the role reminded one critic of Charlie Chaplin.[44] His voice, however, was warm, flexible and expressive. Yet the presence of his own prompter was noted with some disapproval as was the fact that Selma d'Arco seemed to be holding herself in check so as not to detract from Joseph's dramatic effectiveness.[45]

The same day a telegram from Ottavio Scotto at the Hotel du Louvre in Paris had arrived at Joseph's rooms in the Hotel Métropole (Brussels) asking him to go there to finalize the contract for a performance of *Roméo et Juliette* in French at the Colón, Buenos Aires. Joseph was in Paris three days later.

On 22 April Joseph took part in a memorable *Pagliacci* at La Monnaie. As Canio he was not averse to appearing in a plain and even faintly ridiculous costume. He disarranged his hair in the final tragic scenes of the opera to reveal a balding skull. It was a Gala Performance in aid of the Olympic Games performed before the Belgian Royal Family.

> 'I was singing Canio,' Joseph remembered. 'I was in good voice and good condition. The performance went very, very well until we reached the last scene. There I took a knife from the table threatening Nedda and saying to her "I must know the name! What is your lover's name?" I took the knife and was about to plunge it into her, but unfortunately the knife was razor-sharp so I had to let it slide up through my hand to avoid hurting Nedda – I cut myself badly.
>   There was a lot of blood, but I seized the opportunity and smeared the blood on my face and clothes so that I looked like a butcher! The children in the auditorium were crying and a cold shiver ran through the whole theatre.'[46]

It was an artistic triumph but Joseph retained the scar for the rest of his life. In Antwerp his Cavaradossi on 24 April was a triumph. However, two later performances had to be cancelled due to Joseph's illness.

With his three-month contract in Belgium over at the end of April 1925, Joseph began to prepare for his forthcoming guest appearances in Buenos Aires at the Teatro Colón early in July.

In the middle of May, he was back in Brussels at La Monnaie where he opened on the 17th. Two days later his London agent, the American Sidney Hecht ('Sid'), husband of the soprano Selma d'Arco, telegraphed him regarding the negotiation of future contracts. Hecht had been writing earlier to Ottavio Scotto, the manager of the Italian opera company with which Joseph was to appear at the Colón. The date of sailing from Genoa had been brought forward by nine days to 2 June. Hecht endeavoured to persuade Scotto to compensate his client for loss of earnings, including fees for two farewell concerts in Scotland and a day at Hayes to make some new gramophone records.[47]

Joseph, his wife Karin and Sidney Hecht travelled by train to Genoa, sailing First Class on the *Duca d'Aosta* on 2 June at 3 o'clock in the afternoon along with the other (mainly Italian) members of the Scotto company. After seeing them off Hecht took the train for Milan and next morning called on Signora Bonini who received him graciously and enthused about Joseph's South American engagement. She said Scotto was a decent fellow and on the level. All Milan knew about Joseph's 'great success in Belgium.'[48]

Back in Paris Hecht heard Hackett, Queena Mario and Defrère sing *La traviata* in the barely half-filled Gaieté Lyrique: 'Since I heard Hackett your stock has gone up fifty points. He cannot sing *La traviata* to please me. Wise tells me that he had heard several of the operas and that the houses are always poor. Wise says you are the best he ever heard. . . . Harold Holt told me that

As Canio in Leoncavallo's *Pagliacci*, Stockholm 1919

the McCormack concert for tomorrow has had a very poor advance sale. He blames it on the hot weather.'[49] Hecht was also in touch with Joseph's agent in Belgium regarding Belgian engagements for the following autumn.

Twelve days later Hecht wrote with news of a business venture. He had established a new firm, Hislop, Hecht & Brown Ltd, with offices at Victoria Street (London). The company was being registered and business stationery printed. The business was an agent for Arco Sealit, a patent asbestos roofing sealant manufactured in Italy by Selma d'Arco's family.[50]

Joseph rehearsed on board the *Duca d'Aosta*, while from London Sidney Hecht continued to send selective extracts from the newspapers:

> The press is the worst I have ever read. See what they say: *Lindi* 'A very ordinary Cavaradossi. High notes are the best but in the lower register has a tendency to wobble badly and cut his phrases. Why does this man shout so? He should have learned at rehearsal that Covent Garden acoustics do not require such roaring. A very awkward and unfinished figure. A strong voice but . . . where are the great tenors?' *Borgioli* 'A small weak voice and did not seem sure of himself'. *Lappas* 'He added another to the list of disappointing tenors'. There you are, Joseph, three men down and two to go: Lo Giudice and Lauri-Volpi. I understand that Volpi is coming the third week and will do *Andrea Chénier*.[51]

Meanwhile, leaving Europe at the height of summer, the *Duca d'Aosta* had called at Gibraltar before heading out into the Atlantic. There, on 12 June the ship crossed the Equator, an occasion marked with daytime frolics and evening festivities.

Sailing south the ship berthed at Rio de Janeiro, Santos, and then in Montevideo before the Scotto company disembarked at Buenos Aires. It was in mild winter weather on 25 June that Joseph and Karin booked into the luxury Plaza Hotel.

The 18th Colón Opera season began on 1 July 1925 with Verdi's late masterpiece, *Falstaff*. Public reaction was extremely favourable: 'It has been many years since so musical, so well-balanced and such an integrated version of an Italian opera was presented. The event deserves special mention.'[52]

Under Tullio Serafin the orchestra, composed of local players augmented by instrumentalists from Europe, gave evidence of long and careful rehearsal. Cesare Formichi took the title role, Claudia Muzio was Alice, Leone Paci was an incisive Ford, while Adamo Didur showed that even in a part as small as that of Pistol, a good actor and singer can make an impact. Singing opposite Joseph was Laura Pasini as Nanetta. A critic observed that 'Joseph Hislop, a young tenor new to Buenos Aires, who played Fenton, sang his part (with that of Nanetta, the only lyrical roles in the opera) with great taste. His voice is of pleasing and refined quality.'[53]

Claudia Muzio and Tullio Serafin signed Mrs Hislop's autograph album and, as Karin was expecting her third child, Cesare Formichi added in

French that he hoped 'the little Caesar becomes a great artist like his father Joseph, but with a superb basso profondo voice!'[54]

Dispatches came fast and furious from the garrulous Sidney Hecht. 'Lauri-Volpi appeared in *Andrea Chénier* last week and here is what the press says: *Observer* "A clear and strong voice but without special beauty. Sounds too forced and without sweetness." *Standard* "Went suddenly and violently out of tune during an important passage." *Westminster Gazette* "Would have pleased his hearers more if he had not forced his high notes so persistently." '[55]

On Sunday 5 July Joseph made his South American debut as Alfredo in *La traviata*. He was scheduled to share the role with Beniamino Gigli, who was to sail from Europe in a week's time. 'The tenor José Hislop did the role of Alfredo more than justice' commented *La Prensa* (6 July 1925). 'His voice has none of the extremes of power or passion. However, he sang with taste and acted convincingly.' Claudia Muzio impressed once again with the beauty of her voice and her intelligence, while Giuseppe de Luca sang Père Germont with a stature which had not been seen at the Colón for many years. A young Gabriel Santini conducted. Afterwards de Luca and Santini also added their names to the autograph album, de Luca ending his saluta-tion. 'I finished the signature with a pencil (the pen ran out). It's a real pig's breakfast!'[56]

Four days later came Roméo, Joseph's most successful role in Argentina, with Ninon Vallin as Juliette, de Luca as Mercutio and Ezio Pinza as Fra Laurence. The opera was sung in French and conducted by Pietro Cimini. *La Nación* (10 July 1925) was enthusiatic about Joseph:

> a singer who confirmed the good impression he made in other roles by the effectiveness of his singing and acting, finding his greatest success in the duet of Act II. Without jolting or astonishing the audience Hislop showed that he has first class vocal quality. His lyric tenor, a little *spinto*, almost seamlessly soft and beautiful, charms the ear and breathes life into the role.
>
> In his open-throated *mezza voce* he is the equal of the best tenors of our day, and it cannot be doubted that within a short space of time we will see him shine in the front rank of international tenors if he continues to study with the single-mindedness which his interpretations demonstrate. His singing of the romanza 'Lève-toi, soleil' and the duet of Act IV are specially memorable.

La Fronda (10 July 1925) was equally approving. 'The young tenor Hislop performed with extraordinary success. On only few occasions have we heard an interpretation of Roméo played with greater dignity, understanding of the character or stage-presence. Very elegantly costumed, dramatically realistic, he sang with poise and security, justifiably sharing the applause given to Madame Vallin.'

Yet another waspish epistle arrived from Sidney Hecht:

> This week, thanks to Dua, I heard Volpi in *Andrea Chénier* and Borgioli in *Rigoletto*. Volpi has a fair middle but screams and forces on his top. He

reminds me of Dua's imitation of Caruso! He sings persistently off-key and his voice is full of tremolo. I cannot imagine how he ever succeeded in getting across at the Metropolitan. . . . In *Rigoletto* . . . Borgioli looked well, but his singing was very mediocre. His voice is very small and in the top he uses a nice girlish falsetto. . . . In *The Telegraph* Robin Legge says that England will never succeed in having real interest in Opera until they avail themselves of the fine artists that England has herself produced and who are compelled to earn their laurels and fees in other lands. He says among other things that no country can boast of producing such great tenors as John McCormack and Joseph Hislop.[57]

In Buenos Aires a second *La traviata* was presented on Saturday, 11 July. On the 14th *Roméo et Juliette* was repeated in honour of the French National Festival in the presence of the French diplomatic corps. This was a particularly successful performance, enthusiastically supported. A third *La traviata* on the 17 July was followed by a repeat of *Falstaff*. Four days later, Joseph made his debut as the young lover Rinuccio in Puccini's *Gianni Schicchi*.

The leading part of Gianni was sung by the finest exponent of the role, Giuseppe de Luca, marvellously made up. The parts of Lauretta and Rinuccio were sung by Laura Pasini and Joseph 'two delightful singers who were applauded by the public for their duet'.[58] 'The audience at the final curtain burst into applause and de Luca, with Laura Pasini and Joseph Hislop and all the rest of the company, had to come forward three times to the footlights (and even a fourth time with Maestro Santini). A very thorough success. The superb theatre was completely packed.'[59]

Joseph had sent complimentary tickets for *La traviata* to the editor of the Buenos Aires English language newspaper, *The Standard*. 'It was a ripping performance and we enjoyed your singing immensely. Perhaps when you are giving *La bohème* you would be good enough to remember me again? Our congratulations upon the reception that the public gave you and which is an honour to you and the Auld Bonnie Scotland for the people of Buenos Aires are a very critical audience.'[60]

On 8 August Joseph again sang in *Gianni Schicchi*. A week later he sang Fenton again before making his South American debut in *La bohème* on 16 August. He repeated that role on the 23rd, his final performance at the Colón. Mimi was sung by Frances Alda, with whom he had sung at the Biltmore Hotel (New York) in December 1921. Giuseppe de Luca played Marcello, Ezio Pinza was the Colline and Thea Vitulli the Musetta. Gabriel Santini conducted. 'To Mr Hislop,' Alda later wrote in Karin's autograph book, 'with the best of good wishes and a happy remembrance of a charming performance of *La bohème*.'

On 18 August a tumultuous reception greeted the arrival of Edward, Prince of Wales. The following evening, he attended the Colón Opera to hear Gigli and Claudia Muzio in Catalani's *Loreley*, in a house crammed with the elite of Buenos Aires society. During the intervals the audience of

3 000 (which included Joseph and Karin) repeatedly cheered the Prince. At midnight there were more celebrations in Joseph's hotel where the Prince danced for some time. Naturally the Scottish tenor and his wife made a point of being introduced.

Soon after his final performance on 23 August, it was time for Joseph to return to Europe. Waiting to see him and Karin off was Signor Fossati, the Master Chief of Claque from La Scala (Milan) whose return fare to Buenos Aires was paid for by a grateful management every year. He had met them when they arrived and now stood with a bouquet of flowers which he presented to Karin. From the deck of the liner Joseph and Karin watched the silhouette of Buenos Aires slip away. They were taking home a large bundle of fan-mail pleading for signed photographs and a young green South American parrot called 'Jock' which loved to perch on his master's shoulder and whistle as he sang!

So ended another chapter of the achievement in a career damaged by Joseph's failure to clinch a deal with the administration at La Scala two years previously, a good offer by any standards since it would have opened the gateway to the New World which he craved and which would be denied him. Nevertheless Joseph continued to enrich his vocal and dramatic technique. He was gradually enlarging his repertoire, though not perhaps as rapidly as some tenors. He worked hard to compensate for his La Scala misjudgement by winning golden opinions all over Europe. At the end of the day, however, such successes could never compensate for his failure to establish a more permanent working relationship with Arturo Toscanini.

References

1. Stockholms Dagbladet, 18 February 1922.
2. Svenska Dagbladet, 21 February 1922.
3. Svenska Dagbladet, 1 March 1922.
4. Eves, G. op. cit.
5. The first British singer to take a leading role at La Scala was the English soprano Elizabeth Billington (1765–1818) who appeared there in the late 1790s.
6. Il Corriere della Sera, 12 April 1923.
7. The Daily Sketch, 2 June 1923.
8. The Times, 2 June 1923.
9. Unidentified newspaper, 2 June 1923, NLS.
10. Unidentified newspaper, 2 June 1923, NLS.
11. The Daily Sketch, 2 June 1923.
12. The Sheffield Telegraph, 9 June 1923.
13. Unidentified newspaper, 2 June 1923, NLS.
14. Unidentified newspaper, 2 June 1923, NLS.
15. Svenska Dagbladet, July (?) 1923, NLS.
16. The Manchester Evening News, 13 October 1923.

17. ibid.
18. ibid.
19. The Manchester Evening News, 26 October 1923.
20. John Steane, *My Ideal Rodolfo*, BBC Radio Three, 12 July 1989.
21. Anecdote told to author by Joseph Hislop jnr.
22. Unidentified London newspaper, 9 February 1924, NLS.
23. The Times, 9 February 1924.
24. Anecdote told to author by Joseph Hislop jnr.
25. Unidentified Stockholm newspaper, 'Stjärnspel och Stjärnsmall', 5 April 1924.
26. The Westminster Gazette, 9 June 1924.
27. The Sunday Times, 8 June 1924.
28. The Monthly Musical Record, 1 July 1924.
29. The Times, 7 June 1924.
30. The Sunday Times, 8 June 1924.
31. The Times, 10 June 1924.
32. The Times, 14 June 1924.
33. La Libre Belgique, 14 February 1925.
34. ibid.
35. La Gazette de Liège, 17 March 1924.
36. L'Express, 17 March 1925.
37. Le Journal de Liège, 17 March 1925.
38. La Gazette de Liège, 18 March 1925.
39. ibid.
40. La Meuse, 18 March 1925.
41. ibid.
42. Léon David (1867-1962), Edmond Clément (1867–1928).
43. Le Journal, 31 March 1925.
44. Le Matin, 5 April 1925.
45. Le Métropole, 6 April 1925.
46. Berg, Ulf Börge (1972) 'Carusos kronprins', ALB.
47. Letter 6 May 1925.
48. Letter 6 June 1925.
49. ibid.
50. Letter 15 June 1925.
51. Letter 22 June 1925.
52. La Prensa, 2 July 1925.
53. ibid.
54. Autograph album, 5 July 1925 (in private possession).
55. Letter 5 July 1925.
56. Autograph album, 5 July 1925.
57. Letter 11 July 1925.
58. Il Giornale d'Italia, 22 July 1925.
59. ibid.
60. Letter 19 July 1925.

6   Opera (1925–1937): 'You sang like a god yesterday'

'FAMOUS TENOR'S MUSICAL PARROT' read the welcome home given to Joseph in January 1926 by *The Birmingham Post* (7 January 1926) under a photograph of the young green parrot called 'Jock' perched cheekily on his master's shoulder. Joseph was tired after his long voyage from Buenos Aires and the excitements of the Teatro Colón, but now his thoughts were turning to North America. From the Royal Crescent Hotel in Brighton, where he had gone for a short break, Joseph wrote to his friend the Swedish director, Harald André, then in America:

> I cabled you yesterday as follows 'Hecht has written Gatti-Casazza offering me for next season. Please see him and say all you can'. Hecht intimated in his letter that I would be quite glad to sing during the first season for a lower fee than we hoped to get eventually and which Hecht claimed I was worth.
>
> I simply must get back to America. It is quite ridiculous for a singer of my class to cut such a wonderful continent from my vision. The concert field offers such vast scope for me in America but, as my heart is in Opera, and furthermore, as the Metropolitan or the Chicago houses are the only real ways of coming back, we must impress on their directors that I am worth twice as much money as they might think of offering. The principal thing is to get back and to be well presented during my early appearances.[1]

While waiting for developments in the USA, Joseph sang for the first time in France, at the Opéra-Comique in Paris. Opening on 26 March 1926 in *La bohème* with Yvonne Brothier as Mimi, he was probably the first British tenor to sing the part of Rodolfo in France. 'It is no exaggeration to say that the audience was overcome by the magnetism of his remarkable voice' wrote one critic. 'Warm, powerful, easily produced as only the Italians can, Mr Hislop's voice reminds one nostalgically of Caruso's.'[2] Joseph sang in Italian, the rest of the cast in French. 'Mr Hislop's voice is robust. He sings with open tone up to F natural and the higher notes expand strongly into full, powerful resonance' observed Pierre Maudru.[3]

Putting on make-up at the Opéra Comique, Paris 1926

The Daily Express (27 March 1926) reported that 'Joseph Hislop, the first British artist to sing at the Opéra Comique, in Paris, scored a brilliant success in the role of Rodolfo in *La bohème* this evening.' 'The theatre was packed,' the report continued. 'After "Che gelida manina" came a burst of applause which continued for some minutes. In spite of repeated shouts for an encore the conductor refused to give one. After the first act Joseph had to take half a dozen curtain calls.'

He stayed in a hotel near the L'Avenue de l'Opéra and, in what free time he had, enjoyed the company of the conductor Georges Lauweryns and the Russian-American basso, Edward Lanko, sampling the delights of the well-known Italian restaurant, Poccardi.[4] On the greyish-yellow billboards of the Opéra-Comique the name 'HISLOP' was written in large letters. Life was full of activity for Joseph. 'Look, here's a telegram which I've just received from Barcelona,' he told a journalist, 'and here is a contract for a tour of South America next season. As you can see, this copy has already been signed by my manager. But on this one my signature is still absent. One has to choose wisely.'[5] In the event he did not sign.

A second performance of *La bohème* followed on 31 March; then on 3 April Joseph opened in *Werther* with Lucy Perelli as Charlotte, Lauweryns again conducting. Louis-Charles Battaille found that Joseph's thin and rather bony physique gave an impression of

> dryness and coldness in his personality which he softened from time to time by a warm tone and a charming *mezza voce*. His rather hard vocal production did not leave him enough freedom in his higher notes which he compressed and reached only with the application of much force. Nevertheless, his timbre is easy on the ear, especially when he allows the quality of the voice to be heard. Mr Hislop can certainly class himself as one of the good Massenet tenors.[6]

His French accent was also admired.

After six performances of *Werther* his last appearance in Paris was as Mario Cavaradossi in *Tosca*. Floria Tosca was played by Madeleine Sybille, with Henri Albers as Scarpia.

Joseph's first recordings by the new electric process took place at Hayes in May 1926. 'O Mimi, tu più non torni' from *La bohème* (DB 939) and 'Solenne in quest'ora' from Verdi's *La Forza del Destino* (DB 939) were both conducted by George Byng and sung with the baritone Apollo Granforte.

Writing in *The Gramophone* (October 1926), Compton Mackenzie rated the recordings as 'a really first-class disc. I doubt if Hislop ever sang better on any record, and the voices suit each other to perfection. The recording is something like the best vocal recording to date.' Herman Klein added that both were

> sung by artists with voices well matched in timbre and strength. One perceives the complete understanding between the two men, the intention to support each other where the voices unite, the effort to make them blend rather than spoil their quality by shouting. The result is an excellent record of both pieces, alike in the singing and the making, while the orchestral accompaniment is quite on the same level of merit.[7]

What neither reviewer could know was the struggle Joseph had to get his share of the microphone from Granforte who insisted on singing as loudly as possible. Only Joseph's perfect timing enabled him to counter the giant voice of the baritone with electrifying high notes.[8]

In the same month came one of the finest Hislop recordings. 'Salut, demeure' from Gounod's *Faust* (DB 944) was made in June coupled with 'Pourqoi me réveiller?' from *Werther* (DB 944). 'The opening of "Salut, demeure" is the loveliest example of *mezza voce* that has been heard from a British tenor since the palmy days of Edward Lloyd,' wrote Herman Klein.[9] 'The whole air is supremely well sung and the high C at the end is magnificent.. . . Ossian's song ("Pourquoi me réveiller?") from *Werther* (Act III),' he continued, 'is one of the most touching pages in the opera and its melancholy charm is abundantly realised in the present instance, thanks to Joseph Hislop's reposeful method and fine tone, supported by the graceful *arpeggiando* of an excellent harpist. The entire record is mechanically fault-less.' In more recent times Lord Harewood added that the piece 'exhibits an aristocratic style and brilliant top A sharps. A fine souvenir of a distin-guished artist.'[10]

Before giving some concerts in Oslo in November Joseph was inter-viewed by the Stockholm press and asked if he liked being world-famous. 'There's always pressure,' he answered thoughtfully, 'continuous awareness so as not to let myself or the audience down. It involves constant work, uninterrupted study, practice and self-control. But it's wonderful to journey round the world singing.'[11]

Soon after, he was off to Barcelona. Travelling by train through Paris, Toulouse and over the Pyrenees, Joseph reached the Catalan capital where the ex-bullfighter and tenor Miguel Fleta reigned supreme. 'El divo FLETA' as the Barcelona press described him,[12] the master of *messa di voce*, was then singing Meyerbeer's *L'Africana* and *Tosca*. During an opera Fleta would accept the calls for an encore by launching into a series of popular Spanish songs. Joseph recalled that, 'after a performance of *La Favorita*, he came on stage and sang Spanish songs at the piano. They tried to persuade me to sing Scots songs after my performance, but I did not think that for that public they would be comparable in effect to Spanish songs sung by Fleta.'[13]

Joseph's debut at the Líceo (Barcelona) was to have been in *La bohème* on 18 November. However, he was prevented from appearing through ill-health. He was scheduled to sing *La traviata* with Gilda Dalla Rizza and his old friend Riccardo Stracciari three times in December. However, what one local paper called 'repentina indisposición' (sudden illness) again forced him to withdraw.[14]

During this period of enforced rest Joseph was able to observe a number of other singers, among them the tenor Alessandro Bonci, who had been in the Chicago Opera Company with him in 1920. 'When Bonci,' Joseph wrote later, 'the world-famous tenor, in middle age and past his best, did not sustain one or two high notes long enough to please the gallery, their boos, whistles and cat-calls hurt him so much that he left Barcelona the following day.'[15]

Joseph returned to Edinburgh to recuperate on 20 January 1927, staying with Karin at the Caledonian Hotel. To an *Evening Dispatch* (21 January 1927) reporter he repeated his weariness at such constant travelling. 'I'm tired, and no wonder. Missed the train from London last night. Been travelling all day.' He changed an approaching yawn into a sigh. 'It's good to be home,' he murmured, staring into the fire, 'but, och, I'm tired!'

A fortnight later, on 10 February, Joseph finally made his long delayed debut at the Líceo (Barcelona) as Rodolfo with the Argentine soprano Hina Spani as Mimi and the baritone Apollo Granforte, with whom he had recently recorded, as Marcello. *La Vanguardia* (11 February 1927) found that Joseph had 'a voice of wide compass with a timbre pleasing in all its registers, executing the high notes of the role with ease, and sustaining them with great taste, for which he was frequently applauded during the whole performance. Mr Hislop, moreover, is as excellent an actor as he is a singer.' A matinée and a last evening performance of *La bohème* brought his contract in Barcelona to a close. Shortly after his last performance he returned to his hotel room and at one in the morning wrote to his mother in Edinburgh.

> Sang and finished my last performance an hour ago. I am glad I came down here again. Just to prove that I could do the job. It is over and that's that.
>
> It has been a very trying time as my general strength has not been quite up to the work. However, having got through this has taken a considerable amount of a rather overpowering load from my mind. I leave tomorrow for Brussels where I will arrive late on Monday evening. I shall sing there on Wednesday.
>
> I am happy to be able to leave with my colours flying because this is perhaps the most trying theatre I have ever been in. I had a most flattering press. Bonci, the famous tenor, had to leave after two performances because of the disapproval of the public, while Ada Sari (you remember, she was on tour with me) was whistled and hissed off the stage. She sang only one performance. It's a great life![16]

The fate of Bonci and Sari had engraved on Joseph's mind the importance of the claque, who in Spain could be especially dangerous. This was because of the proviso in some clauses stating that if the standard of singing by the artists did not reach that expected by the principal conductor or the public, the contract could be cancelled and the artist dismissed – powerful ammunition in the hands of rival singers and their claques!

Joseph appeared next at the Théâtre de la Monnaie in Brussels, first as Mario Cavaradossi on Thursday, 24 February, and on the following Monday as Rodolfo. Three more performances of *La bohème* and two of *Tosca* were given in March, during one of which Joseph was commanded to the royal box and highly complimented by the King and Queen.[17]

Then to Copenhagen at the Theatre Royal during April when he sang *La bohème* and *Tosca* twice each. During the former the audience, which included the Royal Family, clamoured so much for 'Hislop' (whom they already loved from his Tivoli concerts) that the inflexible rules of the house were broken and he appeared in front of the curtain after each act at least three or four times.

Once again it was Joseph's characterization and vocal style that surprised the opera-going public. He would begin by sketching in the character with broad, deft touches, gradually tightening and refining the impersonation as the work progressed towards the climax. At the same time he conserved his great vocal powers for the thrilling 'peaks' of the action. In this he was typical of the *lyrico spinto* tenor capable of rising from purely lyric to dramatic and heroic expression in the opera. It was observed that he underplayed and husbanded his vocal resources, saving his greatest intensity for the dramatic climaxes. His style of acting was unfamiliar to Copenhagen opera audiences. He played Rodolfo larger than life to begin with, with touches of comedy. But in the final scene of Mimi's death his acting had unusual power.[19]

As in *La bohème* he sang *Tosca* in Italian. Here the critics considered that the role gave only limited scope to his talents. In addition, with his slight figure, he was thought not to have captured the full heroic stature of Cavaradossi.[20] Moreover, the suspension of disbelief was rudely shattered when 'the shot painter had to rise from the dead not less than three times during the deafening ovation!'[21]

During his final appearance at the Theatre Royal as Cavaradossi on 7 April, Joseph's agent presented him with a Knighthood of the Dannebrog – a decoration which had just been awarded by King Christian of Denmark for his outstanding achievements in the field of music. This was a considerable honour, especially for a foreigner, and Joseph was enormously surprised and pleased.[22]

From western Denmark Joseph travelled home to Sweden to appear at the Royal Opera in Stockholm for the first time in three years. Starting with *La bohème* on 19 April 1927, he sang Cavaradossi a week later before Prince Gustav Adolf and Princess Ingrid. Anna Edström was Tosca and Carl Richter played Scarpia. After a second *La bohème* Joseph sang Canio in *Pagliacci*.

After the second act of *Pagliacci* an unexpected ceremony took place. The Director of the Opera, John Forsell, presented Joseph with a large laurel wreath decorated with blue and gold ribbons on behalf of the management. The staff gave him a golden lyre, a gesture which delighted the audience.[23] Three days later he was also honoured by the King of Sweden with a Knighthood of the Vasa, First Class (again, a rare distinction for a foreign subject).

This sealed Joseph's bond with the people and culture of Sweden and was to give him a position of honour for the rest of his life. Though decorated by two monarchs, his achievements found no such official recognition in Britain. After the Second World War, when he might have been awarded some kind of honour in the UK, he was already a Swedish citizen.

A recording session for The Gramophone Company followed on 20 June when Joseph joined Piero Coppola who had last conducted him in Oslo in 1919 in *Rigoletto*. At the Small Queen's Hall, Coppola directed the orchestra for Joseph and the delicate china figurine voice of the soprano Lotte Schöne in 'E il sol dell'anima' (DB 1127) from *Rigoletto*. From the skittish opening of the duet Joseph injected a tender lyricism, finely-spun phrasing and a mature fullness of voice.

June 1927 found Joseph back at Covent Garden for one solitary appearance in Britain. His absence from the London season was lamented. *Tosca* on 21 June with Göta Ljungberg (a fellow pupil of Dr Gillis Bratt) and the incomparable Mariano Stabile as Baron Scarpia 'brought the welcome return of Mr Joseph Hislop to the stage of Covent Garden,' wrote *The Times* (22 June 1927):

> and his performance made one wonder why the management had left his engagement to the last week of the season. His is a beautiful voice, with plenty of power where power is needed, in the first duet with Tosca, in the cries of 'Vittoria' in the second act and in the climax of 'E lucevan le stelle' but also a voice of quality without effort.
>
> His singing was lyrical and easy throughout and was marred only by one passage in the first act not perfectly in tune. It seemed to be a momentary accident and a slight one. The soft passages in the final duet showed a feeling for fine phrasing that is rare.

This was praise indeed, for the artists engaged by the London Opera Syndicate that season had included Aureliano Pertile, Francesco Merli and Fernand Ansseau.

Although America still rankled in his mind, Joseph also instructed his Danish agent Richard Rydberg (based at Copenhagen's Summer Tivoli) to negotiate with the Berlin theatrical agent Otto Mertens to secure engagements for him at the Staatsoper and in Vienna, as follows:

> I have received a letter from Mr Hislop in which he asks me to make a contract with the State Opera in Berlin according to the conditions proposed in your letter of 11 January, namely 1 400 marks per performance, including rehearsal.
>
> Of his repertoire I can indicate the following:

Italian	*French*	*Swedish*
Bohème		Bohème
Roméo	Roméo	Roméo
Tosca		
	Faust	Faust
Butterfly		Butterfly
Rigoletto		Rigoletto
Traviata		Traviata
Falstaff		
Aida		Aida
Mefistofele		Mefistofele
Cavalleria		Cavalleria
Pagliacci		Pagliacci
	Manon	Manon
	Werther	
	Carmen	
		Martha

Mr Hislop is at this time studying *Lohengrin* and *Tannhäuser* in the German language, and is willing to learn further and other of the above roles in

German. The most convenient time for Mr Hislop would be in October, November or December of this year, before a great American tour.[24]

At around this period the immensely popular Austrian tenor Richard Tauber was apparently receiving 2 000 marks per concert, but Joseph's insistence on a fee of 1 400 marks per performance (including rehearsals) was not acceptable to Berlin. Numerous communications passed between Rydberg and Mertens, the former pressing for a definite commitment and the latter explaining delays in the negotiations. According to Mertens, the German Stage Society had ruled that no artist, no matter what his importance, should receive a fee greater than 1 000 marks per performance and 200 marks for rehearsals. 'The most important question is that Mr Hislop be introduced in Germany at a first-rate opera house. I think that in a short time the rulings of the German Stage Society will be done away with, and if Mr Hislop has good successes he will surely be paid more.'[25]

Financial matters were eventually settled. The next problem was that of dates. Mertens conveyed Professor Bruno Walter's conviction that only a 'permanent engagement' was of real value to his theatre. He wondered what Mr Hislop's opinion would be concerning a proposed six- or eight-month contract with the Berlin Municipal Opera.[26] After spending some time resting on the west coast of Sweden in a small bungalow at the salty summer paradise of Brottkärr, Joseph sailed to Copenhagen to see Rydberg. However, the idea of being tied contractually for as long as eight months in Berlin did not appeal to him and the engagement was for the time being abandoned.

Joseph then left for England where he had just over a week to refresh himself for two important Covent Garden performances of Gounod's *Faust* with the great Russian bass, Feodor Chaliapin. He later remembered this interlude:

> I took a suite at a hotel in Margate, and, together with my Italian accompanist, Alberto Sciarretti, got down to practise. While we were working one day who should breeze in but Antonio Scotti, the great baritone from the Metropolitan Opera. . . . Although he had sung during nine seasons at Covent Garden and 30 at the Metropolitan he still retained a very strong Italian accent and, when hearing him knock, I called out 'Come in', he entered with a cheery ''Ow are-a you, caro Peppino?'
>
> We naturally went to dinner afterwards and, knowing from the experience of our many performances together that he had not much voice left, I asked him if he was going to sing in the following season at the Met. Whereupon he replied 'Gatti-Cassazza, 'e ask-a me, would I like to sing the next season and I answer 'im, "So long I 'ave the arms and legs, *I sing!*"'[27]

From Margate Joseph made his way back to London to prepare for his appearance at Covent Garden on Friday 22 June 1928 in Gounod's *Faust* with Chaliapin whose electrifying interpretation of Mephistopheles was eagerly awaited by the British public. As it turned out, the scheduled French conductor was ill and had to be replaced by Eugene Goossens, one of the most experienced orchestral directors of his age who had worked before with both Joseph and Chaliapin. Goossens later remembered that, the morning of the performance, he

> had a short piano rehearsal with Chaliapin, who had just arrived from Paris, and discovered that the great man was, as usual, very shaky in the matter of both words and music. He covered up his inaccuracies in both respects by pleading fatigue, but I recalled that some time before, when we had made gramophone recordings together, his French was found to be very sketchy. In note-values he was notoriously inaccurate, and always led conductors at the opera a merry dance in this respect.[28]

To heighten the tension, The Gramophone Company had decided to record live highlights of the *Faust* performance in the Royal Opera House. For this purpose three microphones were placed in the footlights under the proscenium arch, one in the middle (opposite the conductor), and one at each side of the stage. This meant that the thunder of kettle-drums, for example, would drown the soloists as they moved away from the footlights.

The Opera House was packed from floor to ceiling. In the programme the management requested the audience to observe silence during the performance so as to accommodate the recording engineers. There was an air of intense excitement as the curtain slowly went up.

Playing the elderly Faust, Joseph sang with youthful vigour. Chaliapin then appeared but quite failed to create any effect but one of benevolence. The duet which closed the first scene ended with Chaliapin coming in late and sliding off-key at 'A moi les plaisirs.' He bulldozed his way out of trouble by seizing the initiative on the final note, disregarding the beat of the conductor. Only Joseph's iron nerve enabled him to come in on time and so emerge without loss of face from the musical confusion on stage.[29]

In the wings there was consternation. 'When I was leaving the stage after the first scene,' remembered Joseph, 'I ran into Colonel Eustace Blois, the Director of the Opera House and Colonel Williams, the manager of the International Section of HMV, two tall, handsome English gentlemen. I walked up to these two worried men and, pretending to be very annoyed, said "If that big Russian bass says a word too many to me I shall send for a pair of steps, climb to the top rung and kick him in the pants!" That took the worried look away from them and all was well.'[30]

Goossens later recalled that, after what Herman Klein described as 'the dance portion of the Kermesse', Chaliapin missed a lead and, forgetting his words, started extemporizing with some impromptu "la la's". His floundering was obvious to the audience, especially when, to cover it up, he came downstage and started conducting the orchestra, trying to give the impression that I was not playing the music to his liking. I kept on serenely, with undeviating tempo, and paid no attention to him, till he was shortly engulfed by the corps de ballet!'[31]

From the other side of the footlights came a very different impression: 'The whole production got slower and slower, until, finally, in the second scene, Chaliapin, roused to a devilish fury, leaned towards the footlights and made a gesture of violent disapproval towards Mr Goossens. "Plus vite!" he hissed but Mr Goossens refused to hurry. Again Chaliapin brandished his arms at the conductor and with a look of hatred strode away from the footlights. Everyone gasped. The opera, which had been intolerably dull, had suddenly come to life.'[32]

Goossens remained unshakeable when, during the second act, the Russian again erupted and tried to conduct him in the quartet. Chaliapin, infuriated, strode off into the wings at the end of the scene shouting ' Lights, Lights,' as he thought that the stage was too dark; *The Daily Mail* (25 June 1928) correspondent commented that the conductor must have had the most exciting five minutes of his life during the Katerina serenade. Goossens later recalled that Chaliapin's musicianship and French diction were consistently wanting throughout the performance.

Small wonder that Faust seemed very old and tired, and mooned about with rather meaningless gestures. As one patron remarked, 'One felt that nowhere in the opera was he quite happy'. 'Mr Hislop's Faust', wrote Harold Hobson in *The Daily Telegraph* (23 June 1928), 'was in more senses than one overshadowed by the evil genius of the plot. The Scots tenor sang sweetly and well and "Salut, demeure" (which was beautifully accompanied), brought him special congratulations.' It was suggested that his lacklustre interpretation of the acting side of the role may have been deliberate. Perhaps, after all, the effect was intentional and really a feather in Mr Hislop's cap.[33]

Later one of Chaliapin's Russian pupils brought Joseph a translation of the great bass' diary entry for 22 June. It read, 'Tonight I sang with a *real* tenor not a painted doll'.[34] Joseph was delighted with the compliment. He had got on well personally and professionally with Chaliapin. And in spite of all the public controversy the opera was repeated on 26 June with the same cast and conductor. Some years later Joseph was asked to serve on the committee that was formed in Paris to organize a celebration for the anniversary of Chaliapin's 50th year on the stage. He presumed this was at Chaliapin's request. Unfortunately the Russian bass died before the celebrations could take place.

Goossens, for his part, was quite unruffled by the affair in spite of the uproar in the press. Eight days later he and Chaliapin were recording together in the Queen's Hall as if nothing had happened!

The 'Salut, demeure' which emerged from the live recording at Covent Garden was in later life one of Joseph's proudest achievements on disc.

While he would complain that in some of the duets with Chaliapin the kettle-drums were too close to the microphone, nevertheless, he would always point to the high C at the close of this aria as being a perfect example of effortless timing and production.

At the Royal Swedish Opera on September 1928, Joseph made his debut as Don José in *Carmen*, a role he only ever sang again in Melbourne, Australia and in Riga, the capital of Latvia.

December brought two fine recordings made with John Barbirolli at the Small Queen's Hall: 'Che gelida manina' (DB 1230) from *La bohéme* and 'Addio alla madre' from *Cavalleria Rusticana* (DB 1230). Barbirolli had

As Don José in *Carmen*, Stockholm 1929

now known Joseph for a number of years, having been a cellist in the Covent Garden orchestra at the time of the tenor's debut in 1920.

The following year (1929) began with more performances at the Royal Opera in Stockholm. Then it was time for a very special engagement. Joseph's first (and last) appearances in opera in the city of his birth, Edinburgh.

The occasion was unique for another reason. The composer Donald Tovey, Professor of Music at Edinburgh University, had written an opera, *The Bride of Dionysus*, in collaboration with the poet R.C. Trevelyan. In 1914, when the work was near completion, it was to have been produced in Germany, but the outbreak of war put an end to that proposal. It was not until 1918, in fact, that Tovey finished what was then widely anticipated as his masterpiece. Its first performance by the Edinburgh Opera Company was now eagerly awaited by critics, conductors and composers from the great opera centres of Europe (Vienna, Prague, Berlin). No expense had been spared on the production. The scenery and costumes were by Charles Ricketts RA, who had recently been associated with many highly successful ventures. With some slight previous acquaintance with extracts from the opera, the 60 professionals of the University Reid Orchestra were complemented by the 119 enthusiastic and dedicated amateurs of the Edinburgh Opera Company whose numbers were strengthened by professional and semi-professional principals.

The producer of *The Bride of Dionysus* and of the other three works to be presented (Gluck's *Orpheo ed Euridice*, *Pagliacci* and *La bohème*, the latter two starring Joseph) was the American former heldentenor Charles Hedmont. Affectionately known in the Edinburgh Opera Company as 'Daddy' Hedmont, he was a producer of inflexible determination. From the start there were violent differences of opinion over Hedmont's handling of the production of Tovey's opera. His approach was considered by Professor Tovey to be heavy-handed and old-fashioned and Hedmont eventually resigned, leaving the production in the care of a well-known local concert artist, Mona Benson.

Taking advantage of the presence of the national and international press in Edinburgh for the occasion, Sir Thomas Beecham promoted his idea of an Imperial League of Opera. 'Edinburgh,' announced Sir Thomas during the interval from the stage of the Empire Theatre on 24 April, 'is still short of 300 members to secure its annual festival of opera under the Imperial Opera League.' The aims of the League were on the one hand to give greater opportunities for the development of British artists and on the other, to attract back to Britain all those first-rate artists who were at present singing in every country but their own. He added that the finest Scottish tenor ever was an unwilling exile. 'He read in an Edinburgh paper the other day that it was the first occasion on which Mr Hislop had appeared in his native country in an operatic role. If that were true, it was an astounding circumstance, and one which could only occur in this country. If Mr Hislop sang abroad it was not because he particularly wanted to, but because there were opera houses there.'[35]

After the end of the opera Joseph was called upon to make a speech. He endorsed what Sir Thomas had said (as had done on the Monday night after the second act of *La bohème*), appealing for the support of his fellow citizens.

Joseph had originally planned to bring his long-time accompanist, the American Spencer Clay, to conduct him. When the former proved unavailable, Joseph insisted on having one of the finest young British conductors, John Barbirolli. Joseph gave three performances in all, two of *La bohème* and one of *Pagliacci*. He sang in Italian while the rest of the cast used English. 'His voice rang out in easy fullness at the top of those melodic curves that Puccini has so generously provided' (wrote *The Glasgow Herald*, 23 April 1929), 'but it was also tender, quietly rich and full of colour where intimacy is called for. There was the same fullness of detail in the acting which had a subtlety of meaning seldom to be enjoyed in operatic performances.' After the last *La bohème* the principals and conductor were enthusiastically applauded with cheers, handkerchiefs and programmes.

Such a Canio had never been seen on an Edinburgh stage, although in September 1909 Caruso had sung 'Vesti la giubba' (and indeed 'Che gelida manina') at the McEwan Hall. 'This great Scottish singer never takes the stage but he immediately transforms a dead space into a picture that is living and tense,' *The Edinburgh Evening Dispatch* (25 April 1929) commented. 'He has been gifted with a very striking pair of eyes that are mobile to catch and reflect the essential mood of the dramatic moment, and his hands lend an enchantment of eloquent gesture that renders his messages magnetic.'

And then, as quickly as they had come, the echoes of his voice died away and Barbirolli, Beecham and Joseph Hislop were gone, leaving opera in Edinburgh a very fragile bloom indeed.

Following their collaboration at the Empire Theatre Joseph and Barbirolli recorded continuously at the Small Queen's Hall from May to July, producing seven first-rate operatic recordings which included 'E lucevan le stelle' (DA 1063) and 'Recondita harmonia' from *Tosca*, 'Vesti la giubba' (DA 1062) and 'No, Pagliaccio non son' (DA 1062). The 'Flower Song' from *Carmen* was not issued (as Joseph disapproved of his performance), but was later transferred from a private white label recording specially pressed by HMV (now EMI). Two Wagnerian recordings, 'The Prize Song' from *Die Meistersinger* (DB 1351) and 'The Grail Song' from *Lohengrin* (DB 1351), both sung in English, were warmly recommended by Herman Klein.

'The Prize Song' becomes in his hands a veritable love-song, glowing, like the morning it celebrates, with the warmth of sunshine and newly-awakened passion. The tone is vibrant and full, the feeling well controlled, the diction such that one hears every syllable. In the *Lohengrin* 'Narrative' a more sedate note is properly struck, but with a voice no less haunting in its beauty. In both pieces the cantilena is sustained with effortless smoothness and an art free from needless *portamento* or any other kind of exaggeration. The orchestration is admirably treated, under the careful guidance of John Barbirolli.[36]

An interesting footnote comes from the actor Grenville Eves who wrote that 'during the last war, in the autumn of 1943, I was stationed in Glasgow, and went to see my friend Richard Tauber, then appearing in his operetta, *Old Chelsea,* at the Alhambra Theatre. As we were having tea at Richard's hotel the BBC broadcast Joseph Hislop's record of "Lohengrin's Narration", to which we both listened intently. "That," said Tauber, "is one of the most beautiful of voices. The musicianship and interpretation are on the highest level."'[37]

As for 'The Prize Song', the distinguished concert tenor, the late Canon Sydney MacEwan, remembered his friend Count John McCormack commenting to him: 'Sydney boy, nobody sings "The Prize Song" better than Joe.'[38]

A landmark in Swedish opera came when Joseph returned to Stockholm in November 1929. He gave two performances each of *La traviata* and *Tosca* before taking part in the Swedish première of Puccini's *Manon Lescaut* (sung in Swedish) at the Royal Opera in front of the King and Queen. The La Scala (Milan) company had recently had a great success with the opera in Berlin, so Sweden decided to follow suit. Joseph sang des Grieux in this acclaimed first production with Greta Söderman as Manon (with whom he had sung in the 1916 revival of Massenet's *Manon*). 'There was passionate temperament and the joy of singing in every note sung by this Manon and her des Grieux,' wrote one critic.[39] Joseph made 'the strange, erotic idealism believable,' commented another.[40]

After seven nights of *Manon* and two as Canio (with Greta Söderman, conducted by Nils Grevillius) in *Pagliacci*, Joseph, Greta Söderman and Grevillius recorded excerpts from *Manon Lescaut* in a Stockholm hotel (as the recording studios were on strike!) Six recordings in all were made, fresh and full of pathos. As Edward Greenfield commented, this was 'Hislop at the age of 45 singing vividly and with great passion.'[41] These were the last operatic recordings Joseph made.

He returned to Sweden in 1930 to appear at the Royal Opera in *Manon Lescaut* on 5 February and *Carmen* three days later. By 15 May he had crossed the sea to Copenhagen where, at the Royal Danish Opera House, he sang one performance as the Chevalier des Grieux in *Manon Lescaut*. At the end of the opera he was called in front of the curtain five times.

Greta Söderman with Hislop at the Swedish première of Puccini's *Manon Lescaut*, Stockholm 1929

Meanwhile Helmer Enwall, of the International Concert and Theatre Agency, had been in contact with Herr Simon of Wolff and Sachs in Berlin to reach agreement with the Staatsoper for a number of Hislop guest appearances. On this series of negotiations, progress ground to a halt early on, with a note from Herr Simon: 'As a result of financial burdens the Staatsoper is not in a position to consider the engagement of any new members or guest singers. Apart from that, it is not allowed to take on any artists who cannot sing in German.'[42] Enwall added cynically, 'I think this is a remarkably unfair ruling, when you consider that all Italian singers in Berlin are allowed to sing in Italian!' (At this time a converse movement was underway in Britain and America to sing everything in English.)

Joseph would have been expected to sing not only *Tannhäuser* and *Lohengrin* in German (which he was quite prepared to do as he had been in 1928), but also *La bohème*, *Pagliacci* and the rest of his Italian and French repertoire. There was a suspicion that the Germans were really operating a closed-shop for political reasons. This obligation on British singers probably explains why Joseph's operatic repertoire was some 30 operas smaller than Gigli's, for example, who was able to sing everything in Italian.

Back home in Britain, opera continued in stops and starts, with much foreign guesting and precarious funding. Joseph was asked what he thought about the state of opera in Britain. 'I am wholeheartedly in support of Sir Thomas Beecham. He has done more than any man in this country to foster the cause of grand opera and in so doing he has spent a fortune.'[43] Beecham, a passionate apostle of opera, bemoaned the fact that

> Germany has 135 opera houses and 210 permanent orchestras. Italy, poor old Italy under the yoke of Mussolini, 70 opera houses. Paris five in the city alone. London, with 8 000 000 people, has not an opera house, not a permanent institution.
>
> It is the most difficult thing in the world to find a singer, but there are great English singers. They are to be heard, but it is in every other country under the sun. Opera properly done is the most appropriate medium of conveying not only music but other arts to the unsophisticated mind of the average person.[44]

By March 1929 Beecham was bankrupt and at a meeting of his creditors it emerged that since 1927 he had spent more than £15 000 in furthering the Imperial League of Opera, of which he was a tireless advocate, but was very much a voice in the wilderness.[45]

Meanwhile the ever-thorny question of Joseph's future plans arose. He expected to sing in Stockholm. On this subject a letter arrived from John Forsell, Director of the Royal Opera in Stockholm and Joseph's old friend and colleague, as autocratic in his decisions as ever: 'My dear Mr Hislop, welcome home and welcome to us! Mr Grevillius tells me that you don't mind changing *Aida* for *Faust*. I will, however, ask you to stick to *Aida*, partly because we probably will get a better audience and partly because I have promised an excellent Norwegian singer, a Miss Amundsen, to sing with you in the title role'.[46] The next three weeks were spent in preparation for four performances at the Royal Opera House (Stockholm) of *La bohème*, *Aida*, *Carmen* and *Tosca*.

His agent in Paris, Theo Ysaye, pressed him to take up the offer of performing *Werther* in Bordeaux on 18 April, even though the director at Bordeaux was only prepared to offer minimal terms. On the back of Ysaye's letter Joseph scribbled two telegrams in pencil. The first read 'If you consider conditions good will take your advice and accept offer Gala performance. What are maximum capacity receipts?' Later he drafted a second message: 'Unfortunately suffer bad cold now, afterwards many engagements keep me busy Sweden until 10 April. This does not give me sufficient time study *Werther* which not sung since 1926. Under circumstance dare not promise sing *Werther* 18 April. Can you postpone until following week. Terribly sorry inconvenience caused.'[47]

By 1934 Joseph's hopes of appearing again in opera in Britain faded. Sir Thomas Beecham had formed a new syndicate to administer Covent Garden and had spent considerable sums in modernizing the theatre. For the 1934 season, however, he chose to reverse his former policy of nurturing home-grown talent and imported most of his leading singers from abroad.

During late April preparations were made for the Italian Season which was to begin on 30 May with a performance of *La bohème* under Gino Marinuzzi whom Joseph had known in Mary Garden's Chicago company. Joseph had high hopes of being engaged as Rodolfo, but in the event the part was given to Angelo Minghetti.

On 1 May, British Equity sent a letter of protest to the Prime Minister over the employment of six Viennese in the chorus. The letter spoke of 'grave disaffection in the ranks of the profession' over the granting of work permits to foreign singers. Joseph wrote on 6 May to his friend, the producer Harald André at the Royal Opera in Stockholm.

> I should very much like to express some of the disgust that I feel for the unprincipled conduct of Beecham. I have tried to get into touch with the wicked baronet but he has as usual retired behind a barrage of silence. He does not reply to letters.
>
> Judging by the Press you will notice that whatever Beecham does in the theatre is lauded to the skies. The Jewish producer Otto Erhardt, with all the new lighting etc, seems to pass unnoticed. That Beecham and Co are such damned fools is past belief. Naturally I feel rather bitter for being left out, but what can one do![48]

With the exception of a single *La bohème* in Stockholm on 27 September 1935, Joseph did not appear again on the operatic stage until the unforgettable moment in October 1937 when he sang his final four evenings at the Royal Swedish Opera.

La traviata came first on 12 October. The next morning Joseph received the following note from his pupil, the tenor Jussi Björling. 'You sang like a god yesterday. You delighted the ear and the eye. You were just wonderful. The papers think that you were finer 20 years ago, but I believe you are today more impressive than ever! Joseph, it was a marvellous evening.'[49]

Nine days later came *Faust*, then a last *La bohème* with a lingering 'Che gelida manina'; Joseph's own hand was cold with melancholy. Lastly, to complete the circle, the opera in which he had made his debut in September 1914, a final *Faust* in which Sigurd Björling as Mephistopheles offered him the secret of eternal youth.

So came to an end a glittering career on the operatic stage for the former chorister and photoprocess engraver, a career which had catapulted Joseph all over the globe, in which he had partnered the finest international artists as no British tenor had done or has done since.

It is a matter for regret that in his prime Hislop was not invited to sing at Covent Garden more often and that his extraordinary talent was not better appreciated at home. Stockholm audiences heard him in opera on almost 200 occasions, Naples on 30, London on a mere 23. Thus the finest international operatic tenor Britain has ever produced ultimately failed to win the highest accolade which his talent, experience and application so richly deserved.

Because Britain had no established system of identifying and training opera singers Joseph had had to start his career relatively late. From that point he was haunted by the need to achieve success quickly as time was against him. This forced him to take on a punishing workload and to price himself over-aggressively. Besides these factors he was held back by the fact that he was not Italian and had to learn operas in Swedish, Italian and French, which explains why his repertoire was relatively small.

References

1. Letter 1 January 1926, Swedish Royal Opera Archives.
2. Le Soir, 28 March 1926.
3. Comoedia, 28 March 1926.
4. Våra Nöjen, 9 April 1926.
5. ibid.
6. Le Courier Musical, 1926 p. 249.
7. The Gramophone, October 1926.
8. Anecdote told to author by George Donald and Joseph Hislop jnr.
9. The Gramophone, November 1927.
10. *Opera on Record*, Alan Blyth (ed.), Hutchinson 1979, p. 504.
11. Svenska Dagbladet, 29 October 1926.
12. La Vanguardia, 16 December 1926.
13. Eves, G. (1970) 'Joseph Hislop', *Recorded Sound*, April, No. 38.
14. La Vanguardia, 19 December 1926.
15. Eves, G. op. cit.
16. Letter 20 February 1927, NLS.
17. The Monthly Musical Record, 15 April 1927, p. 117.
18. National Tidende, 8 April 1927.
19. Social Demokraten, 4 April 1927.
20. Politiken, 4 April 1927.
21. Social Demokraten, 4 April 1927.
22. Dagens Nyheter, 8 April 1927.
23. Svenska Dagbladet, 29 April 1927.
24. Letter 13 March 1928.
25. Letter 14 April 1928.
26. Letter 15 May 1928.
27. Hislop, J. (1969), 'Some Reminiscences of my life', *78 rpm* February, No. 4.
28. Goossens, E. (1951), *Overture and Beginners*, London, Methuen & Co., p. 255.
29. see recording CR21001 – 1.
30. Hislop op. cit.
31. Goossens op. cit. p. 256
32. The Daily Express, 23 June 1928.
33. The Daily Telegraph, 23 June 1928.
34. Transcript in English (in private possession).
    The International Committee for Chaliapin's Jubilee Celebrations (Paris), Chairman Sir Thomas Beecham, was in the process of organizing several events on both sides of the Channel, including a dinner in London. See Letter of 28 November 1937 from M. Sabline, EMI.
    Archives: F I Chaliapin, Hayes No. 76880.

35. The Scotsman, 25 April 1929.
36. The Gramophone, February 1930, p. 410.
37. Eves op. cit.
38. Letter to author, 10 August 1985.
39. Stockholms-Tidning, 23 November 1929.
40. Stockholms Dagbladet, 23 November 1929.
41. *Opera on Record* 3, 'Manon Lescaut', London, Hutchinson 1984, pp. 211–12.
42. Letter 22 September 1930.
43. The Edinburgh Evening News, 23 January 1931.
44. The Times, 2 October 1928.
45. The Monthly Musical Record, 2 March 1931, p. 85.
46. Letter November 30 1931, Swedish Royal Opera Archives.
47. Letter 5 December 1931.
48. Letter 6 May 1934, Swedish Royal Opera Archives.
49. Letter 13 October 1937, NLS.

7 Opera Tours (1921–1933)

Of all Joseph's varied endeavours perhaps the most unpredictable but the most exciting was touring with a large opera company, travelling many hundreds of miles for single-night performances. To be a member of a travelling company living and working together, often in cramped quarters, with improvization and crisis a way of life, was invaluable experience for the emerging tenor. Probably the most enjoyable part of the touring life was the spirit of camaraderie which inevitably built up among artists who knew they had to rely totally on one another, jointly savouring triumphs or suffering humiliations.

Joseph's first taste of touring came when he joined Antonio Scotti's Second Transcontinental Tour in the autumn of 1921, shortly after Enrico Caruso's death. The Scotti tour was to cover some 6 000 miles, presenting 15 operas in 14 cities of the United States and Canada. The scenery and effects were from the studios of the Metropolitan Opera (insured and bonded by Scotti), while the orchestra of 65 players, the 58-strong chorus and 24 ballet dancers had all been recruited from full-time Metropolitan Opera personnel.

A fortnight after he landed in America Joseph boarded the distinctive sleek yellow Pullman carriages of the Scotti Opera Company as it left New York via Chicago to pick up members of the Chicago Company on 5 September. Then the train set off on a week-long journey to Seattle to perform in the city's Metropolitan Theatre. Joseph appeared as Cavaradossi on the second night with Scotti as Scarpia; the local girl, Alice Gentle, always popular in her native Northwest, revealed for the first time the full measure of her superb gifts. Scotti was a rapacious, cold-hearted, uncompromising – yet courtly – villain.[1]

According to the press Joseph sang with admirable musical comprehension and disclosed a tenor voice of exceptional quality and volume, reaching the climax of his interpretative endeavours in a moving and impassioned rendering of the aria 'E lucevan le stelle'. His opening, 'Recondita harmonia', was excellent and in the duets with Alice Gentle he again proved to be a vocalist of uncommon charm.[2]

From Seattle the Scotti Company sped south along the Pacific coast to San Francisco to fulfil a two week engagement at the Exposition Auditorium. Seating 8 000 in a wedge-shaped hall with a balcony, it was not ideal for opera. Over the two weeks the Company took $27 000; seat prices ranged from $2 to $6, the higher rates being charged on Gala performances or when the American soprano Geraldine Farrar (who had been romantically linked with Scotti) sang.

Joseph appeared as Rodolfo opposite the Mimi of Queena Mario in a Saturday matinée on 24 September. Playing Marcello was Scotti and the Musetta was Anna Roselle. Fulgenzio Guerrieri was the conductor. 'I never saw a lovelier Rodolfo and Mimi than Joseph Hislop and Queena Mario', wrote the critic in *The San Francisco Examiner* (25 September 1921); 'silhouetted by the half-light, they looked like proud lovers in a Rembrandt painting. I have seen a score of Rodolfos in my life, but not one who looked the young poet better than Hislop. And he sang like a lover. That is to say, he is an artist to the fingertips.'

Joseph's black costume caused some comment in the audience. He explained the reasoning.

> You expect, probably, to see me in full, checked trousers, velvet jacket and flowing tie. Well, I have played the part in such nondescript attire. But the black garment is really a costume of the period around 1830. . . . Remember too, that the poet Rodolfo speaks of having a rich uncle. He gets a little money now and then and can rise above the nondescript in clothing. Another point is that the black costume I wear supplies a contrast for that of Marcello.[3]

Among the public relations exercises carried out by members of the Scotti Company in San Francisco was a wireless telephone concert given by Queena Mario, Joseph, the baritone Mario Laurenti and Myrtle Schaaf. The quartet stood in a sound-proof booth and sang into a wireless microphone above their heads so that their voices could be transmitted to listeners 1 000 miles away and to 50 liners out at sea.

On being asked for advice to young aspiring singers, Joseph replied that a singer should feel the vibrations of the vocal chords throughout the entire range of the voice. The resonance of the G string of the violin should be heard in every tone.[4]

On Monday 26 September Joseph sang Rodolfo again with Queena Mario in a double-bill with *L'Oracolo* by Leoni, the latter with José Palet and Scotti who won another triumph with his realistic and intense impersonation of the sinister Chim Fang. Joseph was thought to be in splendid voice, singing with lyric fervour and compelling pathos.[5] His voice, though not of the clarion type or of heroic dimensions, was thought to be exactly suited to the role and to the music that is assigned to the young writer of verse. 'It has sweetness and warmth in its quality, and its charm was indisputable'.[6]

The Duke of Mantua in *Rigoletto*, San Francisco 1921

Riccardo Stracciari was Rigoletto to Joseph's Duke of Mantua the following evening, with Angeles Ottein as Gilda and Alice Gentle as Maddalena. In the local press a cartoon character, Doc Pheeney, was shown aspiring to rival Joseph. Joseph's final San Francisco appearance was during a Gala

Performance on Sunday 2 October when he sang Act III of *La bohème* with Queena Mario.

Then it was south again, past Monterey and Santa Barbara to Los Angeles where the Company stayed for a week, appearing at the Mason Opera House where their presentation of *Aida* was a triumph. In *La bohème* too, 'the intelligence displayed by Joseph Hislop as Rodolfo was an outstanding factor. He showed the reserve of real artistry, giving to the role a definite new character. His singing was lyrically fine. His voice does not astonish by any brilliance but is used with discretion.'[7] Scotti as Marcello employed his skill as an actor to telling effect.

A second wireless concert was arranged on the roof of Hamburger's on 6 October from a radio station installed by engineers from the Leo J Meyberg Company, consisting of a five-watt phone set with a day range of 1 000 miles. Joseph sang 'La donna è mobile', Queena Mario 'Voci di Primavera' and Anna Roselle of New York 'Musetta's Waltz'.

A final performance of *Rigoletto* on 8 October with Riccardo Stracciari, Joseph and Agnes Ottein finished the Scotti Company's Los Angeles offerings.

The Pullman carriages headed north again past Las Vegas to Salt Lake City, the Mormon capital of Utah, where Scotti presented *Carmen* and *La bohème* on 10 October (the latter with Joseph, Scotti and Queena Mario). Then east to Denver where a few aspects of their performance of *Manon Lescaut* on 11 October – delayed for over an hour by a railroad accident – were found to be 'quite laughable'.[8] However, the Denver audience found *Tosca* to be sung superbly, brilliantly, gloriously by Joseph, Scotti and Alice Gentle. Joseph won instant favour in the first act and reached new heights in the letter aria in the final act. He had 'youth, an attractive appearance, a glorious voice and gave the impression of a highly developed intelligence.'[9]

Further east went the Scotti train. First Omaha (13 October), then Kansas City, (where Joseph had sung exactly seven months previously), on the 14th and 15th. 'Its locomotive seeming to chase the two tattered white flags at the front, when the special Missouri Pacific train from Omaha eased in to Kansas, the station business manager sent the Pullman into a siding to give the artists (Scotti, Agnes Ottein, Stracciari and the others) time to sleep. Joseph, a tall, slender man in grey business suit and brown hat, carrying his own bag and raincoat (refusing aid), alone got off the train. Striding briskly, he commented that the success of the company had been acceptable elsewhere, and walked up the stairs 'just like any human being'. He could have been any typical dapper businessman.'[10]

Although Queena Mario sang Mimi on 15 October while suffering from a severe case of laryngitis, her singing showed no trace of throat trouble. Greek Evans was the Schaunard, Anna Roselle the Musetta. As Rodolfo, commented one critic, Joseph:

sang as few tenors ever sing, with his heart in his chest and his brain in his head. Almost perfect voice production permitted him to make lyric moments melting and dramatic moments vocally tremendous. His last rush across the stage with the realization of Mimi's death upon him was the sort of acting that Wagner wanted for his music drama.[11]

Following a production of *La bohème* in Davenport on 17 October, *The Davenport Democrat* (17 October 1921) noted that Joseph had 'been called "the successor to Caruso", his fine voice having certain warm qualities that suggest the famous Italian.' From Davenport to St Paul where Joseph sang Rodolfo on the 20th in a matinée performance. Two days later, the yellow Pullmans of the Scotti troupe slipped into Milwaukee.

In an interview with *The Milwaukee Journal* (22 October 1921) Scotti gave his considered verdict on the much-debated question of 'Caruso's Successor'

Scotti was suave and courtly. His clear-cut face and bright, dark eyes clouded over as one spoke of Caruso. His friend of years. "I can't talk of him. It is too close. But this talk of someone taking his place, that is nonsense. No one will ever fill his place in America. It is bad judgement even to suggest it. He was too many sided in his art. He had worked so long to make the place that he filled and it is now impossible for anyone to occupy it."

In Milwaukee, the Scotti Company presented *La Navarraise* with Alice Gentle and Morgan Kingston and *La bohème* with Queena Mario, Joseph, Scotti as Marcello and Anna Roselle. Joseph's 'gorgeous' voice took the house by storm. 'It is such a superb organ', commented *The Milwaukee Journal* (22 October 1921), 'of such luscious quality, of such unlimited power and produced with an ease that we had almost come to believe a lost art. He is moreover an actor of distinction, who absolutely looked like a poet, a thing as interesting as it is novel.'

Next a day's stop at Toledo, before moving north to Toronto in Canada where Joseph appeared with Queena Mario in a matinée of *La bohème* on 26 October. Toronto had recently heard Frances Alda and Giovanni Martinelli sing the love duet at the close of the first act. Joseph and Queena Mario stood the comparison well:

To Mr Hislop the chief honors of the production were awarded. . . . He has a vibrant voice, smooth, finished vocalisation and an expression that can scale the heights of passionate love. Mr Hislop brought the duet to a rapturous climax with the 'O Soave Fanciulla'. The impression he made was so great that the audience broke in upon the duet before it was finished. Hislop proved great. A most satisfying artist.[12]

Although he had a fairly heavy cold which he managed to conceal, for *The Toronto Star* (27 October 1921) it was Joseph's innovations in costume which intrigued. 'Rodolfo looked different from others we have seen. Hislop admits that he changes the garb in almost every town where he sings, keeping, however, to the traditional vogue of 1830. He declines to wear the bald pate and the chin fringe of whisker and as a result he looks like a Scots theologian posing as a Bohemian. Until he sings and then the cold attic studio vibrates with a tenor voice of wonderful beauty and power.'

In Montreal on 28 October 'it was the young tenor, Mr Hislop, who set everyone talking. With a voice of perfect equality throughout its entire scale, a voice of appealing timbre, smooth, warm and of ample strength, with natural histrionic ability and a stage presence of more than usual magnetism.'[13] Queena Mario was singing Mimi while Riccardo Stracciari was the Schaunard.

Three days later the Scotti Company was in Washington at the National Theatre for an afternoon performance of *La bohème* before an audience that filled every seat and all available standing room. It was an audience, also, appreciative to the point of enthusiasm. 'Applause began before the last note of each number died away.'[14] Queena Mario was on home ground, having appeared in Washington in previous seasons with the San Carlo Opera. The production as a whole was applauded, as was Joseph's 'tenor voice of sweetness' and the fact that he sang with ease and finish.[15] From Washington the Company went to Baltimore. The Second Transcontinental Tour of the Scotti Opera Company ended in New York, where it had begun, on 2 November.

During the kaleidoscopic, ever-changing vistas of this first long transcontinental tour, Joseph had made many friends in the operatic fraternity and had thrilled not a few hearts across the footlights. This collaboration with artists from the Metropolitan thus led to happy memories but no engagement in New York.

Operatic touring did not come Joseph's way again until 1927 when he went to Australia and used his position as an international artist to promote the idea of Australian opera. While working this concert circuit Joseph was invited to adjudicate at an audition in the Theatre Royal (Sydney) for over 200 aspiring opera singers from whom he was able to select six as suitable for further training.[16]

In an interview with *The Sydney Morning Herald* (26 October 1927) Joseph urged Australian music-lovers to organize annual three-month seasons of opera in Sydney and Melbourne. 'You have the voices here. That you have a musical standard I have discovered from my concert experiences.'[17]

During his 1931 tour of Australia he continued this theme in a long article in the *Melbourne Herald* (27 June 1931), entitled 'Grand Opera as an Australian Industry'. Joseph posed the question

> What does opera do for a city like Melbourne, which is growing out of the utilitarian stage of all newer cities into a realization of the value of things that cannot be weighed and measured? It gives it very definitely an orchestra, a very necessary thing. For, however one admires the excellence and the

ingenuity of tinned music, it is to actual music as artificial silk is to the real thing. An opera house plays a tremendously important part in the community.

In August 1931 a three-week season of opera took place at The Theatre Royal (Melbourne) under the auspices of J.C. Williamson, whose representative, Claude Kingston, saw Joseph's participation in the venture as an important step in the work of establishing native Australian opera:

> Professor [later Sir] Bernard Heinze, then Ormond Professor of Music at the University of Melbourne, decided with a fine contempt for economic obstacles that time was ripe for Australians to run a grand opera season of their own. The Firm agreed. So Bernard and I formed a company and, rather timidly, asked Hislop if he would come in. He consented without a moment's hesitation and flung himself into the venture boots and all.[18]

In *Carmen* he played a haggard Don José 'but his eyes were glowing with a dangerous light'.[19] Joseph was the only artist to sing in French, his Carmen (Alice Orff-Solscher) singing in German, and the Escamillo (Franco Izal) in Italian. The Australian principals and chorus used the English version in an extreme example of an old-style 'polyglot opera'.

The other productions were *Faust* and *Tosca* where the same language arrangements obtained. ' "Ich liebe die nacht", sings Orff-Solscher, and Hislop answers in French, while Izal storms in Italian'.[20] Understudying Joseph was Charles Nicis, a Russian tenor. 'When Hislop's throat was bad Nicis had to come on in the third act of *Tosca* without any rehearsal and another night take Don José after hurried preparation'.[21]

During one performance of *Faust* (sung by Nicis) 'Mr Hislop's wife and young daughter occupied a box. The great tenor was with them and received an ovation from a packed house.'[22] 'It was a complete answer to those croakers who said Australians couldn't produce and didn't want Grand Opera,' commented Claude Kingston. 'He proved it if only by the work he did to help lay the foundations of Australian home-grown Grand Opera when champions of the idea were being widely dismissed as crackpot visionaries.'[23] Years later he added significantly that 'I believe our permanent opera organisations of today owe more than they know to that long-ago season staged under immense difficulties, in which Joseph Hislop, that fine tenor from Edinburgh, played a conspicuous part.'[24]

The culmination of this very successful venture was that Joseph was asked to come out to Australia permanently. 'I have been offered', he confided on his return home to Sweden, 'the post of Artistic Director with the Melbourne Opera. At the same time I would look after the "primo-amoroso" department.'[25] He was on the point of taking the decision to emigrate when the Second World War intervened.

By now Joseph had also established himself in quite different parts of the world. In mid-February 1930 he had embarked on an operatic tour, this time to the Baltic capitals where he had large ready-made audiences in the Swedish-speaking communities in areas formerly under Swedish rule: Finland had been Swedish until 1809; Latvia until 1712. Swedish language and culture still remained influential in the Baltic states. To Baltic audiences familiar with the extrovert style in voice and gesture of Latin tenors, Joseph's practice of building an operatic character from the inside out was enigmatic. Yet he impressed by the conviction and realism of his performance.

In Helsinki Joseph was to appear with the Finnish Opera in a number of his favourite roles. He was 'magnificent' as Rodolfo (in spite of an orchestra which threatened to drown the singers)[26] and manly as the Duke of Mantua (although the foggy weather seemed to have affected the clarity of his voice and rehearsals were uncomfortably brief).[27]

As Cavaradossi his singing was 'virile and magnificent'.[28] His 'totally human' portrayal of Canio in *Pagliacci* resulted in demands for an encore of 'Vesti la giubba' (sung the second time in Swedish).[29] His performance in *La traviata* deeply impressed the audience.[30] The final verdict on his guest appearances was given by full houses and stormy applause.

Ten days later, on 18 March, Joseph was in Riga, capital of Latvia, to give five performances at the National Opera. He seems to have been the first Briton to sing there and as Cavaradossi was found to be a musician of quality, well-trained but with some dryness in the middle register, perhaps caused by his heavy performance schedule or the strain of travelling, but with plenty of 'force where force was needed'.[31] His main characteristics were 'style, clarity of purpose and naturalness of execution'. Another critic remarked enigmatically that he 'possesses a lyric tenor of darker Rimbaud shade'.[32]

His portrayal of Cavaradossi was different from what Latvians had been used to: 'it was more restrained, direct, with less bravura or excessive heroism'.[33] The orchestra, however, was often unable to adjust its volume to match the quiet intensity of the interpretation. As for the Tosca of the soprano Maria Ullmann, it had improved, wrote J. Cirulis, 'but why does she try to force and sing louder than the bassoons?'[34]

Riga audiences were familiar with Gigli and Miguel Fleta, but Hislop was unlike them. 'In every phrase he looked for the musical content, paying more attention to the inner reality of the music and less to external effect,' wrote J. Zalits.[35] 'His voice does not overwhelm with its strength or width of compass, but with its special colour, its even flow and its fullness of tone. It is not a lyric voice *par excellence* but it is lyrical in a dramatic way with a dark timbre and a powerful resonance. His anguished singing will never be forgotten.'[36]

In *Rigoletto* on 20 March Joseph was joined by the Soviet soprano Valeria Barsova, a soloist from the Bolshoi Opera with a three-octave range. His Duke of Mantua was as unfamiliar as his Cavaradossi. He played the part neither with aristocratic pride nor with the authority of an all-powerful ruler. 'His voice is good and of wide compass, most rich in the upper register. His timbre lacks attractive gentleness. The tones are too deep in the cavity of his mouth.' He avoided the expected 'sweet intoxicating and long-held phrases' but immediately established a rapport with his Russian Gilda.[37]

Subsequently Valeria Barsova as Violetta in *La traviata* 'unleashed many a rocket of sound, shooting single high notes like bullets of light.'[38] She sang in Russian while Joseph used Italian, surely one of the most extreme linguistic contrasts. He played Alfredo as an elegant Frenchman. 'The great passionate outburst in the party scene in the third act was most effective and the charming treatment of *mezza voce* was particularly pleasing.'

It was in Bizet's *Carmen* on 25 March that Joseph's voice was shown off to best advantage. 'His mezzo type of tenor is more suited to the dramatic role of José than to the lyrical singing in *Rigoletto* or *La traviata*. He made the greatest impression in the second Act with a brilliantly sung "Flower Song,"' wrote G. Brusubarda.[39]

After performances of *Tannhäuser*, *Turandot* and *Boris Godounov* by local artists, Joseph returned to Riga for a final *La traviata* on 28 March before leaving for a holiday in Sweden.

In the first week of 1933 Joseph was back in Helsinki to sing one performance of six different operas: *La bohème*, *Aida*, *Carmen*, *Roméo et Juliette*, *Faust* and *Tosca*; the first three were conducted by his colleague in Stockholm, the composer Armas Järnefelt.

After some lapses in vocal quality and intonation, singing above the note, Joseph settled into his Rodolfo, demonstrating his familiar qualities of naturalistic acting and great variation of tonal colour and dynamics.[40]

The leaders of Finland's artistic community were in the auditorium to see Joseph in *Aida*. His Radames impressed by its simplicity and absence of vocal and dramatic artifice. 'He sang straight into the hearts of the audience, giving a deeply personal portrayal of the part. . . . He saved his greatest vocal resources for the last act and played the part, not so much manly and heroic as Finnish audiences had come to expect, but as a mature and civilised prince, and his "crystal clear voice" contributed to the characterisation.'[41]

In *Carmen* Joseph combined dramatic with lyrical singing. In his characterization of Don José it was his attention to detail that impressed – from the underplaying, the offhand touches of the first act to the violent passion of the ending.[42]

Gounod's *Roméo et Juliette* saw Joseph avoid sentimental exaggeration. He sang in French but at times the part seemed too high for him. He strained for the high notes in the first act and seemed to be in danger of using too much falsetto (as observers reported that Richard Tauber had as well)[43]

When Joseph appeared two days later as Faust the critics found his interpretation of this role to be traditional, that of the Paris Opera. Nevertheless he performed with taste and intelligence.

With *Tosca* Joseph said farewell to Helsinki, reinforcing his dramatic and vocal quality to a capacity audience before travelling on to Reval (Tallinn) in Estonia to give *Tosca*, *Faust* and *Carmen*.

A touching incident took place during his stay in Tallinn.

> I arrived in the city and had just checked into my hotel. I was feeling unsettled in this country which I had never been in before. Suddenly the telephone rang. The person at the other end of the line introduced himself in French and asked if I would like to meet an old friend of mine called *Kutz* at a plastics factory.
>
> I was rather hesitant but curious at the same time, as it all sounded very plausible. I went to see him and imagine my surprise when I met my old friend the Englishman Albert Coates, world-famous conductor, previously director at the opera in Petrograd and now the most distinguished musician in all Russia. We had a very enjoyable evening. Amongst others I was introduced to a young Russian lady whom my friend Coates called 'cousin'.
>
> Next day this became clear to me when a small party was held in the lady's house. Her mother, still quite young, was married to an English diplomat, a relative of Coates. Hence the name 'little cousin'.
>
> But in this charming family I had yet another surprise. Apparently, unknown to me, I had contributed to the happy union between the English diplomat and the Russian widow after the loss of her officer husband during the war. The Englishman had evidently been too shy to propose in the conventional manner. When he could not find a way of doing so he decided to send his beloved a gramophone record. It was 'When the dawn flames in the sky, I love you' by Cadman (on the other side 'For You Alone') and it was sung by my unwitting self.
>
> The phrase 'I love you' recurs over and over again in all possible combinations. It had clearly had the right effect and they now had both wanted to thank me personally. It was a most enjoyable evening and, as you can guess, I was persuaded to sing 'the proposal' for the happy couple.[44]

In Tallinn as Cavaradossi, Joseph's occasional tendency to sing above the note (nearly half a tone) was remarked upon, as well as the velvet quality of his voice and his dramatic skill.[45] The auditorium was only half-full due to the presence in Reval of an opera company from Berlin which had attracted away the German-speaking inhabitants. The local Russian-speaking public, for their part, preferred to patronize Russian artists.

Theodore Lemba, writing in *Palvaleht* (29 January 1933), noted the baritonal timbre of Joseph's lower notes, the well-blended smoothness of the voice in general, which betrayed his training in *bel canto*, and his warm *mezza voce*. When he came to review *Faust*, Lemba remarked that in the cavatina Joseph's 'high C rang brilliantly'. To Lemba the British tenor appeared to be compensating for a voice that was not naturally as beautiful as that of many an Italian tenor by intensifying the emotional and dramatic interpretation accordingly.[46]

In all the countries he visited the Hislop voice was acclaimed as something rich and strange, with a unique beauty. There were failings, the occasional coldness of tone, a baritonal quality not always appreciated, a tendency sometimes to sing *above* the note or to build up the characterization only loosely at first. Yet in the final analysis it was Joseph's positive contribution to each opera that made the most lasting impression: his cultured virility of voice production based on the 'sweet attack' and sung 'in line' in the Italian manner; a governing sense of style, and above all, dramatic truthfulness that did not shrink from abandoning superficial effects in favour of internal authenticity.

References

1. The Seattle Post-Intelligencer, 14 September 1921.
2. ibid.
3. The San Francisco Chronicle, 26 September 1921.
4. The San Francisco Bulletin, 27 September 1921.
5. The San Francisco Chronicle, 27 September 1921.
6. ibid.
7. The Los Angeles Daily Times, 6 October 1921.
8. The Rocky Mountain News, 12 October 1921.
9. The Denver Post, 13 October 1921.
10. The Kansas City Star, 14 October 1921.
11. The Kansas City Star, 14 October 1921.
12. The Toronto Globe, 27 October 1921.
13. The Montreal Daily Star, 31 October 1921.
14. The Washington Star, 1 November 1921.
15. ibid.
16. Stockholms Dagbladet, 6 March 1928.
17. The Sydney Morning Herald, 26 October 1927.
18. Kingston, C. (1971), *It don't seem a day too much*, Sydney, Rigby Ltd, p. 153.
19. The Melbourne Herald, 3 August 1931.
20. The Illustrated Tasmanian Mail, 19 August 1931.
21. ibid.
22. The Illustrated Tasmanian Mail, 12 August 1931.
23. Kingston op. cit. p. 153.
24. ibid. p. 154.
25. Stockholms Tidningen, 5 December 1931.
26. Uusi Suomi, 20 February 1930.
27. ibid.
28. Suomenmaa, 22 February 1930.
29. Unidentified Helsinki newspaper, 5 March 1930.
30. Unidentified Helsinki newspaper.
31. Pedeja Bridi, 10 March 1930.
32. Segodnia Vecherom, 19 March 1930.
33. ibid.
34. Latvis, 23 March 1930.
35. Jaunakas Zinas, 19 March 1930.

36. ibid.
37. Latvijas Kareivis, 22 March 1930.
38. Pedeja Bridi, 22 March 1930.
39. Segodnia Vecherom, 24 March 1930.
40. Uusi Suomi, 10 January 1933.
41. Uusi Suomi, 13 January 1933.
42. Uusi Suomi, 16 January 1933.
43. Uusi Suomi, 19 January 1933.
44. Stockholms Tidningen, 31 March 1933.
45. Revalsche Zeitung, 28 January 1933.
46. Palvaleht, 29 January 1933.

8 Individual recitals (1921–1941)

Compared to the opera singer transformed by make-up, costume, lighting and scenery, the recitalist stands alone, vulnerable, with only his technique and artistry to pacify or charm a sea of faces. While the former may have the more memorable combinations of artists, the latter relies on routine professionalism, sometimes with minimal rehearsal, turning a concert into a triumph of invention over adversity.

One of the most bizarre solo appearances Joseph ever made took place early in 1921 in Chicago. He had been invited to sing at a prestigious Scotophile function in the city on 1 January, immediately following the celebrations of Hogmanay. A procession entered the Second Regiment Armory headed by a MacDuff clan Chief escorting Joseph and Karin to the strains of the 'Barren Rocks o' Aden' played by two pipers. First he sang 'Bonnie Mary of Argyle', then 'My love is like a red, red rose', and finally 'La donna è mobile' as an encore. Joseph was presented with a silver loving cup engraved with the legend 'Let Italy have her Caruso, Ireland her McCormack. Scotland has her Hislop!'[1]

Three months later Joseph turned from singer to claque-master. After the Chicago Opera had finished its season at the Manhattan in 1921, Joseph took a busman's holiday and with his agent Paolo Longone accompanied the baritone Titta Ruffo to New Jersey where the latter was to give a concert. Noticing Ruffo's distressing nervousness and knowing that a great number of the audience were Italian, Joseph took a chance, stood up and in a loud voice, called out: 'Viva nostra Titta Ruffo'. The audience responded immediately with an ovation. Ruffo flushed with pleasure, and a broad grin spread over his face. He proceeded to sing like an angel.[2]

Joseph left America on 4 May, sailing on the *Adriatic* to meet his wife who had gone before him to their children in Devonshire where he planned to take a long rest and play a lot of golf. The fifteenth hole was just 15 feet from his garden gate.

He turned down an offer to sing in Havana (Cuba) but did make one interruption to his holiday – a Sunday appearance at the Royal Albert Hall on 12 June to an audience of 4 000. Accompanying him was Harold Craxton in the inevitable 'Che gelida manina', 'Bonnie Mary of Argyle' and the Lament from Cilea's *L'Arlesiana*. Also on the programme were the pianist Frank Laffitte and the cellist Lauri Kennedy.

Two months later Joseph was at Hayes to record for The Gramophone Company, his first recordings since his 1916 session for the French engineers of Pathé Frères in Stockholm. To the accompaniment of his genial American secretary Spencer Clay he made five takes of 'Bonnie Mary of Argyle' and one of Balfe's 'Come into the garden, Maude', but none of them was issued.

In the autumn of 1921 Joseph was in America again for the Scotti Transcontinental Tour. When the tour ended Joseph began a series of concerts on 14 November in rather insignificant venues which were originally scheduled to take him on to 1 June of the following year. Had he completed it, the tour would have kept him away from his life-blood, the operatic stage, for almost seven months. The purpose of the lengthy concert series was to keep his bank-balance healthy but also, and perhaps more importantly, to maintain his availability as long as possible should an offer arise from the Metropolitan Opera House.

During his free time in New York recovering from the constant travel of the Scotti tour, Joseph was able to enjoy a very broad range of entertainment, including Al Jolson appearing in 'Bombo'. Among the composers active in New York at the time were Rachmaninoff and Richard Strauss. Heifetz was scheduled to appear at Carnegie Hall later in the month and the conductor Albert Coates after him. The legendary bass, Feodor Chaliapin, had also just sailed in from Communist Russia, although many of his subsequent concerts were to be cancelled due to indisposition.

A very curious event took place on Sunday 20 November, at the Lumière Studio on 5th Avenue. A large painting, 'The Voice from Beyond', was unveiled by Mme Alberto Sciarretti depicting a wraith with the face of Enrico Caruso rising from the grave. During the ceremony the tenor, Cantor Rosenblatt, sang and Alberto Sciarretti, Joseph's accompanist, played.

Thanksgiving, 24 November, was a day of demonstrations by the rival fans of Geraldine Farrar and the newly arrived Czech soprano Maria Jeritza (known as the Gerry- and Jerry-Flappers) who took part in extravagant public support for their idols.

An even more significant day was Sunday 27 November when some 25 000 music-lovers turned out to hear ten concerts, the one by Chaliapin evoking a continuous and often overwhelming roar of enthusiasm from 5 000 compatriots. Also that afternoon the Met held a Caruso Memorial Concert at which Geraldine Farrar, Frances Alda, Galli-Curci, Gigli and

Giovanni Martinelli (among others) performed. Elsewhere that evening John McCormack entertained some 6 000 people with 20 songs at the Hippodrome.

On the following morning Joseph appeared at the Biltmore Hotel with Gatti-Casazza's red-haired New Zealand wife, the Metropolitan Opera's Frances Alda, along with Raoul Vidas (violin) and Spencer Clay at the piano. Joseph's first number, 'Una furtiva lagrima' at once won his delighted hearers, who demanded an encore. The concert ended with 'O Soave Fanciulla' sung by Joseph and Frances Alda.

Six days later Joseph's idol Titta Ruffo made his Met debut as Don Carlos in *Ernani*, while Chaliapin appeared for the first time as Boris Godounov the following evening.

Joseph, by contrast, gave his final North American concert in Winnipeg, Canada, on 25 January, where he appeared under the auspices of the Men's Musical Club with Spencer Clay. His 'My love, she's but a lassie yet' brought the house down on Burns Night when Joseph disclosed an unexpected fund of humour and command of imitative effects.[4]

When he returned to England in April 1922 Joseph parted company with his agent Thomas Quinlan and signed up with Lionel Powell and Harold Holt. Powell was an extrovert showman; Holt a solicitor by training. Together they made a formidable partnership, managing Sir Thomas Beecham, for example, as well as the Chilean pianist Claudio Arrau.

On 7 May 1922 Joseph was in London at the Queen's Hall in Sir Henry Wood's Sunday afternoon concert. According to *The Times* (8 May 1922)

> Most people who came were moved to forego the first fine summer day in order to hear Mr Hislop sing. They were not disappointed, except that he did not sing very much. His is a singularly beautiful voice, almost entirely free from the usual vices of tenors. There is hardly a trace of throatiness or of lingering unduly on high penultimates. It all comes out easily, distinct and vocal at every moment.
>
> He sang operatic numbers with the orchestra, beginning with 'Celeste Aida' which, including the high B natural at the end, left no doubt that here was a great operatic singer. Those who had not heard him before must have been surprised that an organ with so much warmth of tone, so much expressiveness and so much richness could come from the cold North.

Joseph's first records of Scots songs were made in the middle of May with Spencer Clay and included 'The Herding Song' from Lawson's *Songs of the North*, 'Afton Water' by Hume, Marjorie Kennedy-Fraser's 'An Eriskay love lilt' and 'O my love's bonny' arranged by George Short. An Edinburgh organist and music teacher, Short was employed by the Edinburgh music-sellers and concert agents, Methven Simpson. He was to play an important role in Joseph's Scots concerts, accompanying him almost exclusively over the next decade and arranging tirelessly, publishing some of these arrangements in three volumes dedicated to Joseph.

On 28 June 1923 Joseph sang at the Albert Hall in a Dame Clara Butt Concert to the accompaniment of Ivor Newton, with Selma Kurz, Kennerley Rumford and the American Quartet (the last all pupils of Jean De Reske).

On 1 July the American baritone John Charles Thomas appeared with Joseph at the Albert Hall. (Thomas would later join Joseph in *Faust* at Covent Garden in 1928.) The pair shared another Albert Hall concert on 30 September which received a barbed review from *The Monthly Musical Record* (1 November 1923):

> One is labelled tenor, the other baritone, but that is to convey a difference in their range and styles which is not apparent. . . . Both know their business and are pleasantly self-confident. They bank on a good cantabile (strange that there should ever be divorce between singing and cantabile, but there is in these civilised days!). Both make much of a feeling of easy fervour, which may on occasion sink into sentimentality. Hackneyed music was chosen by the one and the other, though Mr Thomas condescended even more than Mr Hislop, and in his second group unblushingly flourished a couple of out-and-out pot boilers. But for the most part the two accomplished young fellows were like as two peas.

Joseph returned to London on Saturday 20 October to take part in the second Chappell Popular concert with Isobel Baillie and Muriel Brunskill before going north again to Liverpool to partner the Polish soprano Ada Sari, the contralto Phyllis Lett, the baritone Eric Marshall and the Serbian violinist Bratza. 'Like Prospero's isle,' remarked *The Times* (22 October 1923), 'the Philharmonic Hall last night was full of voices; the hall resounded with the rage of encores.'

On February 1924, Joseph appeared in another Chappell Popular Concert at the Queen's Hall with Isobel Baillie, Myra Hess and Eric Marshall. Joseph's programme, which included 'Tombe degl'avi miei' from *Lucia di Lammermoor* and 'In Summertime on Bredon', satisfied the concert demand for contrasts of mood and style. At the podium was Eugene Goossens (who in 1928 would conduct Joseph in *Faust* at Covent Garden).

Three days later Joseph recorded a batch of Scots songs with Clarence Raybould at the piano and showed a rich vein of vitality, 'Hislop is in fine fettle', wrote *The Gramophone* (November 1924),'and enjoys himself enormously in the rollicking "My love, she's but a lassie yet", a kind of vocal Highland fling, and in the charming "Corn Rigs".' Both these Burns songs had been arranged by George Short.

A well-received London concert took place when Joseph appeared with the soprano Evelyn Scotney and the pianist Ignaz Friedman at a Special Sunday Concert on 18 May in the Royal Albert Hall with Percy Kahn as accompanist. Joseph sang the romanza 'Ma se m'è forza perderti' from Verdi's *Un Ballo in Maschera*, an opera which depicts the assassination of

King Gustav III of Sweden in 1792; he also recorded the same aria in December at Hayes (see p. 71).

Later in the year Joseph signed a contract with the Colón Opera in Buenos Aires for the July 1925 season. He agreed to play two parts new to him, Rinuccio in Puccini's *Gianni Schicchi* and Fenton in Verdi's *Falstaff* – both ardent, lyrical young lovers. To prepare for this new challenge he persuaded the well-known composer and vocal coach Manlio Di Veroli to accompany him on a family holiday to Wales, where he had rented a large country house near Colwyn Bay.

Together, Di Veroli (later to be the vocal teacher of the Welsh tenor and comic, Harry Secombe) and Joseph gave two concerts in North Wales. The first, on 17 August, was at the Pier Pavilion (Colwyn Bay). Joseph sang the first performance of Di Veroli's 'Lighted Lamps'. One of the boxes was occupied by Karin and their two bright little children, the latter applauding their father's efforts with great vigour. Then, early in September he appeared with the soprano Dora Labbette at the Pier Pavilion (Llandudno) accompanied by the Pier Company's Grand Orchestra before a large and appreciative audience.

By Saturday, 4 October, Joseph was back in London at the Queen's Hall. The next day John McCormack followed him onto the same platform. *The Daily Sketch* (6 October 1924) noted that 'one or two of his songs, if I may outrage the McCormack devotees, did not give me the same intense pleasure that Joseph Hislop's rendering has given me. But then, Hislop, too, is a very great artist.'

Ten days later Joseph received a bundle of manuscripts of tenor songs by British composers from the secretary of the British Empire Music Festival, asking him to select a winner. 'Should there not prove to be any one song that you consider worthy of the Gold Medal, which you are so kindly giving, perhaps you know of a song written by a British composer that is still unpublished and is worthy of the medal and would award it to that.' None of the songs, however, appeared to be of the requisite standard.

On 17 October Joseph was at the Usher Hall in Edinburgh with the pianist Wilhelm Backhaus and the imposing figure of soprano Florence Austral. Percy Kahn accompanied Joseph and Miss Austral in the duet from the close of Act I of *Madama Butterfly*. 'He has everything that goes to the making of an almost ideal Italian tenor', wrote *The Scotsman* (18 October 1924), 'and his singing provided a series of triumphs.' In Glasgow the next day Joseph was complemented on having 'a fine, powerful tenor voice, rather hard than sensuous.'

Sunday, 23 November saw Fritz Kreisler's first concert that season at the Royal Albert Hall. In the evening Joseph and Martha Baird the pianist gave a recital at the Queen's Hall followed by a lavish Powell-Holt dinner in honour of Amelita Galli-Curci and attended, among others, by Backhaus,

HISLOP

Concert with Percy Kahn, c. 1924: cartoon by Nerman

Sunday 23 November 1924, at the RAC Club, London. *Back Row:* Lionel Powell, Wilhelm Backhaus, Fritz Kreisler, Joseph Hislop, Harold Holt. *Front Row:* Frieda Hempel, Dame Clara Butt, Amelita Galli-Curci (courtesy of Harold Holt Ltd)

Kreisler, Clara Butt and Frieda Hempel. As concert-managers, Messrs Powell & Holt certainly treated their artists with style.

Some days before the dinner Joseph had met Lionel Powell and Galli-Curci for a round of golf at the Coombe Hill Golf Club in Kingston-on-Thames and her photograph duly appeared in the newspapers swinging a golf club. No doubt there were reminiscences of *Roméo et Juliette* in Chicago when the guests took to the table at the RAC Club. Yet another press photographer captured an expanse of white tablecloth loaded with food and wine.

Kahn accompanied again at the third Annual Concert of the British Empire Music Festival in the Royal Albert Hall on 10 December in the presence of Princess Louise, Duchess of Argyll. The other artists were Dame Clara Butt and the fine English bass, Robert Radford. Joseph sang Stanford's 'Windy Nights' (with words by Robert Louis Stevenson) and Aitken's 'Sigh no more, ladies', continuing in a second group with 'The Lea

Rig' and 'My love she's but a lassie yet'. The programme was closed by the Central Band of the RAF and the pipers of the Scots Guards. With this patriotic conclusion Joseph's musical activities for 1924 came to an end.

After Christmas in Gothenburg Joseph was back in Edinburgh by 23 January for the 1925 Lumsden Scots Festival, appearing with Edna Thornton, the principal contralto of the British National Opera Company. In the days that followed he also gave concerts in Glasgow and Dundee.

Using the challenging new electric recording process, Joseph recorded two very popular Scots songs in October – the evergreen 'Bonnie wee thing' and Sir Walter Scott's 'MacGregor's Gathering' accompanied by Percy Kahn. *The Gramophone* (March 1926) was not impressed. 'Joseph Hislop makes a brave effort to forget his operatic history. That experience does not help a man to sing Scots songs. I don't like the trace of sentimental sobs in the second verse. This is disappointing, and worse still is his cadenza in this verse. No! This is the wrong style altogether, friend Hislop. "Bonnie wee thing" is better, but he is still singing out too much to the far gallery, not to his love on the brae.'

Compton Mackenzie, however, disagreed. 'I see Joseph Hislop got into trouble for his performance of "MacGregor's Gathering". I suppose it is too operatic, but still, legitimate or not, I had a real good thrill out of it. And I protest that a Highlander has ten times as much drama in him as a Lowlander.'[5]

Sidney Hecht, Joseph's personal manager and friend who constantly plotted and schemed to promote his client's reputation, had for some time been trying to get William Blackwood of the Associated Press to use his considerable influence to further the Hislop name in the international press. In December 1925, Blackwood sent Joseph five songs, three by Gunby Hadath, which he believed had 'great possibilities' if set to some 'decent music'[6]

Electrically recorded versions of 'An Eriskay love lilt' and the 'Herding Song' were recorded by Joseph with Percy Kahn at the piano at the beginning of June 1926, eliciting this dismissal from C. M. Crabtree. 'The popular "Eriskay love lilt" by this noted tenor might have been remarkable. Personally I find it almost devoid of sensitiveness and not nearly tender enough. The other song is a beautiful one, and well, if not outstandingly well, sung.'[7]

On the afternoon of 12 June Joseph was at the Crystal Palace to sing in *The Messiah* at the Handel Festival. Before a large audience (which included the American tenor Charles Hackett), Flora Woodman, Margaret Balfour and Horace Stevens took the platform with Joseph and Sir Henry Wood. Marcato in *The Monthly Musical Record* (1 July 1926) wrote that the last day was remarkable for Sir Henry Wood's passionate endeavours to force the choir to sing the well-known music . . .'with more variation of tempo, with more verbal expressiveness, and sometimes excessively quickly'. *The Times*

(14 June 1926) complimented Hislop: 'His honeyed voice and quiet expressiveness suited the solemn character of the tenor solo.'

The end of June found Joseph giving four concerts at the Tivoli Concert Hall in Copenhagen, full for the first time that season, with the audience of 4 000 gripped by 'Hislop-hysteria'; one evening almost ended in panic![8]

He sang Puccini, Leoncavallo and two songs by Tosti, finishing with 'En Drøm' by Grieg. At the end Joseph, 'thin as a rake', embraced the short and portly conductor, Otto Olsson, rather like Laurel and Hardy![9]

A welcome rest followed at Brottkärr in Sweden, then back to Wales. At the National Eisteddfod in Swansea's Victoria Park Joseph sang in the final concert on 7 August before nearly 20 000 people with Percy Kahn at the piano. Tosti's 'Ideale', 'Che gelida manina', 'At Night' (Rachmaninoff), two Scots songs and 'Vesti la giubba' meant that, in the words of the press, 'time and again this lovely tenor was encored.'[10] The concert ended close to midnight.

The Sir Henry Wood Promenade Concerts in the Queen's Hall featured Joseph on 27 August, again with Sir Henry Wood. Muriel Brunskill sang Bach's 'Jesus Sleeps' 'with good tone and a sense of style. Mr Joseph Hislop gave us the best singing we have had this season in Beethoven's "Adelaide",' said *The Times* (28 August 1926).

By 1 September, Joseph returned to the Proms singing Handel's 'Angels, waft her to the skies' from *Jeptha*. 'In spite of not being in good voice, Mr Hislop showed a fine sense of style and an all too rare finish in his phrasing. The recitative was exceedingly well done, with a full sense of its dramatic power.'[11]

Another Prom included Joseph on 9 September, and on the 22nd, Aubrey Brain (horn) and Clifford Curzon (piano) joined Marjorie Burt and Joseph, who sang 'O Paradiso' from Meyerbeer's *L'Africana*.

In September 1926 Joseph also recorded four songs at the Small Queen's Hall with Percy Kahn, Marjorie Hayward (violin) and Nifosi (cello). These were 'I heard you singing' (Eric Coates), 'Nightfall at Sea' (Montague Phillips), 'At Dawning' (Cadman) and 'For you alone' (Geehl), the song he had used for his test recording in 1914. Commenting on the first two *The Gramophone*(May 1927) enthused that they 'give opportunity for tremendous effect to a great operatic tenor. Hislop rises fully to this opportunity.'

More Proms featured Joseph on 2 October with the 'Flower Song' from *Carmen*, and on 8 October. On the afternoon of the last night of the Proms the traditional Chappell Ballad Concerts were replaced by a series of Matinée Prom Concerts also given under Sir Henry Wood. Joseph sang 'Celeste Aida' and the *La bohème* duet 'O soave fanciulla' with Dora Labbette, so making his last appearance in England for 1926.

At the end of the month Joseph was in Oslo with Percy Kahn under the auspices of the flamboyant concert agent Rulle Rassmussen whom the violinist Henry Temianka once described as 'a grand old rogue and Norway's leading impresario'.[12]

Joseph's first concert with Percy Kahn was in Bergen on 21 October followed by two in the University Hall, Oslo; an appearance at a cinema in Tønsberg, near Oslo; and a final concert in the capital at the Logens Store Sal where he met the violinist Jascha Heifetz.

During his operatic appearances at La Monnaie (Brussels) in 1927, Joseph was invited to the Royal Palace to give a concert before Queen Elizabeth of Belgium, the Duke and Duchess of Brabant, the Princesses Martha and Astrid of Sweden and the eminent Belgian violinist Eugène Ysaye. Among the 20 or so items on Joseph's programme were many Swedish songs.[13]

Thursday 12 April found Joseph at the Regina Theatre in Aarhus on Jutland, accompanied once again by the portly Otto Olsson. Typical of a Hislop concert was the variety of languages used: he sang in English, French, Italian, Swedish and German and turned even trifles into works of art.[14] Those who believed the English could not write songs were confounded by Joseph's interpretation of Stanford's 'Windy Nights' and Armstrong Gibbs' 'Five Eyes'. One critic noted that the strong limelight in the theatre appeared to inconvenience the singer while a slight hoarseness was heard from time to time.[15] The greatest impression was made by his operatic numbers from *La bohème*, *Rigoletto* and *Pagliacci*. A nice touch came at the end when Joseph pulled a flower from the bouquet he had received and placed it in his accompanist's buttonhole![16]

During May he appeared in four concerts at the Auditorium in Stockholm accompanied by Adolf Wiklund. His farewell concert on 31 May was packed out with an enthusiastic audience who applauded both the intimate items on the programme as well as the more showy operatic numbers, ending with Grieg's supremely poetic 'En Drøm'. Joseph was heaped with applause and flowers and forced to sing encore after encore.[17]

Joseph's next recording session took place at the Small Queen's Hall in mid-June, once more with Percy Kahn, Marjorie Hayward and now Cedric Sharpe on the cello. Several exquisite Scandinavian songs were produced: 'Evigt dig till Hjärtat Trycka' (Sjögren), 'Mens jeg venter' (Grieg) in Norwegian, and the powerful but notoriously difficult 'En Svane' by Grieg in which Joseph used a wide range of dynamics to startling effect. Herman Klein writing in *The Gramophone* (October 1931) commented on Joseph's interpretation:

> Joseph Hislop is by now probably known to thousands of admirers abroad as against hundreds in his native land. That is wrong, of course. . . . In Stockholm, where the Scots tenor made his debut and also in Italy and South America, he has long been a favourite. He sings Grieg's songs in the original Norwegian, and sings them well. Here are two that are known everywhere and

lose nothing of their delicious local colour at his hands. Yet, while admiring the refinement of his style, I find his tone at times too soft and veiled in proportion to the amount of its carrying power. His *mezza voce*, for instance, does not travel like that of Slezák or Schipa. Nevertheless I would not have the entrancing 'Swan' (En Svane by Grieg) sung with less contrast than it is by Hislop, who evidently revels in its gentle sweetness. It shows him to be a greater artist than he was when I last heard him, and I prefer his musical whisper in music such as this to all the sonorities of the heavy type that the microphone is often made to convey.

Three other songs were recorded at this time: 'When swallows homeward fly' (Abt), 'Let us forget' (White) and 'Bird songs at eventide' (Eric Coates).

'Afton Water' and 'Bonnie Mary of Argyle' were later recorded by Joseph and Piero Coppola at the Kingsway Hall, the former replacing his acoustic version of 1922. '"Afton Water" is really beautiful,' wrote *The Gramophone* (February 1928). 'It is rarely one hears such a song sung quite so imaginatively. It is just as rarely that one welcomes, as here, a new tune to a good folk-song (and I imagine this is a new tune, it is certainly not the familiar one). Notice that the former accompaniment was by piano whereas now it is orchestra, and well worth while. "Bonny Mary of Argyle" is very good, but is, I think, a little cheapened.'

Then came recordings of 'Mary' and 'My love is like a red, red rose' made at the Small Queen's Hall with Kahn, Hayward and Sharpe. 'Hislop is one of the few singers who can make us resigned to red labels, even for the simplest ditties,' C. M. Crabtree pointed out in *The Gramophone* (February 1929). 'All honour to Scotland! And here he gives us two songs almost at his best, though perhaps a little strained. The first, one of the loveliest of all Scottish folksongs. Is any song more typically Scottish than "My love is like a red, red rose", with its wide, free range?'

Joseph gave few concerts in Europe for almost two years. Then in mid-July 1928 he crossed to Copenhagen to appear in popular evening concerts in the Tivoli Concert Hall, accompanied again by Otto Olsson. He gave four concerts and at his farewell appearance was overwhelmed by applause and cheering, bouquets of flowers and expressions of regret that he would not be heard there again until the following summer.[18]

The end of 1928 was remarkable for eight recordings of songs. It began with a September session in Stockholm with an orchestra conducted by Joseph's old friend Nils Grevillius where four Scandinavian songs were recorded: 'Du sover bløtt' (Lundvik), 'Mademoiselle Rococo' (Melartin), 'Söntag' (Järnefelt) and 'Jungfrun under lind' (Peterson-Berger). He also made several takes of 'Melodi' by Rangström and 'Brita-Lills vaggvisa' written by his friend, the bass Emile Stiebel (both accompanied by Adolf Wiklund), although neither of these titles was issued.

Two George Short arrangements followed in early December: Burns' 'Corn Rigs' and 'My love, she's but a lassie yet' together with an unsuccessful repeat of his 1914 acoustic version of Tosti's 'Goodbye'. Then two days later with an orchestra under G. W. Byng he recorded the very popular 'To the Children' by Rachmaninoff. This was later issued along with his 'The Grey House' ('La Maison Grise') from Messager's *Fortunio*, eliciting the following commendation from Herman Klein in *The Gramophone* (December 1929): 'Both are suitable songs for a Christmas audience of children and, sung in this charming manner, they should be able to attract as big a crowd of youngsters as the Christmas tree itself. The voice is delicately modulated, and in the Russian song assumes a truly touching quality.'

In the late autumn of 1928, Joseph's plans to secure a contract with the Staatsoper in Berlin fell through after prolonged negotiations. Accordingly he set off for a short concert tour in Norway, with the composer and conductor of the Swedish Royal Orchestra, Adolf Wiklund, as accompanist. In Oslo the press was already describing him as 'Prince Charming':

> Slim and with his usual flexibility and the slightly blasé and coquettish elegance so characteristic of him, he had his audience in the palm of his hand as always before. Being the irresistible tenor Don Juan that he is, he knows well all the seductive tricks and exactly how to win an audience. But the point is, that behind the routine of the famous star singer the serious artist has remained sound and unspoiled.[19]

His programme at the University concert hall (the Aulean) included a new departure, 'When I am laid in earth' from Purcell's *Dido and Aeneas* (normally sung by a woman), together with Hildor Landvik's 'Du sofver blött' (Thou art not dead, thou sleepest only) and Adolf Wiklund's own 'Silkeskö' (Silken shoe). According to *Den 17 de Maj* (20 October 1928), 'Chaliapin, Leo Slezák and Hislop are often mentioned side by side as the three greatest singers of the present time', adding of Joseph's performance that 'there is every reason to believe that we have never heard anything better in this country'. Jens Arbo, writing in *Morgenbladet* (20 October 1928) added that 'there was sunshine in his lyrical tenor with its warm, soft timbre.'

By mid-February 1929 Joseph was in the UK, singing in a concert at Bristol's Colston Hall in aid of The Bristol Police and Fire Brigade Widows and Orphans Fund.

Back again to Sweden for a farewell concert at Stockholm's Auditorium with Adolf Wiklund on 26 March, Joseph showed his linguistic versatility by singing two German lieder (Schubert's 'Frühlingsglaube' and Brahms 'Der Tod, das ist die kühle Nacht'), Swedish and Norwegian songs, as well as 'Ah! Fuyez, douce image' in French and 'O, Paradiso' in Italian.

A favourite recording was made by Joseph in May of Messager's 'The Grey House' with an orchestra under John Barbirolli. He also made two takes of 'Goin' Home' (a vocal arrangement by William Fisher based on the theme of the slow movement of Dvořák's New World Symphony) but they were not issued. A week later Barbirolli joined him for Burns' 'Of a' the airts' and 'Turn ye to me' (arranged by Gibilaro), two eminently successful recordings.

In mid-June 1929 Joseph was back in Copenhagen at the Tivoli Concert Hall singing to packed houses giving the 'Flower Song' from *Carmen* and 'Che gelida manina'. The weather that evening was as warm as the welcome he was given. He sang 'with golden tone, romantically virile.'[20] The hall being full, several hundred people stood outside, quite filling the square. After each item the applause raged through the hall, men and women clapping, stamping their feet and singing all at once.[21] Joseph met the applause with a smile, and once he took out his watch. It was late, but the audience shouted for more. He sang eight encores. It was described as Hislop-mania![22]

Interviewed by the local press after the concert, Joseph acknowledged that his income from concerts and opera work was considerable. 'Yes, I do earn a lot. It must be approximately Kr 250 000 a year. But I also spend a lot! Don't misunderstand me: I have neither horses nor a mistress. I don't drink and I don't smoke but travelling is expensive and on top of that I have a passion for paintings.'[23]

Then Scotland beckoned. Edinburgh's annual Lumsden Scots Festival began on 23 January 1930 with Joseph, Helen Ogilvie (an Edinburgh soprano singing leading roles with the Carl Rosa Opera Company) and Arthur Fear (a principal baritone of Covent Garden). The violinist Daisy Kennedy (wife of Benno Moisevitch) played pieces by Kreisler and Brahms, and George Short once again accompanied:

> Mr Hislop was in splendid voice and his renderings of "Ye banks and braes" and "Of a' the airts" immediately roused his hearers to a high pitch of enthusiasm. The aria "Your tiny hand is frozen" was sung with wonderful artistry and magnificent tone, the high C at the finish ringing out all over the hall. Then came a string of encores, till Mr Hislop, who is always generous with his public, had to appear with his watch in his hand.[24]

Joseph privately felt that time was against him. He had started his operatic career relatively late in life, at the age of 30. It was this sense of being driven that forced him to take on more work than he should have done. The more he felt time was running out, the harder he worked, realizing that, paradoxically, the pressures he was putting on his body and his voice would inevitably cut short his singing career. He also suffered from home-sickness and this made him prefer short-term contracts to long engagements with opera companies far from home. The obvious answer was concert after concert combined with short sallies into opera.

Thus Joseph returned to the treadmill. Concerts followed in Lund and Malmö in the south of Sweden. Some time before, Joseph's friend, the eminent bass Emile Stiebel, had asked him to take on a young, talented pianist he knew of who needed experience in accompanying. After agreeing, Carl Tillius joined Joseph for a concert at the Liseberg pleasure gardens in Gothenburg on 6 June 1930. Joseph's programme included several new pieces: Dvořák's 'Songs my mother taught me', Respighi's 'Stornellatrice' and Järnefelt's 'Lina'.

More recordings were made in February 1931 with an orchestra under Lawrance Collingwood. 'Land o' the leal', 'The bonnie banks o' Loch Lomond', 'Ye banks and braes' and 'O sing to me the old Scotch songs'. Then two English songs, 'The Lea Rig' and 'My Mother'. Commenting on these C.M. Crabtree wrote in *The Gramophone* (July 1931) that 'there are no tricks, except perhaps a top note towards the end of "Lea Rig", but the broad contrasts are rather extreme.' He also considered that 'Ye banks and braes' was 'not entirely free from Hislop's tendency to exaggeration and sophistication'[25] In the following year a set of three more Scots songs was recorded by Joseph, 'Jessie, the flower of Dunblane', 'The Island Herdmaid' (arranged by Marjorie Kennedy-Fraser) and 'Annie Laurie'.

'Scots songs are, of course, very differently treated by that international operatic tenor, Joseph Hislop,' wrote Crabtree in *The Gramophone* (June 1933). 'Some of his fellow-countrymen are enthusiastic about his style in their songs, others cannot do with it. We must leave them to fight it out. All I can say of his "Jessie, the Flower of Dunblane" and "Annie Laurie" is that the sophistication is not extreme; but the impression is that the songs are rather more subservient to the singing than the singing to the songs.' His last-ever recording of a Scots song was made in March 1933, Marjorie Kennedy-Fraser's 'An Island Sheiling Song'.

A unique recital took place in February 1933 when, having ended his stint at the operatic commitment in Estonia, Joseph returned to Finland where, in Turku, he gave a concert accompanied by the pianist Simon Pergament-Parmet. In the Hotel Hamburger Börs he caused quite a stir with his deep voice, slender figure and dark Latin good looks. Joseph was 'an artist who radiated intelligence and had a good sense of humour', observed *The Turun Sanomat* (2 February 1933); 'There are few artists born who like Mr Hislop combine a wonderful voice with a great dramatic talent.' At the end of his concert at Turku he sang a song (Merikanto's 'Kuin hiipuva hiillos') in Finnish to the delight of an enraptured audience.

Joseph returned to England late the next year to give more concerts. On 29 September 1934 during the BBC Proms, Joseph sang with the soprano Ninon Vallin whom he had last partnered in Buenos Aires at the Colón in 1925.

A year later Joseph appeared at a December afternoon concert at the London Palladium accompanied by Gerald Moore, subsequently broadcasting for the BBC 'Songs and Arias' at the end of the month. Of their few appearances together Gerald Moore recalled: 'We were on friendly terms and I admired him for he retained his vocal quality and assured technique into his advanced years. He was one of the most prominent tenors of his era.'[26]

When in late June 1936 he broadcast with the BBC the programme included 'Hiawatha's Wedding Feast' by Coleridge-Taylor and 'The Pied Piper of Hamelin' by Parry. One member of the BBC Choral Society which participated with Joseph was a young tenor, Peter Pears. Many years later he recalled the effect on him of Joseph's singing. 'He was singing a piece which I had not heard before, "The Pied Piper" by Parry. He sang it beautifully, although I do not think it was a great piece. Apart from this I never heard him sing, except on record, but I certainly admired both his voice and performance.'[27]

A final chance for the public to hear again the Hislop method in action came in October 1941 when Joseph gave a strongly-targeted recital in the smaller hall of the Concert House in Stockholm, accompanied by Vivan Wennberg. The programme was staunchly pro-British, including English, Scots and Irish songs, Vaughan Williams' 'On Wenlock Edge' and even 'The Little Damozel' by Ivor Novello. In neutral Sweden at the height of the war he was making a powerful statement of his commitment to the land of his birth and its fight for freedom and independence. His stance echoed the words he wrote home to Edinburgh at the height of the First World War: 'I am in touch with the authorities in London. We intend doing propaganda work for British music.'[28]

In spite of having taken Swedish nationality during the Second World War, Joseph remained at heart firmly in touch with his spiritual roots, the traditions of his youth and the rich cultural heritage into which he had been born. To the end he retained in his speech a pungent Scots accent, almost as a living anchor.

References

1. Untitled Chicago newspaper, 2 January 1921, NLS.
2. MS notes for BBC Radio 3 broadcast 'Titta Ruffo', 15 July 1956 (in private possession).
3. *The New York Times*, 3 December 1921.
4. *The Manitoba Free Press*, 26 January 1922.
5. *The Gramophone*, April 1926, p. 502.
6. Letter 4 December 1926 (in private possession).
7. *The Gramophone*, February 1927, p. 379.
8. *Ekstrobladet*, 1 July 1926.
9. ibid.
10. *The South Wales Daily Post*, 9 August 1926.
11. *The Times*, 2 September 1926.
12. Teminaka, H. (1973), *Facing the Music*, New York, David McKay & Co., p. 221.

13. Stockholms Dagbladet, 18 March 1927. The Monthly Musical Record, 1 April 1927, p. 117.
14. Politiken, 4 April 1927.
15. Aarhus Amstidende, 13 April 1927.
16. ibid.
17. Stockholms Dagbladet, 1 June 1927.
18. Dagens Nyheter, 21 July 1928.
19. Oslo Aftenposten, 20 October 1928.
20. Politiken, 20 June 1929.
21. Unidentified Copenhagen newspaper, 20 June 1929, NLS.
22. ibid.
23. Svenska Dagbladet, 22 June 1929.
24. The Edinburgh Evening News, 24 January 1931.
25. The Gramophone, November 1931.
26. Letter to author, 28 August 1986, NLS.
27. Letter to author, 16 September 1985, NLS.
28. Letter 20 August 1918, NLS.

9 Concert tours (1920–1923)

The first British concert agent to take Joseph in hand was The Thomas Quinlan International Musical Agency Ltd. In September 1920 Joseph reported to Thomas Quinlan at Chandos Street, Covent Garden, ready for the opening concert of his first British tour. This was to be a Corbett Concert in Middlesborough Town Hall on 22 September. Heading the bill was Madame Emma Calvé announced as 'the world's greatest Carmen'.[1] The other artists were Alfred Cortot (piano) and Isolde Menges (violin), the latter deputizing for Jacques Thibaud who had suddenly been taken ill in London. Harold Craxton was the accompanist.

The view of *The North-Eastern Daily Gazette* (23 September 1920) was that Joseph's voice was wonderfully even throughout its extensive range and of great power, together with a thrilling vibrant timbre exceedingly effective in his intensive passages. At the Victoria Hall (Bolton) it was also remarked that the most remarkable characteristic about his voice was its great power, the famous tenor air from *Rigoletto* being perhaps his greatest achievement, because it brought out so many arresting qualities of tone and colour.[2]

From Bolton the party crossed the Irish Sea to Dublin. There it was said that the pianist and the male vocalist possibly pleased the audience the more because it had to be announced that Madame Calvé's diamonds, clothes and music had gone astray en route.[3] As for Joseph, his frank, unaffected manner, his freshness and good tone had immediate appeal.[4] After appearing in Belfast, the artists crossed back over the Irish Sea to Leeds.

Emma Calvé was replaced by Kirkby Lunn. Jacques Thibaud joined them at last. The audience found Joseph to possess, 'a robust tenor voice of great range and brilliancy'.[5] At Huddersfield Town Hall it was the sympathetic timbre of the lower and middle registers that impressed Joseph's listeners, as well as the tricks of modern Italian opera – from the half-notes turned to a sob to the passion surging picturesquely to the penultimate note.[6] In Newcastle it was the beauty, ease and power of his voice which emphasized the lovely quality and rare artistry of the new British tenor.[7] He was requested to sing six additional items in Manchester, and at Sheffield's Victoria Hall he revealed his exceptionally fine quality and range.

Then it was over the Border to Scotland, Joseph's first professional adult appearance in his home town, in the Usher Hall, no longer with Cortot but Alexandre Siloti, the Russian pianist who had been a pupil of Liszt and Tchaikovsky. He has 'a wonderful voice, beautiful in quality and powerful, yet without any suggestion of the baritone, which in tenors too commonly accompanied power'. Such at any rate was the opinion of *The Scotsman* (18 October 1920). 'He is indeed a marvel,' enthused *The Scottish Musical Magazine* (1 November 1920), 'and it is almost safe to say that no such star has sailed into the vocal firmament for years.'

In the west of Scotland Glasgow's music-lovers in St Andrew's Hall were equally appreciative. *The Glasgow Herald* (19 October 1920) observed that he had 'a powerful voice and all the passionate style of a real Puccini tenor. He sang with marked intelligence and with a clearness of articulation that were rare indeed.' Then to Nottingham where *The Nottingham Journal and Daily Express* (22 October 1920) music critic sensed from Joseph's singing of 'Che gelida manina' and 'M'appari' from Flotow's *Marta* that the accomplished tenor was also a skilled actor.

Joseph was absent through illness for the following three concerts at Liverpool, Birmingham and Bristol. He did appear, however, at the Kingsway Hall in London on 30 October for a last recital with the masterly violinist Jacques Thibaud. There it was 'the British artist who carried off the leading honours, since the large audience went quite wild over Mr Hislop's singing.'[8]

In the spring of 1921, when Joseph had finished his appearances at the Manhattan Opera (New York), he set out on a 20-concert tour of North America with the Uruguayan cellist Oscar Nicastro and the Italian pianist Alberto Sciarretti. His first concert was on 10 March at the National Theatre (Washington) when he presented a programme of Italian arias, English songs, French, Swedish and Norwegian classics, Scottish ballads and songs of the Hebrides. In the appreciative audience were members of the Swedish Legation and Vice President and Mrs Calvin Coolidge.[9]

At Symphony Hall (Boston) the following evening a small but appreciative audience insisted on Joseph singing a number of encores. He had a voice of excellent quality, commented *The Boston Herald* (12 March 1921). His command of breath was commendable; his intonation was sure. But as an interpreter he was thought to be curiously uneven. He sang 'Celeste Aida' as though Radames were leading his troops to battle. However compelling he might have been in opera, as a concert singer he 'had much to learn'. *The Boston Globe* (12 March 1921) admitted he 'had a big, rich voice, excellent diction and a good operatic style of singing' but advised Joseph that if he wanted to please American concert audiences his best bet would be a mixture of operatic arias and Scots folk songs.

Having crossed north into Canada Joseph next appeared at the Grand Opera House (Hamilton) on 14 March where he was advertised as offering a programme mainly of Scots songs drawn from a repertoire of 70 titles. By now *The Hamilton Spectator* (15 March 1921) detected hints of strain in his voice. Nevertheless he was given a warm welcome by the many Scots in the auditorium. After further concerts at Toronto in the Massey Hall two days later and then in Boston, Joseph sang next at Springfield (Massachussets). In a programme once more designed to appeal to expatriate Scots, he was found to be a singer in 'the full-throated, round-mouthed Italian style.'[11]

Joseph helped to create a sensation at the gigantic New York Hippodrome on Sunday, 3 April. Evidently the audience was moved to cheers, not only by the beautiful singing of the Scots tenor, but also by the band of 100 pipers, whose extraordinary skill in handling their bagpipes seemed to be as much appreciated by the general public as by the hundreds of Scots people present.

Next came a long journey to Kansas City in the mid-West where the St Andrew's Society had engaged Joseph to raise money for the construction of an old folks' home. At his two and a quarter hour concert on 14 April he delighted his audience with Scots songs and astounded them with operatic numbers, leaning nonchalantly against the piano for the final encore as no other artist had been known to do.[12] Joseph acted as master of ceremonies at the event and appeared as 'a braw, fresh-coloured lad' with a voice whose 'dramatic colouring is pure, the pigment of genuine emotion'.[13]

North then, for a concert in Chicago, where the Scottish Old People's Home at Riverside was the beneficiary of his appearance at the Auditorium, the scene of his former triumphs, on 18 April. The well-known Kiltie Band was also on the bill, making its first appearance since the war (when it had been employed in recruiting), as were 100 Scottish dancers. Joseph was found to have a voice of lyric as well as of beautiful dramatic quality.[14]

Then to the Orchestra Hall in Detroit on 21 April where he was to share the programme with the Scottish Choral Society under the auspices of the St Andrew's Society and the Clan Campbell. Joseph found the manners of the mid-West more hearty and genuine than the polished indifference of the Eastern states. He liked their rough and ready ways. They reminded him of home. Talking about modern popular music he commented that 'jazz is rasping to the nerves. . . . Music, real music, is a tonic. It soothes and refreshes. After the hustle for money and what money can buy, music is just what the tired businessman needs.'[15] *The Detroit Free Press* (22 April 1921) observed that his voice was of large range, even throughout the registers, and of robust type. Unhappily only 40 or 50 people came to Orchestra Hall to hear Joseph and Leonard Cline, writing in *The Detroit News* (22 April 1921) blamed poor publicity and the languid spring weather. 'He has a wonderful voice, a voice of great power, although he himself is far from robust physically, and of exquisite purity and resonance. For one of his encores Mr Hislop sang a Scots ballad, "MacGregor's Gathering", a corking piece with lots of vim and this was perhaps his most popular offering.'[16]

The final stop was Buffalo at the Elmwood Music Hall on 29 April, with all proceeds going to the Church Home repair fund. The correspondent of *The Buffalo Express* (30 April 1921) was struck by Joseph's poetical face and manner which 'reflected the nature of the Scot with his background of mysticism and sturdy strength.' Joseph for his part insisted on visiting the Church Home. There he talked with the old men, making them chuckle over his stories, some told with a broad Scottish accent. He played with the orphanage children and told them folk-tales of Scotland and of England. At around four in the afternoon the next day he came and sang. Toddlers of three and women of 80 surrounded him; Joseph had a word for all. On leaving they followed him out on the verandah, with two venturesome youngsters on the running-board for a final hug and kiss.[17]

A large Buffalo audience attended what was to be his final American concert that season. He impressed with his personal magnetism and charm of presence, his simplicity and sincerity. During the evening a basket filled with spicy carnations was presented to Joseph with the card of Mrs Wilhelm Carl Berling who, as Ingeborg Suneson, had sung Juliette to his Roméo at the Royal Opera in Stockholm. She had also been a student in the Opera School with him.[18] In spite of the brave face he put on for the public Joseph was not well. A bout of 'flu had left him in bad shape and by the time of the concert he was so ill that he could hardly see the conductor.

A week after he got to New York Joseph received a letter from his agent Thomas Quinlan in Paris saying he had just returned from Australia where he had formed a syndicate composed of some of Australia's wealthiest men. He considered Joseph to be the ideal man for the launch of his musical operations the following year: 'I am quite sure that it is the right moment for you to enter Australia, because John McCormack will not go back there. I absolutely recommend you to do this regardless of Covent Garden or anything else next year, because I know jolly well Covent Garden can't pay you £3 000 or give you the same chance of making a continent to yourself, such as I am offering.'[19] Early in January 1922 Joseph reluctantly left the United States. He had become homesick and tired of waiting for his career in the US to take off.

His first Scottish concert since October 1920 took place in the St Andrew's Hall (Glasgow) on 13 April 1922 with the violinist Daisy Kennedy, future wife of Benno Moiseiwitsch, and Spencer Clay at the piano. While he had a very warm reception from the large audience (which filled even the platform), critical reaction was mixed. 'He has not come on since his first appearance in his native land', complained *The Bulletin* (14 April 1922),

> but then he had nothing to learn in the matter of technique, and his lack of real passion, which makes the Caruso comparison ridiculous, is not to be made good by growth in artistry. The voice is strong, flexible and, except in one short space, grateful. Nearly everything he does is technically perfect and when he lets himself go he reaches all but the highest level obtained by operatic artists. This loftiest pitch was exemplified in the great aria from the last act of *Tosca*, 'E lucevan le stelle', and in 'La donna è mobile', given as an encore. 'Mary of Argyle' was a failure. The 'Celeste Aida' was beautifully sung, but not so as to impress anyone who has heard Frank Mullings.

His first recital at Edinburgh's Usher Hall on 4 April was postponed for seven days and when he did appear he was still suffering the effects of a heavy cold. But the 'most distinguished tenor of the day' need not have worried, according to *The Edinburgh Evening News* (19 April 1922) . 'Since his last appearance in the Usher Hall Mr Hislop's voice, while retaining its lovely quality, especially in the *sotto voce* passages, has gained greatly in power. There was a richness in the lower notes which was quite as fine as the magnificent ringing tones in the higher register. Throughout its whole compass the voice is beautifully placed; the breath control is perfect while the enunciation is a model to all singers.'

The Usher Hall was more crowded than it had ever been that season, and in the course of the evening enthusiasm rose to a pitch seldom experienced even in acclaiming the very greatest artists. During one of his encores Joseph turned and sang to the patrons of the organ gallery. 'One was impressed anew last night,' wrote one member of the audience, 'by the rich, creamy quality of Mr Hislop's voice, which is a pure tenor of quite exceptional beauty and power, and by the smoothness and ease of his delivery.'[20]

On the following day Joseph was entertained to lunch by Lord Provost Hutchison at the City Chambers. Speaking of the beautiful and unique character of Scots songs and melodies, Joseph commented that the Auld Scots singers sang because the scenery of mountain and glen was fair to the eye, because love or sympathy had touched the heart-strings, because they resented oppression or scented battle in the air. Above all, they sang for the love of singing.[21]

The following evening Joseph sang in a special charity concert in aid of the Royal Infirmary and the Lord Provost's Rent Relief Fund. The Hislop family now lived close to the Infirmary in Melville Terrace just over the Meadows. His younger brother Stephen had partly trained at the Infirmary before practising as a doctor of medicine. Appearing with Joseph were the well-known Edinburgh artists Marie Thomson (soprano), Catherine

Mentiplay (contralto), Ramsay Geikie (solo piano) and two accompanists, Paterson Lamb and the indefatigable Spencer Clay. In his programme Joseph sang 'The Great Awakening' by Kramer in which he was accompanied by his former choirmaster, Mr (later Dr) Thomas H. Collinson, who played the organ obbligato. Returning home that night Collinson took out his pen and wrote the following entry in his diary[22]

> Joseph Hislop Concert. All the choristers were taken. Joseph Hislop is simply one of the marvels of the 20th Century, his genius even transforms a poorish song into a thing of beauty and significance. How much more his great operatic scenas! His *mezza voce* is simply fascinating and he sings double forte to high B with ease and confidence. His is the art which conceals art. It is like a dream to think that he was once with us as a tiny Probationer and as a Chorister. Never has there been I believe such an enthusiastic audience in Edinburgh. Mr Keith [Joseph's old schoolteacher] says he wept with emotion at the reception and dear old J. K. is a sturdy old Scot. The boys' shrill cheers could be heard above the huzzas of the audience.

The concert realised £550; the Edinburgh press commented that 'Mr Hislop's heart is as big as his voice is beautiful.' J. Aitken Brown, writing in broad Scots, also contributed a patriotic verse in his praise.[23]

Joseph then journeyed north to the Music Hall in Aberdeen where on 25 April there were extraordinary scenes when an unprecedented, densely packed crowd queued for seats. Joseph had been extravagantly billed as 'the world-famous tenor who is acclaimed as successor to Caruso'. Though some in the audience knew that the parallel could not be pressed too far, Joseph was admitted to have a pure tenor voice of extraordinarily rich and expressive quality. His tone was always exquisitely warm, and even on the highest notes in the *Tosca* aria, completely unforced; Joseph made 'an effective use of a soft sostenuto' while to his unusual capacity for expression he added 'remarkable vividness and dramatic power'.[24]

His Dundee concert two days later earned him the same rebuke. 'Without having heard Caruso, except on a gramophone,' commented *The Dundee Courier* (28 April 1922), 'we doubt if the claim made for Mr Hislop to be that wonderful singer's successor is a wise one. If Mr Hislop's voice does not have the warmth and richness of Caruso's, we are sure that he uses it with equal art and perhaps puts more of the intellectual into his singing.'

A farewell concert in Edinburgh brought the observation from *The Edinburgh Evening Dispatch* (29 April 1922) that though the great tenor did not happen to be called Hislopski, and was trained in a local cathedral choir, his fellow-citizens offered him a rapturous welcome; in a period of less than 12 days he had three times packed the Usher Hall to overflowing, and there were still crowds who would rush to hear him if he agreed to appear again the following week. In the course of a long panegyric 'A.M.' of Edinburgh expressed a current of local popular feeling to the effect that although being 'a master of the operatic style', he had not forgotten his Scottish roots and continued to sing what 'common chiels' could understand.[25]

Perth provided the venue for his last Scottish appearance that spring. There the core of his singing was defined as clear diction, flawless phrasing, a beautiful line of tone, colour and expression, wrote *The Perthshire Advertiser* (6 May 1922). But 'Mr Hislop did not seem to be in the best of form, and sang, on the whole, disappointingly in comparison with his appearance here last spring. The subtle style of vocalisation required for the singing of songs was not quite within his control and the result was a slight untidiness of attack on occasion and a tendency to be a little bit below pitch.'[26]

The first week of October found Joseph in Glasgow again at St Andrew's Hall for the opening concert of the Abstainers' Union with the soprano Dora Labbette and Isolde Menges (violin). Spencer Clay was at the piano. Joseph sang the final aria from Donizetti's *Lucia di Lammermoor* and Liza Lehmann's 'Ah, Moon of My Delight' from *In a Persian Garden* (both of which he later recorded, the latter remaining, unhappily, unissued).

By the beginning of the following week Joseph sang with the Liverpool Philharmonic under Sir Landon Ronald at Philharmonic Hall. He made his first appearance in Liverpool with 'O Paradiso' and a group of songs. Back in the Usher Hall on 20 October, Joseph sang to the accompaniment of George Short, the Edinburgh pianist and arranger. His varied programme was devoted to Scots and English songs and operatic numbers. The pianist Ramsay Geikie was his supporting artist.

The concert party appeared next in Dundee at the Caird Hall where it was observed that there was 'a wonderful delicacy about his head voice, a liquid quality of great charm which he used with the ease which told of perfect command'.[27] More concerts in Glasgow, Perth, Greenock and Aberdeen followed in quick succession. For one critic in Aberdeen Joseph revived the glory of the days of old. To speak only of British tenors, one who had heard most of the prominent artists from Sims Reeves onwards 'could not avoid the conclusion that in Mr Hislop there lived one of the most distinctive of all'.[28] As for the often-repeated 'Caruso' label Joseph's voice was different, the passion more restrained, the art more intellectual, the style more lyrical and less purely dramatic.[29]

After yet another Usher Hall concert on 3 November 1922 where he included the Richard Strauss song 'Breit über mein Haupt dein schwarzen Haar'. He was joined in Middlesbrough on 8 November by Spencer Clay, the mezzo Kirkby Lunn and Mitja Nikisch (piano) at a Corbett concert. 'He possesses a clear, powerful voice with a richness of tone at times reminiscent of Caruso,' wrote the music correspondent of *The North-Eastern Daily Gazette* (9 November 1922).

It was to be full year before Joseph again took to the road on the British concert circuit. On the afternoon of Saturday 27 October 1923 the team of Ada Sari, Hislop, Marshall and Bratza, (who had given their first concert together three days before in Liverpool) gave an International Celebrity Subscription Concert at the Cardiff Empire. On the Sunday back in London at the Royal Albert Hall, Sari, Joseph and Wilhelm Backhaus the pianist played at a Special Sunday concert with Clarence Raybould at the piano. To the Town Hall in Birmingham next for 29 October – this was Joseph's first appearance in the city. He came with the reputation of being among the tenors, quite a considerable host already, who had been acclaimed as new Carusos. That he had a better right to the distinction than most was quickly evident.[30]

However, his first venture in the Caruso vein did not find him in the best of voice. His tone in Donizetti's 'Una furtiva lagrima' was clouded, and he was once a trifle under the pitch of a high note. Better things were to come. It was in Rachmaninoff's 'At Night' that Joseph's quality first asserted itself to the full, and the audience 'knew him for a singer whose merit was not to be assessed by comparisons with any predecessor, however well-meant. A reversion to opera brought "Vesti la giubba" with a sob on its final line not a whit inferior to the famous Caruso effect.'[31] It struck Joseph's listeners that the strength of his voice was in its middle tones, which were warm and round and occasionally took on a golden quality. His high notes made an appeal because they seemed a natural expansion of the middle register. They had not been developed as a thing apart.[32]

At the St Andrew's Hall in Glasgow on 1 November his singing of 'Bonnie Mary of Argyle' was considered to be much too sophisticated.[33] The Usher Hall in Edinburgh also heard him in the 'Flower Song' from *Carmen* and 'Questa o quella'. He finished the programme with an enticing version of 'O soave fanciulla' with Ada Sari as Mimi. Not a single item was allowed to pass without a demand for an encore. This brought the comment from *The Scotsman* (5 November 1923) that 'a good deal of the enjoyment was vitiated by the inordinate length of the programme, still more extended by the unreasonable demand for encores'.

A final Scottish concert took place at the Caird Hall in Dundee on 5 November in front of a very large audience. The large number of encores brought protests from *The Scottish Musical Magazine* (1 December 1923) as this made the concert finish as late as half-past ten. Joseph's final British concert took place on 26 November at the Queen's Hall with Sir Henry Wood and the violinist Jelly d'Aranyi. He sang 'Lensky's Aria' from *Eugene Onegin* and 'Isobel' by Frank Bridge:

> The sorrow of the wind is love's farewell,
> The darkness of the blind I will not tell
> Until the night within my mind is turned to light and Isobel.

References

1. The Bolton Evening News, 17 September 1920.
2. The Bolton Evening News, 25 September 1920.
3. The Monthly Musical Record, 1 November 1920, p. 255.
4. The Irish Times, 28 September 1920.
5. The Yorkshire Post, 2 October 1920.
6. The Huddersfield Examiner, 9 October 1920.
7. The Newcastle Daily Journal, 8 October 1920.
8. The Glasgow Herald, 1 November 1920.
9. The Musical Leader, 17 March 1921.
10. The Boston Herald, 12 March 1921.
11. The Springfield Daily Republican, 1 April 1921.
12. The Kansas City Journal, 15 April 1921.
13. ibid.
14. The Musical Leader, 21 April 1921.
15. The Detroit Free Press, 21 April 1921.
16. The Detroit Free Press, 22 April 1921.
17. The Buffalo Express, 30 April 1921.
18. The Buffalo Express, 30 April 1921.
19. Letter 3 November (in private possession).
20. The Edinburgh Evening News, 19 April 1922.
21. The Edinburgh Evening News, 21 April 1922.
22. Collinson, Dr T.H. (1922), Diary 9-10 NLS, Acc. 8985/67.
23. The Edinburgh Evening News, 21 April 1922.
24. The Aberdeen Journal, 26 April 1922.
25. The Edinburgh Evening Dispatch, 29 April 1922.
26. The Perth Advertiser, 6 May 1922.
27. The Dundee Advertiser, 23 October 1922.
28. The Aberdeen Journal, 2 November 1922.
29. ibid.
30. The Birmingham Post, 30 October 1923.
31. ibid.
32. ibid.
33. The Glasgow Herald, 2 November 1923.

10 Recital tours (1924–1930)

The Hislop concert bandwagon rolled on. Back in Edinburgh's Usher Hall for 25 January 1924, Joseph took part in the three annual Lumsden Scots concerts with Dora Labbette. Although Joseph appeared only twice on the Friday evening and was billed to sing four songs he ended by giving four encores, among which was 'My love is like a red, red rose'. He received an enthusiastic ovation, singing to the accompaniment of George Short who had written the arrangements of some of the songs.[1]

Short and Joseph joined the young Serbian violinist Bratza and the soprano Marjorie Dane to give a concert in Aberdeen on 29 January where the press complained that Joseph had not mastered the 'higher reaches of the art and its austerities'; he needed 'singer's songs that gave free expression to the lyrical impulse'. He had to have 'swelling curves in the melody and climaxes, the stuff for those clear, ringing tones of the upper register' which never failed to arouse the enthusiasm of an audience. When he was called upon to restrain voice or feeling the result was commonplace.[2]

A large crowd in the City Hall (Perth), gave Joseph a magnificent reception on Wednesday the 30th. However, it was noted that he appeared strained. His manager announced that he was suffering from laryngitis; indeed, he seemed to have lost a good deal of the youthful freshness and life which had made such a great appeal on his former visits.[3] There was speculation that his recent operatic engagements in Stockholm had taken their toll. Yet it was with little evidence of strain that he tackled a heavy programme of songs.[4]

By 2 February Joseph was in London for an afternoon concert at the Queen's Hall in the Chappell Popular series. With him were the pianist Benno Moiseiwitsch, Rosina Buckman and Harold Williams. The orchestra was conducted by Eugene Goossens. The great soprano Amelita Galli-Curci appeared at the Albert Hall in late October. On 2 November Joseph shared the platform there with the soprano Evelyn Scotney, his programme largely

136

made up of operatic numbers he never performed in the opera house. His first aria was 'Ch'ella mi creda libero e lontano' from Puccini's *La Fanciulla del West*. He followed this with 'Cielo e mar' from Ponchielli's *La Gioconda*, two arias which he rarely performed and never recorded. The programme ended with a duet which does not appear to have been in the Hislop repertoire until then, 'The Cherry Duet' from Mascagni's *L'Amico Fritz*.

Florence Austral rejoined Backhaus, Percy Kahn and Joseph for a Saturday concert at Alexandra Palace on 8 November. By this period in his career, Joseph was well placed in the Powell and Holt stable, along with Kreisler, Frieda Hempel and Clara Butt.

In the middle of January 1926, Dame Nellie Melba came to Edinburgh to sing in the Usher Hall. 'Goodbye for ever,' she said to the city somewhat melodramatically.[5] Only a few days after her came Joseph, appearing first at the Drill Hall (Carlisle) with the young Serbian violinist, Milan Bratza, and the towering Belgian pianist Walter Rummel. Percy Kahn was accompanying, with concert-manager Arthur Russell of Messrs Powell & Holt in attendance. If Madame Melba was the lady love of the Edinburgh concert-goer, (wrote *The Weekly Scotsman* 23 January 1926, after Joseph's Usher Hall concert), Joseph Hislop was the favourite boy of the family itself. It was a special pleasure that both should have been heard within a few days of each other. *The Scotsman* (18 January 1926), however, regretted that he had not included any Puccini arias in his programme as it considered these to be his forte.[6]

Then to the Caird Hall (Dundee) where 'Bonnie wee thing' was thought to be a perfect expression in Scottish sentiment. However, listeners could not understand the vocal exuberance of the strenuous final high note at its close.[7] Then followed visits to Dunfermline and Perth when similar remarks were expressed by a record review in *The Bulletin* (27 January 1926).

On 1 February the concert party arrived at the Albert Hall (Stirling). Sir Harry and Lady Lauder were in the audience. Lauder was an admirer of his operatic colleague and the two often played golf together. One of Joseph's encores was 'For you alone', with Bratza providing a violin obbligato.[8]

Sir Harry had been greeted with a burst of applause as he entered the hall. After the concert he went backstage. Joseph introduced Lauder to Walter Rummel, a huge man and very proud. 'My, Mr Rummel,' said Harry, 'I was fair carried away by your playing tonight'.

Rummel smiled gratefully down at the wee man. 'Yes,' added Harry, 'the way your fingers swept over the keyboard was sheer magic'. Rummel pushed out his chest with pride. 'And your timing, just brilliant!'

By now Walter Rummel could hardly contain his satisfaction. 'But one thing puzzles me, Mr Rummel,' said Harry. 'Why is it that a big strong man like you is playing the piano instead of working?' The deflated Rummel, seeing nothing of the funny side, twitched with rage.[9]

The following Sunday Joseph finally appeared at the Royal Albert Hall with the violinist Erica Morini and the indefatigable Percy Kahn. According to *The Daily Telegraph* (8 February 1926):

> Yesterday was a day of atmospheric gloom, not at all the kind of day to promote sudden vocal expression. Yet the experience of hearing Mr Joseph Hislop sing in the Albert Hall seemed to dispel the February fogs and agues, and to fill the mind with the consciousness of something more tangible than reality. There was something so spontaneous in the spirit of this man's singing, something so entirely lacking in artifice, that very soon we found ourselves tuning our hearts to the notes of early spring. Mr Hislop sings as one that would infect the world with singing.

The programme he used for the tour could be described as an exotic pot-pourri: 'When I am laid in earth' (Dido's Lament from Purcell's *Dido and Aeneas*), Massenet's 'Ah, fuyez douce image' (*Manon*), 'J'ai pleuré en rêve' by Hue; Percy Kahn's 'The Willow Tree' and 'Come Buy' by Buzzi-Peccia (from *A Winter's Tale*). *The Daily Telegraph* concluded its review by saying that with Joseph there was none of the grossness of operatic tradition, the outbursts which were best described as 'animal noises'.

Joseph remained in London until 15 February when his wife Karin presented him with a bouncing baby boy, one who would become a talented amateur tenor. Ten days later Joseph, Walter Rummel and Percy Kahn were back at the Usher Hall. In the audience was his old choirmaster Dr Thomas Collinson who, in spite of his negative verdict on Joseph's voice in 1907, had completely revised his original opinion. After the concert he wrote in his journal that Joseph's platform manner had been very casual and plebeian. His voice, of course, was 'A1 pure velvet, and of marvellous compass, Tenor C, 4 foot (quite firm) up to 1 foot C in full chest'.[10] Collinson, who had perfect pitch, described Joseph's seamless two-octave range (up to high C) in organ-builder's jargon.

A week later, on 28 February, Joseph and Percy Kahn reappeared at the Albert Hall in a special Sunday Concert with the Kedroff Quartet of male vocalists and the violinist Zoltan Szekely.

His next short concert tour came in January 1927 at the Lumsden's Scots Festival in the Usher Hall. His fellow soloists were the soprano Flora Woodman, the baritone John Mathewson and the violinist Florence MacBride. George Short accompanied for all three concerts. The hall was full on the Friday evening and also at the 3 o'clock concert on the Saturday in spite of the rival attraction of the Rugby International (when Scotland scored an overwhelming victory over the French).[11] One observer, voicing the feelings of many, wrote that it was only natural that the audience should give special greeting to Joseph who evidently contrived to be always on his best form when singing to his 'ain folk'.[12]

It was *The Edinburgh Evening Dispatch* (22 January 1927) correspondent who gave what is probably the most illuminating account of a Hislop concert. He noted that his concert style was remarkably free from affectation. Indeed, few great artists had less eccentricity or mannerisms; he also always refrained from importing the atmosphere of the theatre into the concert hall. Joseph appeared simple, boyishly alert almost, his complete absence of any staginess at once establishing a sympathetic bond with his audience. One commendable trait was that he kept to his programme as printed, announcing with uplifted hand the titles of his encores.

The programme began and ended with a vocal quartet. Instead of the five songs on the programme Joseph sang nine, five by Burns (including the ever-popular 'Bonnie wee thing'), 'Mary of Argyle', 'Lochnagar' and, as an encore, an old Italian folksong and 'La donna è mobile' (which had to be repeated!) Curiously enough, it was the last-mentioned item which aroused the greatest enthusiasm; after making what was evidently meant as a final disappearance for the evening amid cries of 'Bravo!' and a flutter of waving handkerchiefs, the great tenor had to come back and sing it all over again.[13]

A welcome return to his family roots came on 26 January when Joseph sang at The Playhouse (Galashiels) to a large audience as part of a series of Border concerts which featured Muriel Brunskill, Roy Henderson, Peter Dawson and Frank Mullings. Percy Kahn accompanied Joseph who gave 12 numbers including 'E lucevan le stelle', Tosti's 'L'alba separa dalla luce l'ombra' and groups of English and Scots songs, pleasing the audience particularly with 'Bonnie wee thing'.[14] One commentator noted that a surprising feature of the finished performance was that owing to Mr Kahn's lateness in arrival there had been no opportunity for practising. Nevertheless, Kahn's faultless accompaniments added considerable charm to the whole programme.[15]

On 16 July 1927 came a grand adventure in the Hislop story: the beginning of the J.C. Williamson concert tour of Australia and New Zealand. Joseph and his American/Italian accompanist Alberto Sciarretti sailed out of Tilbury on the P&O liner *Moldavia* bound for Sydney via Gibraltar, Port Said, Colombo and Freemantle. They arrived on 25 August, only a week after the New Zealand soprano Frances Alda, (his Mimi of the Colón in 1925) had made her farewell appearance at Sydney Town Hall.

Among the prominent artists who had visited Australia that season were Dame Nellie Melba (making a farewell tour of her homeland in April) and Jascha Heifetz (in May). In one season Perth, Western Australia, with 100 000 inhabitants, had hosted Galli-Curci, Chaliapin, Percy Grainger, Backhaus and Pavlova.[16]

Interviewed by *The Sydney Morning Herald* (26 August 1927) at the start of longest-ever concert tour, with 50 scheduled performances, Joseph confirmed that Australia as a musical centre was undoubtedly attracting attention among artists abroad. Asked about his programme for the tour, Joseph replied genially that he would sing everything from comedy to grand opera. With regard to the task of selecting new modern songs, he instanced the experience which he and his pianist, Alberto Sciarretti, had on the voyage in going through hundreds of manuscripts at the piano. According to Joseph, the trouble with many modern composers was they were so fond of employing dissonances that they ignored the need for a melodic line, whereas composers like Brahms, Schubert and Hugo Wolf – they knew what the voice meant. 'Der Doppelgänger' for example was so simple and yet the composer had endowed it with vivid colour. Joseph thought that contemporary British writers were doing some fine work and, as for the Russians, he considered them to be wonderful. He planned to sing many songs by Edward Grieg. Ending the interview he added that he did not condemn other forms of modern music, jazz, for example. He thought that jazz had a very stimulating effect because of its pulsating rhythm. But he also thought that if one were obliged to listen to jazz continually it would no longer be stimulating.

At his first Australian concert on Saturday 3 September, Joseph proved his ability to charge the music of diverse schools with a luminous glow which brought its meaning fully home. In 'Vesti la giubba' his upraised trembling hands gave due emphasis to the anguished tones of despair. After 16 songs he was again called for an encore but excused himself because, he said whimsically, he had not quite got over the trip through the Red-Hot Sea![18]

A momentous occasion in Australian history took place early on the following Monday morning. The first All-Empire Broadcast beamed 12 000 miles from Sydney's Station 2 FC between two and five o'clock in the morning.[19] At the age of 68, Dame Nellie Melba broadcast a message to listeners in Britain, who heard her on Sunday evening. Joseph sent his best wishes to his mother in Edinburgh and sang 'Annie Laurie' to the accompaniment of Alberto Sciarretti.[20] Small and energetic, Joseph stood there early in the morning performing his great record success, 'I heard you singing' – the exquisite pianissimo of the final G being carried over two continents and two oceans.[21]

The Sydney Morning Herald (5 September 1927) observed of Joseph's voice that 'he possesses a wide range, with the special advantage of a middle register of exceptional quality.'

After his seventh Sydney concert on 17 September, Joseph travelled south to Melbourne. He began with two concerts at the Auditorium before an appearance on 26 September at the Ballarat Coliseum. Back in Melbourne he was entertained by the Caledonian Society before giving four more recitals at the Theatre Royal, his final concert (11 October) including 'All Hail Thou Dwelling' from *Faust*, 'Celeste Aida', 'Vesti la giubba', 'La donna è mobile', 'Nessun dorma' (from *Turandot* whose première was in 1926) and 'Un dì all'azzurro spazio' from *Andrea Chénier*. This programme brought the comment from *The Melbourne Herald* (12 October 1927) that he 'sang with the manliest of styles, good cantabile, no undue flourishes and no misplaced emotional gulps'; He was also seen to be 'a most expressive actor with his voice, as well as in gesture and facial responsiveness. His was an art which made the tone suit every shade of feeling and every style of music, while his fluency in the graces of ornamentation were a delight to listen to.'

His first Adelaide concert on 15 October began with Beethoven's 'Adelaide' as a graceful tribute. His performance of 'L'Aubade' from *Le Roi d'Ys* included a 'final A, sung in altissimo . . . a gossamer-thread of sound'.[22] A reviewer of his third Adelaide concert remarked that he seemed to have everything: 'a voice with endless reserves of power, an art which makes the tone suit every shade of feeling and every style of music and a personality which at once captured the whole strength of feeling of his hearers'; at the close the little hush before the applause which broke like a hailstorm conveyed the intense feeling of the audience.[23]

His final Adelaide appearance included 'Ah! Fuyez, douce image' from Massenet's *Manon* accompanied on the grand organ and to show his linguistic versatility, a triple group of Russian and Norwegian songs. He also sang 'A birthday' composed by Willie B. Mansom, who had died at the age of 19 in the Great War. Next day he performed in the first of two concert versions of Gounod's *Faust* at the Sydney Town Hall with the Royal Philharmonic Society, singing (as did the Marguerite) in French, while the rest of the company sang in English. This marked the end of his Australian tour.

After the concert Joseph was taken on an expedition into the interior to observe the Aboriginal way of life and to meet a tribe only a few of whose members had ever seen a European. The chief of the tribe invited the party to a splendid dinner where some of his 20 wives served the guests. After the meal was over Joseph sang to the Aborigines. This made a strange impression on the chief. He had been in good humour, lolling around on his straw mat but, hearing the songs, he began to howl, jumped up and to Joseph's horror began to rub noses with him. The interpreter explained that this was a mark of great respect. He said that the chief wanted to give him a precious gift, he could have his pick of any of his wives! Only with the greatest difficulty was Joseph able to make the chief understand that he could not accept such a generous gesture. In the end, shaking his head in disbelief, the chief reluctantly gave up. Instead he presented Joseph with a dog which from that day on became his mascot and followed him all over the world.[24]

Alberto Sciarretti, Joseph and Karin arrived in New Zealand in time for a first concert at the Town Hall in Auckland on 3 November. During a rehearsal, Joseph urged Maughan Barnett, Auckland's city organist, to quicken the tempo. 'That's better.' The glorious aria from Massenet's *Manon* pealed from the organ loft through the empty Town Hall, echoing and re-echoing. His right hand gently swaying, Joseph concluded the aria, saving his voice as much as possible. Over and over again until it was perfect. Then, pausing for a moment, he surveyed row after row of empty seats. 'I want every one of those seats to be occupied,' he remarked. 'I will do the rest.'[25] Indeed, the concert was a great success, the consensus being that refinement and intelligence marked each phrase. Underlying everything was a certain warmth of expression which only a consummate artist could so rapturously suggest.[26] In 'Ah, Fuyez' from *Manon* Joseph was accompanied by an obbligato on the grand organ. His 'fluency in the graces of ornamentation were a delight to listen to' according to a member of the large and critical audience and one of the outstanding features of the 'Aubade' from *Le Roi d'Ys* was 'the grace of the *lento* ornament and a beautiful *portamento*.[27]

During the early part of the second Auckland concert a discharge of fireworks close to the hall was a disturbing factor. Joseph was also suffering from a slight cold. Later, when things had quietened down, the audience could appreciate his singing of 'En Svane', 'The Sea' (by Borodin) and Marjorie Kennedy-Fraser's 'An Island Sheiling Song'. His account of Cyril Scott's 'Lord Randall' was terrifying in its intensity.[28]

From Auckland the concert party journeyed south to see the magnificent thermal springs at Rotorua and Wairakei and the picturesque Maori villages. Then it was over the Cook Strait to South Island where three concerts followed in Wellington's Town Hall. In the first he was accompanied on the grand organ (with chimes) for 'Ah, Fuyez'. In the second, organ and violin played for Joseph as he sang 'O Lord Most Holy' (Panis Angelicus) by César Franck. Then came two Grieg songs ('En Drøm' and 'En Svane') and 'Un dì' (*Andrea Chénier*). The third concert on 17 November was such a success that an extra fourth one was quickly arranged. The audience was apparently in a frenzy of delight. Joseph no doubt made some concessions to a large mixed audience – for instance, when he clawed the air to suggest the cats 'Jekkel and Jessup and Jill' in the song 'Five Eyes.'[29]

By the time he reached Christchurch he had appeared before 21 000 New Zealanders. At the Christchurch Theatre Royal he scored yet more successes, prompting the comment that his voice was 'a gift of the gods'[30] and a fervent wish that he would not employ extreme force for the sake of the preservation of the voice.[31] Stormy applause greeted Hislop and Sciarretti at a third extra concert. Joseph sang Scots songs to his kilted admirers in particular, who were there in force.

Travelling south again Joseph appeared in Timaru at the Theatre Royal on 7 December. *The Timaru Herald* (8 December 1927) agreed that he was an artist of outstanding ability, the possessor of a voice of lyric quality, controlled with exquisite grace, yet capable of a roundness of tone and a fullness of volume, produced with an entire absence of effort or straining: 'He displays an easy grace on the platform and is at times quite unconventional in manner.'

At Dunedin, populated by a large Scottish colony, a family clan from his mother's side met him at the Grand Hotel. John Lunn, Joseph's uncle, was a well-known builder and a member of the City Council. In an interview with *The Otago Witness* (6 December 1927) Joseph spoke about the pressures of being an opera singer. In his opinion the time of Melba's fame had been the golden age of opera. Now a singer, to satisfy a captiously critical audience, had to cast aside kid gloves and put it over with a rapier.

When he reached Invercargill on the southern tip of South Island, Joseph seemed spare, his face almost thin, thus destroying utterly the old idea that tenors had to be fat and eccentric. 'Britain's ambassador of song,' they called him as he arrived at Invercargill station.[33] His practice of speaking to his accompanist and his wife almost simultaneously in Italian and Swedish drew astonishment in Invercargill as elsewhere and attention was drawn to very favourable comparisons made in the Wellington press between Joseph's 'superb power of dramatic interpretation' and the histrionic ability of the Russian bass Chaliapin who had appeared in Wellington not long before.[34]

On 8 December, Joseph and his party left New Zealand and sailed for Melbourne where he was to give a final concert at the Theatre Royal with a strongly operatic programme. Before its largest-ever audience of 5 000[35] he sang in Handel's *Messiah* both on 20 December and four days later when he inaugurated the new Melbourne Town Hall. His Australian and New Zealand tour over, Joseph sailed for South Africa.

Hislop and Sciarretti had been engaged by African Theatres Ltd for some 37 concerts in South Africa and Rhodesia. 'He was not anxious to go to South Africa just now,' Karin Hislop admitted in Edinburgh, 'as he was wanting so much to see the children. We were so sure they would not give the terms he asked that I came away home, expecting he would be following in a week or two. But I had not left Freemantle two hours when the contract came through.'[36] Leaving Melbourne on 25 January Joseph and Alberto steamed west on board the twin-screw liner *Suevic*, arriving in the port of Natal on 17 February 1928 in preparation for a hard schedule of concerts. It was hot and damp, a first real taste of Africa. At the docks that morning the deck of the *Suevic* presented a cheerful appearance with little knots of dignitaries clustering around waiting to welcome Joseph.[37]

The following morning a Caledonian Gathering waited for them in the Mayor's office. Joseph rose to the occasion displaying, in his public presence, his mastery of the media and his ability to say the right thing. 'Tell the people of Durban,' Joseph said, 'that apart from coming to see this lovely country, of which I read so much in the pages of Rider Haggard when at school, I have come to make friends with its people and not to sing at them.' He added that 'a nation which does not devote attention to music and art is doomed, for the spice of life is art.'[38]

Joseph was the first celebrity to have appeared in Durban. One of Joseph's first arias was 'O Paradiso' from Meyerbeer's *L'Africana*, sung as a tribute to the magnificent continent he was in. His opening concerts on 22 and 25 February at the Theatre Royal were a triumph.

Arriving in Johannesburg Sciarretti and Hislop played the Town Hall four times in February and March. Johannesburg was hot as a frying-pan and also dry. Although Joseph thought that the inside of his mouth was going to dry up, fortunately he did not lose his voice.[39]

Then it was on to Cape Town where Joseph and Alberto were asked to sing for the Governor's wife, Her Royal Highness Princess Alice and Princess Helena Victoria. Two more Cape Town concerts followed before tenor and pianist set off for Johannesburg again to appear at the Town Hall. Then by train to Durban once more.

On the way they found the line blocked by a derailment. Joseph recorded the scene with his cine camera, the engine lying on its back like a wounded dinosaur. The accident caused a 12-hour delay and made him late for his concert at the Theatre Royal (Durban) and an incident took place which Joseph seldom tired of recounting. Going straight to the theatre where the audience was waiting and before changing into dress clothes, he stepped before the curtain, panting, as if he had *run* part of the way from Johannesburg. 'Just give me another ten minutes and I'll be with you.' Terrific applause! When that had died down a voice with a strong Scottish accent shouted from the gallery, 'Joe, "Bonnie wee Thing"!' Joseph was quite taken aback but quickly pulled himself together, thanked the gentleman for the charming compliment, adding that he had never been called that before.[40]

'Looking round the crowded Theatre Royal last night,' wrote the *Natal Mercury* (4 April 1928) music critic,

> and listening to the roar and tumult of applause that followed each one of the numbers contributed by Mr Joseph Hislop left no doubt possible as to the extent to which this most dramatic of singers has captured the hearts of Durban. If there is one quality in Mr Hislop's singing which stands out above that singer's many other notable characteristics it is unquestionably his dramatic power.

After a second Durban concert it was back to Johannesburg for an Easter Sunday concert. The verdict of *The Star* (9 April 1928) was that 'Mr Hislop has a dramatic lyricism which enables him to interpret whatever he sings. He has been taken to the heart of the Johannesburg public.'

Joseph also developed a healthy respect for the inborn musicality of the black South African tribesmen. He visited the gold mines and was struck by the native war-dances and the beautiful singing of the tribal choirs (which he filmed). Near Johannesburg the tribes assembled for enormous celebrations, where he found the different kinds of instrumental and vocal music produced to be absolutely astonishing.[41]

Before he returned to Europe, Joseph gave two concerts in mid-April at the Palace Theatre (Bulawayo). From the first he had a very warm reception, singing 'Un di all'azzurro spazio' from *Andrea Chénier* and Lalo's 'Aubade' ('Vainement, ma bien aimée' from *Le Roi d'Ys*), among others.[42] At the Palace Theatre in Salisbury (Harare), Joseph was greeted with a sudden burst of applause after his opening aria, the 'Flower Song' from *Carmen*.[43] ' "Windy Nights" ', wrote a critic, 'was a supreme example of his power of creating verbal life; the ghostly horseman seemed to flit across the auditorium before the eye and outstretched hand of the singer.'[44] A roar of applause continued until he returned and, obliging a request from the back, sang 'Bonnie wee thing' and the fiery, vengeful 'MacGregor's Gathering'.[45] At his second Salisbury appearance Joseph received a tremendous ovation.[46]

Then, on 22 April, he left by train for Victoria Falls, capturing the scene on his cine camera. On the film we see him sailing up-river and then standing in raincoat and sou'wester smothered by clouds of spray compared to which, as Joseph put it, the force of Niagara, which he had seen in 1921, was nothing.[47]

The last South African concert took place at the Orpheum Theatre in Johannesburg and brought the comment from *The Star* (30 April 1928) that 'occasionally a demonstration in a concert hall merits the characterising phrase "wild enthusiasm". The applause heaped on Mr Hislop and Mr Sciarretti in the Orpheum Theatre last night had that frenetic touch. His artistic personality, his magnificent vocal equipment and his keen intellectuality were the factors that attracted a great audience to hear him on his final appearance.'

Joseph returned to Europe and thought little about concert tours until one day in 1929, when arriving at Brottkärr for a three week rest, he found a letter from Alberto Sciarretti.[48] He had previously agreed to act as Joseph's US manager and do the groundwork in setting up a series of Hislop appearances in the States. This was to involve contacting concert agents, Scots societies, opera companies and even Warner Brothers.

Alberto was to go on to Chicago and, if necessary, travel down the Pacific Coast on the route of the 1921 Scotti tour on which Joseph had been so successful. Alberto was to speak to his friend Gaetano Merola who had founded the San Francisco Opera Company six years previously. He was also to approach Warner Brothers, (who had just merged with United Artists and proposed a $12 m film corporation), to suggest Joseph as a singing actor for a new feature film.

However, the Italian had so far done little of what he had promised. 'Do get a hustle on, Alberto,' wrote Joseph impatiently, 'show me and yourself what you can do.'[49] Finally a more positive reply came from Sciarretti who by then had established himself at Carnegie Hall (New York). He enclosed a contract from Daniel Mayer Inc. of Steinway Hall which stipulated that Joseph should come to America provided that at least five concerts were secured at an average fee of $500. Already one engagement had been arranged, at Kansas City on 28 January 1930 at a fee of $750, and two others were pending, Marks Levine of Mayer's being confident of as many as ten concerts in all. At first Joseph did not approve the agreement, but after some adjustments he signed the contract for a six-week US season.[50] A week later Rudolph Vavpetich of Daniel Mayer Inc. received a draft from Joseph for $800 according to the terms of the contract. Vavpetich had mailed circulars throughout the United States and Canada and also to many Scots societies.[51] In time it became apparent that the response would be poor; the minimum number of concerts as guaranteed was not forthcoming and the venture accordingly was abandoned.

So ended this abortive attempt on Joseph's part to return to the United States where he had once been so warmly welcomed across the nation. Just as he had failed to secure fresh engagements at La Scala in 1923 and was also about to be unsuccessful in his negotiations with the Berlin Staatsoper, so he had eventually to abandon any thought of fresh triumphs in the New World.

References

1. The Scotsman, 28 January 1924.
2. The Press and Journal, 30 January 1924.
3. The Perthshire Advertiser, 2 February 1924.
4. ibid.
5. The Edinburgh Evening News, 14 January 1926.
6. The Scotsman, 18 January 1926.
7. Unidentified Dundee newspaper, 21 January 1926.
8. The Stirling Journal and Advertiser, 4 February 1926.
9. Thompson, R. (1975), 'Joseph Hislop', *The Book of the Braemar Gathering*, p. 207.
10. Collinson, Dr T.H. Diary, Acc. 8985/66, NLS.
11. The Edinburgh Evening News, 23 January 1927.
12. The Edinburgh Evening News, 22 January 1927.

13. The Edinburgh Evening Dispatch, 22 January 1927.
14. The Border Standard, 29 January 1927.
15. The Southern Reporter, 2 February 1927.
16. The Monthly Musical Record, 1 May 1928, p. 136.
17. The Sydney Morning Herald, 26 August 1927.
18. The Sydney Morning Herald, 5 September 1927.
19. The Morning Post, 5 September 1927.
20. Unidentified Sydney newspaper, 5 September 1927, NLS.
21. Unidentified Sydney newspaper, 5 September 1927, NLS.
22. Unidentified Adelaide newspaper, 17 October 1927, NLS.
23. Unidentified Adelaide newspaper, 21 October 1927.
24. Helsingin Sanomat (Finland), February 1930 (undated), NLS.
25. The New Zealand Herald, 4 November 1927.
26. ibid.
27. The Auckland Star, 4 November 1927.
28. The New Zealand Herald, 7 November 1927.
29. The New Zealand Herald, 14 November 1927.
30. The Press, 25 November 1927.
31. The Press, 23 November 1927.
32. The Timaru Herald, 8 December 1927.
33. The Southland Times, 5 December 1927.
34. The Southland Times, 3 December 1927.
35. Stockholms-Dagbladet, 6 March 1928.
36. The Sunday Post, 26 February 1928.
37. The Natal Advertiser, 17 February 1928.
38. ibid.
39. Stockholms-Dagbladet, 5 June 1928.
40. BBC Home Service script broadcast, 16 May 1963, NLS.
41. Stockholms-Dagbladet, 5 June 1928.
42. The Bulawayo Chronicle, 14 April 1928.
43. ibid.
44. ibid.
45. ibid.
46. The Rhodesia Herald, 23 April 1928.
47. Stockholms-Dagbladet, 5 June 1928.
48. Letter (New York) 25 April 1929 (in private possession).
49. Letter (Gothenburg) 2 April 1929 (in private possession).
50. Undated letter (in private possession).
51. Letter (New York) 25 June 1929 (in private possession).

11 Recital tours (1931–1934)

Just after New Year 1931 Joseph received good news from J. Nevin Tait who represented J. C. Williamson Ltd, of Australian and New Zealand Theatres, lessees of the Melbourne Auditorium and The Palace Theatre (Sydney). Nevin confirmed that contractual proposals previously made by Joseph for an Australian and New Zealand tour were acceptable; he urged an early departure so as to pre-empt other artists (including pianists Levitski and Mark Hambourg and the popular Australian bass-baritone Peter Dawson) also expected that spring.[1] Thus in the last week of February Joseph, his wife and young daughter sailed from the South of France to begin his second concert tour in Australia.

On 11 April he opened at Sydney Town Hall in front of the Governor. 'Mr Hislop has not a great voice and on Saturday night it was not heard at its best,' commented *The Sydney Morning Herald*'s (13 April 1931) music critic, 'till the programme had advanced some distance. But he uses it with artistic skill and subtlety in portraying diverse moods and shades of emotion.' Joseph began with 'Lohengrin's Narration' and proceeded through English ballads and Scots songs to the numbers from *Frederica*.

In his autobiography the impresario Claude Kingston paints a vivid picture of Joseph on tour:

> Much of my deep affection for the Scottish tenor Joseph Hislop, exasperating though he was in some ways, rests on our association early in the 1930s. . . .
> His platform sense was uncanny. While singing his first group of numbers in a Sydney concert he sensed resistance in his audience, something intangible but, to the experienced performer, unmistakable.
> He always carried a small booklet on the platform to reinforce his memory. This held the words of some 200 songs written on separate sheets loosely fitted into the cover. Hislop began his second group of songs (three English ballads). His hands, holding his booklet open in front of him, moved almost imperceptibly. The 200 or so pages cascaded from his fingers and, scattering, fluttered out and showered the people in the first few rows like snowflakes.

148

The audience laughed and applauded with Hislop joining in the laugh. The sheets were gathered up and passed back to him, and he put them back into the cover. The concert went on but the atmosphere was wholly changed. The ice was broken, the singer and his hearers were now friends. Joe had brought his audience to his feet by judiciously contriving a little 'accident'.[2]

Joseph arrived in Australia at the heels of fate. Dame Nellie Melba passed away in Sydney on 23 February, aged 69. Only a month before Pavlova (with whom Joseph had shared a platform in 1920) had died in The Hague. On the international political stage Gandhi had just been released after ten months in prison. In England, Sir Thomas Beecham faced his creditors.

The accompanist provided was the brilliant young South African pianist, Isidor Goodman, then in his twenties, over whom Joseph attempted to be a hard and temperamental task-master. 'It started at their first concert in Sydney,' recalled Claude Kingston. 'Goodman opened the programme with a piano solo.'

> He received a great ovation. I went around to the artists' room to congratulate him. Hislop was there. He was scowling and I knew why. Goodman was guilty of the same crime . . . as Marie Aussenac had committed against Clara Butt and Kennerley Rumford. He played too well.
> 'No bloody good to me, Claude,' Hislop said, not caring that Goodman could hear every word. 'You've got to get rid of him.' . . . Joe went on and sang his first bracket. The audience gave him a great hand and I hoped he would be more tractable. He wasn't. 'No bloody good to me', he said as soon as he walked into the artists' room. 'You get rid of him.' . . . Joe kept nagging me about it and I kept telling him he would have to live with Goodman and like it. Sometimes Goodman heard these discussions and sometimes he didn't but he knew Hislop was all the time pressing for his dismissal.[3]

A second concert saw Goodman again rewarded with a great spontaneous outburst of applause. Joseph led off with some Italian songs, continuing with English, Scandinavian and Scots songs. He finished with his operatic repertoire which displayed his versatility and brilliance.[4]

During the third concert Goodman unfortunately began playing one song in an unexpected key; however, at the second start he transposed fluently as he went along, and again Joseph scored a great success with his brilliant climax.[5] A feature of the fourth recital was Joseph's singing of a piece new to Sydney audiences, 'You are my heart's delight' from Lehár's *Land of Smiles* (1929). After a final matinée appearance Hislop and Goodman sailed for New Zealand.

Arrived in Auckland, Joseph gave his revised views on jazz. 'Good jazz is wonderful. There is some quality of rhythm and abandon about it which makes it akin to the strong waters of my native country. It is bottled joy. But I do not sing jazz. Ordinary singing takes a lifetime of study to perfect. No one but a genius could sing jazz.'[6]

Three concerts at the Auckland Town Hall found his voice rich and well rounded.[7] During the party's last days in Auckland, Joseph invited some friends and a few newspaper people for late afternoon drinks at the Grand Hotel. Claude Kingston recalled Joseph's sparkling mood:

> Presently he gave a signal. Three waiters came in carrying gleaming silver trays loaded with cocktails and began to serve the guests. Joe walked over and glanced at one of the trays. 'Take them all out', he snapped. 'You've got the olives in the glasses and it's not full measure. I want the glasses filled and the olives on the side.' The waiters looked stunned but they picked up their trays of cocktails and filed out. A few minutes later they came back. Each glass was now filled to the brim and the olives were on side-plates. They served the drinks and then Joe stood up and made an excellent speech, brisk, dry, witty. Having told his guests how much he had enjoyed his visit to Auckland, he thanked everybody for coming and wished them well, then finished off by saying with an impish grin 'And now, my friends, make sure as you go through life that you always get good measure.'[8]

Leaving Auckland they travelled south to Hamilton where, after appearing at the Theatre Royal, Joseph, Karin, Isidor Goodman and Claude Kingston arrived at Wanganui on the Pacific Coast. One criticism of the concert programmes in Auckland had been that Joseph's choice of songs was not what might be called highest grade.[9] In fact, he gave the impression that he was singing 'down' to his audience. The music critic of *The Wanganui Chronicle* (12 May 1931) also found the concert at the Opera House too full of fragmentary items of light character, ending with several Herbert Hughes nursery rhymes which left the audience in an unsatisfied frame of mind. And there were other difficulties. Joseph was under the handicap on stage of being uncomfortable in a cold draught: he put on his overcoat and continued the programme.

The time came to leave Wanganui. Claude Kingston recalled that 'you always knew there would be a fight when Joe's bill arrived.'

> I paid and went away leaving Joe to his battle. The car which was to take us to Wellington came and I had our bags loaded into it. I went back to the reception desk. Joe was still hard at it, demanding that his bill should be reduced, but the hotel clerk would not budge.
>
> And then I noticed something alarming. Joe was growing hoarser with almost every word he spoke. I went outside and sat in the car. After a while Joe came out and got in beside me. We were an hour late in leaving and all through the journey Joe kept up a croaking hymn of hate against 'those bloody robbers in Wanganui'. For the hotel people had stuck to their guns and Joe had had to give up and pay up.[10]

Joseph was piped by the Wellington Highland Pipe Band from the Hotel St George, where he was staying, to the Town Hall. His sore throat showing itself here and there in his intonation, his first Wellington appearance became a pleasant ballad concert with only two operatic items.[11] By the second concert however, his slight vocal trouble had disappeared and Joseph gave his full-throated versions of grand opera, spirituals (arranged by

Burleigh), ballads and folksongs. In spite of appalling weather a large audience turned out for his third and last recital during which he did not attempt any bravura numbers calling for top C, so dearly loved by the public.[12]

Christchurch was the next stop where he was considered to be a heroic tenor and, at the Theatre Royal, held the audience in the hollow of his hand.[13] He even had time to argue for the relevance of the arts. Joseph told an eager reporter that man could not live without aesthetic and cultural satisfaction. 'Pigment and colour for the eye, sound for the ear.'[14]

In Wellington an apprehensive young reporter sent to interview Joseph for the journal *Music in New Zealand* (1 June 1931), found that the great tenor looked a trifle bored. 'His heavy-lidded large eyes expressed disinterest, nearly.' An air of polite resignation enveloped his well-groomed figure. It was on the King's Birthday (3 June) that Joseph sang with the Wellington Philharmonic Orchestra, pleasing the audience in particular with 'The Prize Song' from *Die Meistersinger* and 'All Hail, Abode so Pure and Lowly' (Salut, demeure chaste et pure), both sung in English.[15] After one of Joseph's three concerts in the Melbourne Auditorium, the critic of *The Age* (18 June 1931) noted that Joseph surprised his listeners by the expressive shades and colour contrasts he commanded between the emotional extremes.

Catching the mail train from Sydney, Joseph and his accompanist set off for Brisbane early in July for four concerts at His Majesty's Theatre. But trouble was brewing; the one-sided quarrel which had been simmering right through the tour, between Joseph and his (much younger and taller) accompanist, suddenly burst into life – as Claude Kingston vividly remembered:

> we had adjoining sleeping compartments and I heard Hislop go into Goodman's compartment and say something in an angry strangled voice. Goodman did not reply.
> 'So you won't talk, eh?' Hislop gritted. 'I'll knock your bloody head off.' Fearful that they would come to blows, I went in to keep the peace. Goodman sat there staring at Hislop. Poor Joe's face was white and working but he was powerless against Goodman's refusal to speak. He turned on his heel and walked out.
> He never did break the silence barrier. It did not matter how he snorted and shouted and swore (and he did all these things), Goodman just looked at him and held his tongue.[16]

Brisbane nevertheless was a triumph for Joseph. 'Hislop inspired public imagination with his grace, vitality, humour and strong sense of dramatic effectiveness' announced *The Brisbane Courier* (9 July 1931).

After giving around a dozen performances of opera on the concert platform in Melbourne, Joseph left in mid-September for his last Australian concerts at His Majesty's Theatre (Perth) on the far west coast. By this time he had parted company with his infuriatingly brilliant bête noire Isidor

Goodman and acquired the services of a member of the Melbourne and Sydney conservatoriums, the London-born (and middle-aged) Henri Penn, as accompanist. During his first concert Joseph quickly revealed his easy rapport with an audience. Near the end of his programme he had begun to sing a Puccini excerpt when a hissing spotlight became decidedly annoying. Breaking off the song, he had the nuisance stopped. A burst of laughter followed the applause when he returned to the platform and quietly re-marked, 'Fearfully sorry, but it was so much like frying eggs and bacon!'[17] His second appearance was remarkable for his skilful use of the head voice and the perfectly smooth transition to and from it. The darkened colouring of voice which he commanded at will lent a deeper eloquence to his utterance.[18]

His Australian engagements over, Joseph set sail for South Africa where another round of appearances awaited him with African Theatres Ltd. From Sweden his pianist, the young Carl Tillius set out to meet him. The *SS Themistocles* docked in Durban's Port of Natal on 8 October. Two days later at the Town Hall in Pietermaritzburg he sang before a small but intensely appreciative audience, again placing as the first item on his programme the beautiful aria from Meyerbeer's *L'Africana*, the salute of Vasco da Gama to Natal, 'O Paradise and thou art mine'.[19]

His return to Johannesburg's City Hall on 13 October for three concerts prompted the remark that he was probably unsurpassed by any contempo-rary singer in the matter of 'resourcefulness' in song delivery.[20] A week later the newspapers announced that the Hislop tour was to be cut short as Joseph had received a cable from the Royal Opera in Stockholm requisition-ing his services at an early date. Two more recitals in Cape Town brought the tour to a sudden close.[21] Thus he sailed from Table Bay after only three weeks in South Africa, cancelling projected concerts in Durban early the following month.

Back in Sweden Joseph appeared briefly at the Royal Opera and later sang in Denmark (in Copenhagen's Cathedral) on 17 December. Then south of Gothenburg at the Palladium in Malmö where he gave a concert on 26 December with his old friend and most regular partner in the concert hall and recording studio, the American pianist Spencer Clay.

It was in Malmö that a famous incident took place. Joseph took a taxi from the station to the theatre and on the way began to warm his voice up in the cab. This infuriated the taxi-driver who stopped the car, opened the window and told his passenger that local regulations made it an offence to cause a 'disturbance' in a moving vehicle. Evidently until he got to the theatre, the famous visiting tenor had to hold his tongue.[22]

Once New Year was over he and Carl Tillius travelled north to Oslo, singing at the Aulean on 13 January 1932 in front of the King and Crown

Hislop at Copenhagen's cathedral, 17 December 1931

Prince with his recent partner at Stockholm, the soprano Signe Amundsen. Joseph and Carl Tillius then returned to Stockholm for a concert in the Auditorium on 1 February.

At the end of February Joseph was in London seeing his agent, Harold Holt, now in sole charge of the firm (Lionel Powell having died very suddenly). From William Smith of Methuen Simpson Ltd, Edinburgh came confirmation that the serious concert season was very lean and few worthwhile offers were being proposed.[23] However, more encouraging news came from Harold Holt Ltd at the end of May. 'My dear Joe, I cannot understand why I have not heard from you for so long. I have written you several letters but have received no reply. In addition to the dates I have already told you about, I have today fixed Sunday, 3 July, at Eastbourne with the Municipal Orchestra, at sixty-five per cent. This now gives you four dates in July. I had a long interview with the BBC yesterday and they will be advising me in a few days about your Summer dates.'[24]

Hot on the heels of this letter came another from Ibbs & Tillett confirming an engagement with the Kilmarnock Lyric Choir in the Grand Hall (Kilmarnock) on the evening of 6 December, at a fee of 90 guineas (including the services of Joseph's personal accompanist, Percy Kahn). Joseph was apparently ensuring a steady supply of work by using two agents in Britain.

The month of July was thus spent singing round the English coast: Folkestone, then Eastbourne, (where, in 'Vesti la giubba' he avoided the common fault of hysterical hyperbole).[25] With Percy Kahn Joseph appeared at the South Parade Pier (Southsea) following Fritz Kreisler by a week and preceding John McCormack and Ivor Novello (the latter at the King's Theatre) by three days.

At the Villa Marina in Douglas (Isle of Man), Joseph announced halfway through his programme that he had a dear old friend in the audience (referring to Sir Harry Lauder who, with his party, occupied seats in the front of the stalls). He had been asked to sing his group of Scots songs earlier than usual to enable Sir Harry to hear them before he left the hall for another concert. Joseph then happily gave 'Bonnie George Campbell', 'Bonnie Mary of Argyle' and 'MacGregor's Gathering', all of which roused the audience to a great pitch of enthusiasm.[26] 'Mary of Argyle' was a particular success. Thunderous applause followed the dying note of the song, and Sir Harry Lauder's heartfelt exclamation, 'Bravo, laddie!' was a great tribute to the younger man.[27]

In the encore which followed Joseph bantered a little with the famous comedian, probably in an effort to persuade him to mount the platform. All Sir Harry did was to shake his fist at the singer, as much as to say, 'You young rascal'. It was a most happy interlude for everyone and, on leaving the hall just afterwards, Sir Harry had a hearty send-off from the audience.[28]

Joseph was back in England by mid-November to renew a singing partnership which had begun almost eight years before. Harold Holt had organized a tour of England and Ireland for the statuesque Australian soprano Florence Austral, Joseph, the young violinist Henri Temianka (then in the process of taking Europe by storm) and Percy Kahn. Temianka, today a distinguished professor of music, remembers Joseph at the time as somewhat aloof, perhaps even arrogant.[29] In Liverpool on 22 November, Florence Austral began with the 'Battle Cry' from *Die Walküre* while Joseph followed with Respighi's 'Nebbie' and Tosti's 'Marechiare'. Their programme was considered to be unbalanced, although Joseph shone in his Italian renderings 'in which vocal country he was a naturalised citizen'.[30] In Kilmarnock on 6 December Joseph appeared with the Edinburgh pianist George Short and the Kilmarnock Lyric Choir. Attracting much comparison with John McCormack (who had sung in the town nearly 20 years before), he sang 17 songs for a fee of £85. *The Kilmarnock Standard* (10 December 1932) commented:

> Over his whole wide range, there is an exquisite purity of tone, round and full and mellow, alike in pianissimo and fortissimo passages. While his voice may lack the tremendous power of Caruso's, it is still of great volume and is of amazing flexibility. It has a certain quality of tender expressiveness that one has rarely heard surpassed.

On the following morning he went out for a game of golf over the Barassie links but, as a local reporter discovered, he was not quite such a star on the putting-green as on the concert-platform.[31]

When the International Celebrity Subscription Concerts party met up again at the Theatre Royal in Dublin on the afternoon of 10 December, Joseph underlined to the audience that opera was his true métier, showing fine control of the head voice. In 'Che gelida manina' the optional high C was taken in his stride without any suggestion of effort.[32]

When the tour was over Joseph, ensconced in the Piccadilly Hotel in London's Regent Street, opened the familiar blue envelope from Theo Ysaye in Paris. On offer was a February concert in the Palais de Beaux Arts (Brussels) for the rather humiliating fee of 4000 Belgian francs (travel, accommodation and accompanist all to be paid by the artist). Although Ysaye pleaded hard times in the concert industry as an excuse for the low level of payment, Joseph did not sign the contract.[33] Instead he made his way to home ground where, on 1 March 1933 with George Short on piano and David McCallum (leader of the Scottish Orchestra) on violin, Joseph pleased a large Usher Hall audience.[34] He presented a song, 'The Cornish Witch,' by a young Edinburgh composer present in the audience, Alan Murray (who wrote 'I'll walk beside you'). Liza Lehmann's 'Ah, Moon of my Delight' (which he recorded for HMV but which remained unissued) was included in a final group of songs.

Passing through London long enough to make some recordings at Hayes Joseph gave a concert in Oslo on 24 March with Carl Tillius as accompanist. The press recognized in him the same dandy and charmer they knew of old. Then Joseph took the train to Bergen where he sang at the Domkirke along with Kantor Karsten Solheim.[35] Two more Stockholm concerts followed at the beginning of April and, after a summer at Brottkärr, he reappeared in Copenhagen at the Tivoli concert-hall.

The last three months of 1933 were spent in unique fashion accompanying the legendary Italian prima donna and coloratura soprano, Madame Luisa Tetrazzini, on her final farewell tour of the British Isles. The 'Tuscan Thrush' arrived in Britain during the middle of October, having last been there in 1925. Like Joseph she had sung at Chicago and at the Manhattan Opera in New York and was a favourite at the Met. Although her voice was not all that it had been, she still had what one reviewer called 'magnetic charm and the ability to hit her fabulous clear high notes'.[36]

Joseph replaced John Stuart in the concert party at the Bournemouth Pavilion on 22 October. Ivor Newton was the accompanist, the 14-year old violinist Harold Fielding completing the party in which the 'Mad Scene' from *Hamlet* by Ambroise Thomas was Tetrazzini's scintillating *pièce de résistance*. On the last day of the month Joseph and Tetrazzini were joined by the Viennese pianist Ania Dorfmann at the Town Hall (Leeds). There the impulsive little lady charmed her audience before singing a note, with her effusive greeting and sly allusion to her breathless ascent of the platform stairs; Joseph was described as a fine robust tenor,[37] although a second critic bemoaned his arrogant confidence and all-too-conscious effect.[38] Alessandro Valente replaced Joseph in the next two concerts in Taunton and Torquay. After another Tetrazzini appearance in Plymouth, Joseph was at the Town Hall (Cheltenham) with Ania Dorfmann, accompanied by Percy Kahn.

The Tetrazzini Farewell Tour proper was launched at the Royal Albert Hall with Joseph, the violinist Lisa Minghetti and the pianist Niedzielski. Then to Middlesbrough where the cellist Piatigorski joined Tetrazzini and Joseph who was in splendid voice, and sang with true musical feeling.[39] From Middlesbrough they travelled to Leicester. On the following morning Joseph set off for his mother's home in Edinburgh at 31 Ulster Gardens, close to The King's Park, which he had bought for her not long before.

The tour's first Scottish venue, St Andrew's Hall (Glasgow), saw Joseph received with open arms by his fellow-countrymen. In the audience once again was Sir Harry Lauder who popped round to the artists' room at the interval and persuaded Joseph to add 'Bonnie wee thing' as an encore.[40] Before the concert in the Caird Hall (Dundee), Tetrazzini was presented with a massive laurel wreath decorated in the Italian colours, placed squarely on the platform so that she did not have room to perform. In spite of being in the process of recovering from 'flu Joseph again distinguished himself in Liverpool. 'He is a singer who rejoices in his powers and hides a fine technical accomplishment under the cloak of expression' wrote *The Liverpool Post* (1 December 1933) after the Tetrazzini concert in the Central Hall on 30 November. With some astonishment it was noted that the prima donna could still manage a chromatic run, as in the 'Mad Scene' from *Hamlet*, with perfect pitch.

A few days later the Usher Hall in Edinburgh rang with a welcome of handclapping as Tetrazzini entered, but the enthusiasm of Hislop's admirers got out of hand, resulting in a surfeit of encores and recalls.[41] Then south again where in Birmingham there was genuine admiration of some rich and beautifully produced notes which recalled the diva's most famous days. She was compared to Sarah Bernhardt, while Joseph delighted with his rendering of Peter Warlock's 'Piggesnie'.[42] In Dublin on 9 December Percy Kahn replaced Ivor Newton. There Tetrazzini's voice soared clean and clear as a flute to the top notes. Final concerts followed in Belfast, Newcastle and Sheffield.

Returning to London, Joseph quickly sailed back to Gothenburg for Christmas and on New Year's Day 1934 sang at an Italian opera evening concert with the Gothenburg Symphony Orchestra in the Lorensberg Theatre. Answering a correspondent of the *Svenska Dagbladet* (January 1934) who questioned him about his recent engagements in Britain, Joseph spoke admiringly of Tetrazzini's still brilliant technique. He reminded the Swedish public that Ophelia's great aria from *Hamlet* contained a melody taken from a Swedish folksong which the composer Ambroise Thomas had heard Christina Nilsson sing many times. Subsequently Nilsson sang the role at the première of the opera in Paris.

Early in April 1934, Joseph launched a tour of some 36 Scottish towns in which he had never sung before. Organizing the trip was Captain Illingworth who had worked on the administrative side of *Frederica*. The other artists included the coloratura soprano Marie Gluck, the Swedish pianist Alfred Roth and the violinist Max Jaffa. A large black Rolls-Royce carried the party, uniformed chauffeur at the wheel.

Appropriately enough for a man whose roots were in the Borders, Joseph's Scottish tour began with visits to six Border towns. Although the theatre in Galashiels had been thrown into semi-darkness during the performances, nevertheless he was in excellent voice, notable for its rich, resonant quality from Handel to Verdi, as well as the almost obligatory 'Bonnie wee thing'![43] Down in the Borders the people of Jedburgh were particularly delighted by the final stanza of 'Afton Water'.[44] At the end of the concert Joseph addressed the audience, saying that he was very pleased to be back again among his 'ain folks'. When he saw so many sonsie faces, he felt as happy as a little dog with two tails. 'I just wish', he added, 'to tell you how pleased my fellow-artists and myself are at the appreciation you have shown, which means that in this burgh of Jedburgh there are many lovers of music.'[45]

Berwick, although in England, was at one time part of Scotland and the concert in the Corn Exchange drew a large crowd from the district. Many seats in the next venue, however, the Roxy Picture House in Kelso, were unhappily empty. A quick journey north to the Museum Hall (Bridge of Allan) for a concert on 10 April was followed by another back in the Borders in the Town Hall (Hawick) where the heavens emptied with such tremendous fury and insistence that muted violin passages could scarcely be heard at times by sections of the audience.[46] At the Playhouse (Peebles) Joseph was given a rousing reception, the highlight of the evening being the excerpts from *La bohème* with Marie Gluck.[47]

Next to Kirkcaldy and St Andrews in Fife. Joseph, suffering from a cold, arrived in St Andrews the day before and was able to enjoy a round of golf over the Old Course which, he declared, was the finest he had played on throughout the world.[48] The beautiful weather, the golf and the invigorating breezes had their expected recuperative influence. Joseph showed no traces of indisposition when he appeared on the platform of the Younger Hall to charm the very appreciative audience which had assembled despite the bad weather.[49] In Montrose the local reporter recorded with incredulity that everybody was seated before the concert commenced, and that during the various items scarcely a whisper was to be heard.[50] In Forfar next day, although the front seats were all too empty, there was an enthusiastic warmth in the reception. In Aberdeen, Joseph gave the public a vision of his many-sided art and charmed with his genial presence.[51]

After posing in Inverness in front of their sleek Rolls-Royce at the foot of the statue of Flora Macdonald, the artists proceeded to enjoy a great ovation from the large audience assembled in the Central Hall Picture House. Joseph displayed dramatic power, declamatory force, romantic beauty, humour and virile rhythm.[52]

Joseph's concerts were really what the late Max Jaffa has called a clever piece of 'dramatic planning'.

> The evening started, quite soberly, with pianist Alfred Roth playing some Chopin, which was followed by an operatic aria or two from Verdi's *La Traviata* sung by the guest singer, Marie Gluck – 'Soprano from the Italian Opera Houses' as her billing went. Then it was the turn of Max Jaffa to play the slow movement and finale of the Mendelssohn Violin Concerto.
>
> Now the last movement does whip up the tempo, and of course it raised expectations for the star of the evening, who then came on to sing a group of arias ranging from Handel to Verdi, including several of the favourites.

For his second group Hislop pulled out all the Scottish stops with songs like 'Bonnie George Campbell' and 'My Love, she's but a lassie yet'. But there was more to come: for the climax of the evening he brought back Marie Gluck and they performed the end of Act One of Puccini's *La bohème* from 'Your Tiny Hand is Frozen' right through to the passionate duet which the lovers-to-be sing as they walk off stage.[53]

To Edinburgh, finally, a lamentably small audience at the Usher Hall saw Joseph's last concert appearance in his native city, with the boy pianist Harold Rubens taking over Alfred Roth's solo role. 'If at times his singing was inclined to be a little cold and with a feeling of mere technical brilliance about it, it had to be remembered that his range was wide', commented *The Scotsman* (28 April 1934). This was a sad state of affairs for an artist who in 1922 had filled the Usher Hall three times in the space of twelve weeks.

Early in August 1934 Joseph was back in Scotland to complete his tour, bringing Carl Tillius over with him. This time the soprano was Nancye Mitchell and the violinist, the Russian Sonia Moldowsky. After an enthusiastic reception in Largs,[54] the concert party travelled to Crieff in Perthshire where probably not since an evening years ago, when Barton McGuckin, of the Carl Rosa Opera filled the Porteous Hall to overflowing, had there been such a noted artist on its boards.[55]

In the Picture House (Grantown-on-Spey) Joseph gave two Tosti songs ('Ideale' and 'A vucchella') and brought a whiff of the opera house with the *La bohème* duets, while, appropriately, in the Argyllshire Gathering Hall (Oban), 'MacGregor's Gathering' was given with a passion and fire which roused the audience to a fire of appreciation. Enthusiasm in Elgin[56] was succeeded by rapture at Strathpeffer.[57] The tour appears to have ended on the windy and rocky coast of East Lothian at the holiday resort of North Berwick, not too far from East Linton where his brother Stephen was a well-loved general practitioner.

This was Joseph's final tour, his farewell to the itinerant, gypsy life of the international concert performer. Visiting the small, out-of-the-way towns was a parting gesture of affection to the land of his birth, This modest circuit may have been chosen partly because Beniamino Gigli, the current shining star of the operatic world and Joseph's former colleague at the San Carlo (Naples) and the Colón (Buenos Aires), was then touring the major towns of Scotland. Nevertheless, Joseph was determined to say goodbye to his roots. In spite of his tinge of arrogance and the occasional frostiness in the voice, he still had what Peter Pears, then a young singer at the BBC, was to admire in 1936: 'the sympathetic qualities of Scottish voices'.[58]

References

1. Letter (London) 22 December 1930.

2. Kingston, C. (1971) *It don't seem a day too much*, Sydney, Rigby Ltd. pp. 153–4.
3. Kingston op. cit. pp. 154–5.
4. The Sydney Morning Herald, 16 April 1931.
5. The Sydney Morning Herald, 20 April 1931.
6. The New Zealand Herald, 24 April 1931.
7. The New Zealand Herald, 1 May 1931.
8. Kingston op. cit. pp. 106–7.
9. Music in New Zealand, 1 July 1931, p. 79.
10. Kingston op. cit. pp. 106–7.
11. Unidentified Wellington newspaper, 18 May 1931, NLS.
12. The Evening Post, 19 May 1931.
13. The Press, 25 May 1931.
14. ibid.
15. The Evening Post, 4 June 1931.
16. Kingston op. cit. p. 155.
17. The West Australian, 16 September 1931.
18. The West Australian, 18 September 1931.
19. The Natal Mercury, 12 October 1931.
20. The Johannesburg Star, 14 October 1931.
21. The Natal Mercury, 22 October 1931.
22. Svenska Dagbladet, 5 March 1932.
23. Letter (Edinburgh) 5 April 1932.
24. Letter (London) 26 May 1932.
25. The Eastbourne Gazette, 6 July 1932.
26. Mona's Herald, 19 July 1932.
27. The Isle of Man Examiner, 22 July 1932.
28. Mona's Herald, 19 July 1932.
29. Letter to author, 29 October 1987.
30. The Liverpool Post and Mercury, 23 November 1932.
31. The Kilmarnock Standard, 10 December 1932.
32. The Irish Times, 10 December 1932.
33. Letter (in private possession).
34. The Edinburgh Evening News, 2 March 1933.
35. Unidentified Oslo newspaper, 25 March 1933, NLS.
36. The Doncaster Star, 26 October 1933.
37. The Yorkshire Post, 1 November 1933.
38. The Leeds Mercury, 1 November 1933.
39. The North-Eastern Daily Gazette, 15 November 1933.
40. The Glasgow Evening Times, 21 November 1933.
41. The Edinburgh Evening News, 3 December 1933.
42. The Birmingham Mail, 6 December 1933.
43. The Border Standard, 7 April 1934.
44. The Jedburgh Gazette, 13 April 1934.
45. ibid.
46. The Hawick Express, 29 March 1934.
47. The Peebleshire and South Midlothian Advertiser, 13 April 1934.
48. The St Andrews Citizen, 14 April 1934.
49. ibid.
50. The Montrose Review, 27 April 1934.
51. The Aberdeen Evening Express, 24 April 1934.
52. The Northern Chronicle, 25 April 1934.

53. Jaffa, M. (1991) *A Life on the Fiddle*, London, Hodder and Stoughton, pp. 111–13.
54. The Ardrossan and Saltcoats Herald, 10 August 1934.
55. The Strathearn Herald, 11 August 1934.
56. The Elgin Courant, 22 August 1934.
57. The Northern Star, 18 August 1934.
58. Letter to author, 16 September 1985, NLS.

Part III
NEW DIRECTIONS
(1929–1977)

12   Film and light opera (1929–1934)

An interesting aspect of Joseph's career was his venture into new forms of musical and dramatic art, including the fledgling talking picture industry. The possibility of a glittering extension to his career in this exciting new medium was a refreshing prospect to Joseph in April 1929. A meeting was arranged between his former accompanist, Alberto Sciarretti (now acting as his American agent) and Al Howson, one of the directors of Warner Brothers. Sciarretti emphasised that Joseph 'should not be considered mainly as a singer, but as an actor who happens to be an international figure in the musical world'.[1] Sciarretti was playing to Joseph's strength, his magnetic personality on stage and his ability to act convincingly.

Warner Brothers, however, had problems of their own. The Vitaphone system of sound recording used for novelty shorts (such as the performances of the New York Philharmonic and the tenor Giovanni Martinelli[2]) came under heavy attack from a number of sound-on-film systems. Warner Brothers thus lost any technical advantage to RCA and Western Electric.[3]

As early as March 1929 the situation in British film studios was also very uncertain and indeed ominous, with many companies adopting a wait-and-see policy. As there were only one or two small studios where sound-synchronized productions could then be made in Britain, it seemed that the advent of all-sound films would mean the migration of much British production to Hollywood.[4]

However, by the middle of May The Gramophone Company ('HMV') drew up an agreement with the British and Dominions Film Corporation (the first British company to produce a sound film) for cooperative production of sound films, using the Western Electric sound system. This new British combine united The Gramophone Company's contractual links with many of the world's finest classical musicians and the latest sound film expertise of British Dominions.[5] It was in this context that Joseph was invited to play the leading role in a film based on the life of the Scots poet, Robert Burns, with options on a second film, (an Irish romance, *The Mountains of Mourne*) and a third, a movie version of Puccini's *La bohème*.

Two films had gone into production at the Boreham Wood (Elstree) studios in September 1929, *The Loves of Robert Burns* and, on the same stage, the Whitehall farce, *Rookery Nook*. Herbert Wilcox was director on both pictures; he had equipped the studio at Elstree with Western Electric sound at a cost of £250 000. The director of photography was ostensibly Dave Kesson, who (being an American) was thought to have state of the art technical skills but in the event the Englishman Freddie Young was assigned to oversee the camera-work. Young, (who was later to receive Oscars for *Lawrence of Arabia*, *Doctor Zhivago* and *Ryan's Daughter*) remembers standing up to his waist in the freezing winter water of the River Afton in Scotland during the filming of the location sequence for Joseph's singing of 'Flow Gently Sweet Afton'. The camera crew had been sent north over the Border to look for Highland cattle, only to find that they were always moved south in winter![6]

The Ben Travers farce *Rookery Nook*, with Ralph Lynn, Tom Walls and Robertson Hare, was produced during the day in the British and Dominion Studios, Wilcox relying on the already established theatre production by Tom Walls. *The Loves of Robert Burns*, on the other hand, was made almost entirely at night; Joseph recalled that he had to sing 'Afton Water' at four o'clock in the morning.[7]

Recording for the soundtrack of *The Loves of Robert Burns* took place in November 1929 at the Kingsway Hall in London. The music was arranged by Leslie Heward, who also conducted. (Heward had been on the music staff of the Royal Opera House, Covent Garden, when Joseph sang with Chaliapin in *Faust* in 1928.) The orchestra included musicians of the calibre of William Primrose, the viola player, who also appeared in the Mauchline Ball scene. The records which resulted proved extremely popular.

From the film came 'Loch Lomond', 'Ye banks and braes', 'Bonnie Mary of Argyle', 'Annie Laurie' and 'Afton Water'. Also on the film itself he recorded 'Auld Lang Syne', 'Rantin', rovin' Robin' and 'The Silver Tassie'.

The Russian bass Feodor Chaliapin visited Joseph on the set and watched the filming. Wilcox had managed to persuade him to agree to play the non-singing role of Sancho Panza in a planned film version of Cervantes' *Don Quixote* (a venture which never materialized). It was a chance also for Joseph to relive their 1928 Covent Garden production of *Faust*.[8]

Joseph found that a film actor's life was full of new challenges. As well as the unsocial hours on partial night-shift, the physical environment in the studios was scarcely pleasant. The main corridor was clay with open ditches which were used as cable ducts by the sound engineers. All the technical facilities were highly primitive.[9]

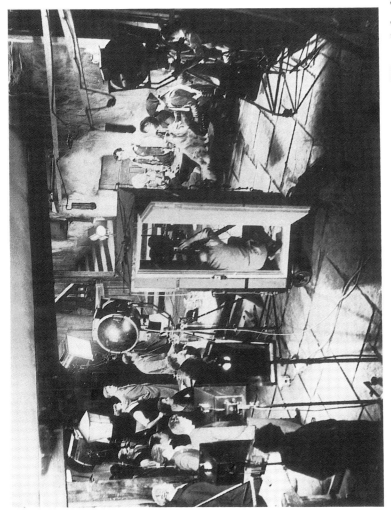

Making the film of *The Loves of Robert Burns* at Elstree in 1930. Herbert Wilcox (left of centre under flood-light), Freddie Young in booth (centre). JH at right.

From the 1930 film *The Loves of Robert Burns*. Hislop as the dying Burns with his wife Jean Armour (Dorothy Seacombe)

The script of the film had been written partly by Herbert Wilcox himself, with dialogue by Captain Reginald Berkeley. Playing Jean Armour, Burns' wife, was Dorothy Seacombe. Eve Gray was a blonde Highland Mary, while the Scots actress Jean Cadell took the part of the poet's mother.

Filming for Joseph finished towards the end of January 1930, after which the Irish-born director Herbert Wilcox planned to start recording *The Mountains of Mourne* almost immediately. However, the news from London following the première of *The Loves of Robert Burns* was not encouraging. While *Rookery Nook* was already convulsing audiences and breaking records at the New Gallery (Regent Street), *The Loves of Robert Burns* was taken off after one week.

One observer described the film as 'a strange, very simple and deeply moving picture. Beauty of sound and beauty of scene flow into and out of

each other.'[10] However, *The Times* (4 March 1930) commented that sentimentality was allowed to run riot over the whole production and even
Joseph's magnificent voice could not make up for the lack of all intellectual,
and even visual, stimulus, the sudden descents into pathos and the constant
recourse to the less subtle and illuminating tricks of camera technique.
Joseph's voice, however, remained to be put down on a credit side which the
reviewer had hoped would have been more substantial. There was also his
acting, which, considering that the part gave him few opportunities, was
remarkably firm and understanding.

Joseph's success as Burns was echoed by Paul Holt. 'Hislop reveals that
he can act finely and sing finely. His personality is remarkable. It must be
said that he is a natural film actor, for he has complete command of
carriage, voice and expression. He is also occasionally subtle.'[11] The opening of the film was universally praised. Paul Holt again: 'The sky is dark and
heavy with storm, the landscape bleak, the sods wet and cold. A marvellous
scene, the most brilliant piece of photography of the year.'[12]

However the personality of Burns in the script was universally con-
demned for presenting the poet as weak and passive. The treatment of the
story was episodic. The film became a pictorial Scottish song recital and
Burns reading. Holt ended his review with the remark that 'at all times it is
magnificently dull.'[13] 'Was it too Scottish for a London audience?' asked
The Daily Mail (10 March 1930).

There was a Scottish première of the film in Edinburgh, launching the
newly constructed Rutland Picture House in Canning Street on Monday 28
April. After the Lord Provost declared the Rutland open, Joseph spoke to
the audience briefly about the making of *The Loves of Robert Burns*. Then the
film itself followed. *The Scotsman* (29 April 1930) critic observed that
Joseph sang with charm and sympathetic feeling. However, he added that a
strongly welded picture could not be made by presenting a number of
separate incidents from a whole life-time. He went on to note that the
audience showed a silly tendency to laugh at serious passages which unin-
tentionally proved amusing. There was such patent insincerity about the
poet's declaration of love to Mary Campbell, coming just after he had
finished with Jean Armour, that this scene, which should have been beautiful, was greeted with loud laughter.

Wilcox later tried to deny any responsibility for the film's failure by
shifting the blame to the leading artist: 'Had I chosen a less indigenous
subject and a greater name star, the story might have been vastly different.'[14]
As a result, neither *The Mountains of Mourne* nor the film version of *La
bohème* were made. The latter project is a matter for particular regret, as it
would have shown Joseph in his true métier.

A second musical form new to Joseph and one in which he believed he had the potential for great success was light opera. In May 1930 plans were being finalized for a Hislop concert tour to Australia. However, in the event he chose to postpone the tour and signed for a London run of Franz Lehár's musical play *Frederica* for a fee reputed to be £1 000 a week.[15] This was to be the British première of a work first performed two years previously in Berlin by Richard Tauber as the German poet Goethe. Joseph brought over to the Gaiety Theatre in London young Carl Tillius as repetiteur. They spent a couple of days in preliminary rehearsal before the première at the King's Theatre, (Glasgow). Then Joseph travelled to Copenhagen once more for a last series of concerts before arriving in Glasgow where *Frederica* opened on 1 September.

Billed as 'The Musical Event of the Season', Lehár's *Frederica* was presented by Laddie Cliff (a former member of the Co-Optimists) and conducted by Jacques Heuvel. Playing Frederica was the soprano, the late Lea Seidl who was universally applauded. She had of course seen Tauber as Goethe in Berlin. 'Of Joseph Hislop with whom I sang *Frederica* I have not such pleasant memories. When I was trying to help him with his acting he said, "I am not going to copy Tauber". So silly!'[16]

The actor Grenville Eves saw Joseph in *Frederica* and in 1943, while he was stationed in Glasgow, went to have tea with his old friend Richard Tauber. He mentioned that he had seen Joseph's London performance: 'Hislop sang it superbly', Eves told Tauber. 'I can well believe that', the latter replied. 'I continued to tell him that Hislop gave his own highly individual interpretation of the role. A tenor, perhaps the only tenor at that time, who did not fall into the temptation of copying Tauber in singing Lehár'.[17] Part of the explanation no doubt lay in the different vocal ranges of the two singers. Tauber, in Joseph's words, had 'no top'[18] (he used a beguiling falsetto for the higher notes), whereas Joseph could sing the top of the tenor range in full voice.

First night reaction was mixed. Joseph received the accolade that he had made the future path of British operetta tenors difficult indeed, for heretofore his like had been unknown.[19] As for *Frederica* itself, the construction of the plot was felt to be unsatisfactory and the sentimentality only too resourcefully exploited: 'A live lamb contributes all the nether comedy there is to this piece, and does its job of work with a spontaneity that mocks at stage technique!'[20]

From the critic of *The Glasgow Herald* (2 September 1930) came clear indications that Joseph was not yet fully at ease with the style of operetta (and the lightness of the acting required):

> In his spoken word there was not sufficient distinction of style, and there were periods in his singing which tended to destroy the illusion. His song "O maiden, my maiden," in the second act, was presented with vocal exaggera-

tions, quietly ecstatic high notes too long held, and followed immediately by a full employment of his great vocal resources

(a characteristic of the recordings he made of the main songs). In fact, Joseph recorded four songs from *Frederica*, 'Oh maiden, my maiden', 'A

With Lea Seidl in Lehàr's *Frederica*, London 1930

heart as pure as gold', 'Wayside rose' and 'Wonderful'. The rich vein of sentimental charm is thoroughly exploited in these recordings made at the Kingsway Hall in September 1930 during the second week of the London run. The listener is given a clear appreciation of the technical brilliance Joseph brought to bear on the vocal side of the role – high notes held in almost a whisper and crescendos of whiplash power. Yet all this paled beside the Ruritanian charm of his leading lady, singing in her delightful Viennese accent.

By the Thursday Joseph had developed a severe cold and his understudy, the tenor Robert Naylor (who had just finished singing in *The Three Musketeers* at Drury Lane the previous week) stepped into the part at an hour's notice, never having rehearsed with the other principals.[21] He sang the rest of the week, receiving warm applause as well as telegrams of congratulation, including one from Joseph which read 'All good wishes and thanks for holding the fort'.[22]

Frederica opened at the Palace Theatre (London) on 9 September, with Joseph recovered from indisposition. The critics were generally favourable, with strong reservations about the plot but admiration for Lea Seidl's charm and highest praise for the music. *The Daily Telegraph* (10 September 1930) agreed that Joseph was vocally in his finest form, and only once or twice inclined to treat Lehár's phrases as though they had the sweep and spaciousness of those of Verdi. Such 'beautifully easy singing, beauty of tone and wealth of purely lyrical feeling' had not been heard on the stage of operetta within memory. Hubert Griffith, writing in *The Graphic* (20 September 1930), had more reservations, feeling that Joseph was 'overshadowed, not only in voice but in personality'. He 'suggested the embarrassment of a curate who is being told a doubtful story'. James Agate in *The Sunday Times* (14 September 1930) echoed Griffith, finding Lea Seidl naturally winsome; 'moreover, she acts almost as well as Mr Joseph Hislop sings, and sings by no means as indifferently as that operatic singer must be said to act.'

In the end *Frederica* – in spite of Felix Edwardes' delightful staging – ran for only 110 performances, finishing its run at the Palace Theatre on 14 December. In spite of a largely enthusiastic press reception, the times were out of joint and Lehár seemed not the man to put them right. With the uneasy peace sliding again towards war, there seemed to be no room at that time for melody or romance.[23] Joseph returned to Gothenburg for Christmas.

At around the same time Sir Landon Ronald, Principal of the Guildhall School of Music, wrote to Fred Gaisberg of The Gramophone Company at Hayes explaining that he had written a new album of songs. 'I got a list of your tenors and the only one who appeals to me at all in the list is Joseph Hislop. He is an old friend and you might tell him that I will be very happy to come and accompany him myself.'[24] 'Regarding the tenors we have at our disposal', Gaisberg replied,

> I agree with you that Hislop is probably the best, although it might be advisable to send a copy to Count John McCormack. If he likes them he would certainly sing them, but he is not very tractable and there will be a large element of chance if we depend on him entirely. Hislop is more tractable and I think we could get him to sing these songs extraneous to his contract and without an advance on royalty, especially as you are accompanying him'.[25]

Two busy sessions for HMV at Hayes produced some 14 recordings, four with the composer Landon Ronald: 'Strew on her roses', 'A pair well matched', 'When I am dead' and 'Down in the forest'. Writing in *The Gramophone* (May 1931) C. M. Crabtree observed:

> I think I am right in saying that our Editor claims that the Irishman McCormack is the best tenor in the world. Next to him I am inclined to place Mr Mackenzie's fellow-countryman Joseph Hislop. They are both of the Italian operatic school, and I have never heard a better Italian. The whole world at least admits them among the best. And here is the Scot on two three-shilling HMV records and I will maintain against any finicking purist that this is real singing. Hislop, one feels can do what he likes with his voice in the way of using it as an interpretative medium, and thrillingly does it.

Crabtree considered 'Down in the forest' to be an especially fine rendering. 'The real lesson for any singer is the old familiar "Down in the forest". The treatment of this is undreamt of, yet one always feels right and notice that Hislop gets on with it at "We will wait no more". I fancy the recording is about as powerful as any, yet it is right, simply because Hislop doesn't sing *ff*, or *f*, or even *mf*, the whole time.'[26]

In the next edition of *The Gramophone* (June 1931) the editor, Compton Mackenzie, printed a devastating demolition exercise on most of Crabtree's judgements:

> It seems to me that Joseph Hislop is singing worse on every record of his I hear. The one I disliked least was 'Down in the forest', but I have heard a dozen singers sing this song better to my taste. However, I read that Sir Landon Ronald rehearsed Mr Hislop for the exact interpretation he wanted, so I shall argue no more about that. I do not know who wrote the words of 'Down in the forest'. Perhaps they were written by Sir Landon himself, in which case the charming song is entirely his, and if he likes Mr Hislop's way of singing it, there is no more to be said.
>
> But Sir Landon Ronald did not write the words of 'When I am dead, my dearest', and I am going to say bluntly that his music is entirely unsuited to the words and that Mr Hislop's singing is even more unsuited to them. The words were written by Christina Rossetti, though there is no mention of her on the record. She and Dryden and Matthew Arnold are all swallowed up in Sir Landon Ronald and Mr Joseph Hislop. 'When I am dead, my dearest' was writen by a woman, who in it revealed in a whispered hint the tragedy behind her cloistered life, and to lovers of Christina Rossetti's poetry this exquisite lyric has a wistful and intimate appeal.

> To hear Mr Hislop yelling the first verse is an extremely painful experience for lovers of Christina Rossetti's poetry. I am not often tempted to pitch a record out of the window, but when I heard Mr Hislop begin to yell 'When I am dead, my dearest' I restrained myself with difficulty, and how Mr Crabtree was able not merely to endure but to enjoy it has defeated my powers of guessing.

Compton Mackenzie admitted that he once admired Joseph's singing:

> I remember that when this Scottish tenor's first records came out some years ago I liked them immensely. One of them was 'An Eriskay love lilt'. Another was 'Flow gently sweet Afton', another was 'The Herding Song', and I remember that our old friend Walter Yeomans remonstrated with me for praising him too highly, and to maintain his point Yeomans argued that so many operatic twirls and twiggles were utterly out of place in such songs.
>
> I admitted that they were unnecessary, but said I was sure that a singer with a lovely voice would soon see how unnecessary it was for him to show off. Alas! Mr Joseph Hislop has cultivated all that was least admirable in his style and forsaken nearly all that was best. John McCormack has been blamed for singing nonsense beautifully. I propose to blame Joseph Hislop for making beauty nonsensical.

For the last three weeks of September 1932, Joseph took the role of Johann Strauss jnr with the soprano Isa Quensel in Strauss' *Waltzes from Vienna* (Wienervalsen) at the Cirkus Theatre in the Djurgården, a promontory of open parkland with restaurants and fairground entertainers, surrounded on three sides by the salt water of Stockholm harbour. Once again the piece, cobbled together as it was from favourite Strauss compositions, was not a suitable vehicle for Joseph's talents, as his awkward figure in the publicity photographs and the short one-month run suggest.

He nevertheless continued to try to make headway in the field of light music. He recorded two songs from the musical *Rose Marie* by Rudolf Friml at the No. 2 studio, Abbey Road, in December 1932 and March 1933, with an orchestra under Clifford Greenwood. In *The Gramophone* (May 1933), C. M. Crabtree comments that, 'It hardly needs saying that Joseph Hislop makes an extremely good record of "Rose Marie" and "Indian Love Call". His diction, however, does not seem too clear to me.' The problem seems to have been not his vocal production and artistry, but his awkwardness at finding himself in a musical milieu and convention foreign to a singer of Grand Opera.

Another attempt in a slightly different tradition came on 7 September 1934 when Joseph opened at the Princes Theatre (London) as Sir Walter Raleigh in a revival of Edward German's nostalgic *Merrie England* (first produced in 1902). This was a role he sang more often than any other in his career – over 300 performances including a long British tour, singing the show-stopper, 'The English Rose'. The 1934 revival was under the personal supervision of the composer. Besides Joseph, the contralto Enid Cruickshank

With Isa Quensel in *Wienervalsen*, adapted from the music of Strauss, Stockholm, 1932

Nancy Fraser Passmore as Bessie Throckmorton and Hislop as Sir Walter Raleigh in Edward German's *Merrie England* (revived in 1934–1935)

was engaged as an imperious Queen Elizabeth. Playing the vivacious Bessie Throckmorton was the young soprano Nancy Fraser, whose mother had taken the same part in the first production and whose father, the genial and diminutive Savoyard Walter Passmore, had been Walter Wilkins, (an actor in Shakespeare's company).

W. A Darlington, writing in *The Daily Telegraph* (7 September 1934), commented that 'best of all, however, was Joseph Hislop in "The English Rose", which gives this very eminent singer a chance to show his quality'. His opinion contrasted strongly with that of *The Times* (8 September 1934) critic who wrote of Joseph that he gave the audience 'the combination, now happily defunct, of a tenor, a drawing-room style of slurring and that dangerous subject, a rose in a garden'. Although the story was generally considered dull and the attitudes outdated, the scenery was lavish, the costumes were designed with great attention to historical accuracy and the cast enthusiastic.[27]

Joseph was now 50. Like most operatic singers he had been frequently away from home, living out of a suitcase. Now from rehearsal into perform- ance, the gallant Sir Walter Raleigh felt himself drawn irresistibly towards the beautiful pantomime star, Nancy Fraser, whose clear, fresh voice blended with his in their Act I duet 'When true love hath found a man'. Off-stage, Nancy Fraser, a girl with strong Scottish connections, was a thoroughly modern woman. She had been brought up in a theatrical family. She was daring and independent. She loved golf, had driven a racing car round Brand's Hatch and even qualified for an aeroplane pilot's licence.

She had come to Joseph for advice on vocal production, as she found that her voice varied in quality over the long weeks of the run. His answer was that a singer needed to have 'a sound technique'.[28] And he set about teaching her. Love slowly blossomed on stage and off.

Merrie England closed in London on 16 February 1935 after more than 200 performances. Two days later, after intense financial negotiations between Joseph and Edward German, a provincial tour began at the Golders Green Hippodrome. A Bohemian romance flowered in a succession of theatrical digs up to Scotland and down through the north of England, the tour ending on 13 May in Birmingham. Ten months after they had first met, Joseph and Nancy stepped out of their professional partnership and into the role of real-life lovers.

In Gothenburg, Joseph's wife Karin had seen the Swedish newspaper reports and photographs of the slim and attractive Bessie Throckmorton standing close to a Sir Walter Raleigh whose hand rested on her bosom.[29] She sensed the coolness between herself and Joseph. Immediately she began to fight back as hard as she could to keep him. Over the next five years, however, their marriage broke down irretrievably.

Through this most difficult period of their lives Joseph continued to work in Sweden, a single *La bohème* in Stockholm followed a September concert in Gothenburg. Then came a radio broadcast with his friend of many years, Nils Grevillius.

In March 1936 he gave a number of performances as Wilhelm Meister in Ambroise Thomas' fairytale opera *Mignon* at the Stora Teater (Gothenburg) with Ingalill Söderman (sister of Greta) in the title role and Joseph's old friend, the bass Åke Wallgren, as Lothario, conducted by Styrbjörn Lindedahl. Joseph was described as Wilhelm Meister performing in 'traditional operatic style with somewhat artificial grandezza'[30]; he did not 'come alive as a character' on stage. 'Hislop was an excellent singer and what he has retained of his voice is only due to his perfect art of singing' commented 'G.N.' in a Gothenburg newspaper.[31]

Joseph was now 52 years old and twenty-two years into his singing career, during which he had made more than nine hundred operatic appearances in leading roles, (averaging over forty operatic appearances per annum), and given some four hundred concerts. However, one cannot help drawing the conclusion that during the closing years of his active stage career Joseph entered into a succession of productions that were largely charming and sentimental in character, giving him little scope to display his true qualities, his convincing acting and powerful singing. Perhaps that is the fate of all romantic leading men: it is difficult to age gracefully. Most baritone roles being set in middle-age, it was possible for baritones to sing leading parts convincingly almost up to the end of their careers. For an ageing tenor, however, the gap between *tenore amoroso* and the smaller (*comprimario*) character roles could be too easily crossed. In the late 20th century opera offers greater variety of role to the tenor. For Joseph and his contemporaries in the 1920s the temptation to linger on in rather spineless leading parts and trade on the rouged profile and studied manly posture was perhaps too great to resist.

References

1. Letter (New York) 5 May 1929.
2. Knight, A. (1959), *The Liveliest Art*, New York, Mentor Books, p. 146.
3. ibid. p. 150.
4. The Glasgow Herald, 26 March 1929.
5. The Glasgow Herald, 15 May 1929.
6. Letter to author, 27 March 1988.
7. Hislop, J. (1963) script for BBC Home Service broadcast, 16 May 1963, NLS.
8. Wilcox, H. (1967), *Twenty-Five Thousand Sunsets*, London, The Bodley Head, pp. 86–7.
9. Letter to author, 16 November 1988, NLS.
10. The Daily Film Renter, 5 March 1930.

11. Unidentified London newspaper, 1930, NLS.
12. ibid.
13. ibid.
14. Wilcox op. cit. p. 86.
15. Göteborgs Handels-och Sjöfarts Tidning, 6 June 1930.
16. Letter to author, 27 February 1986.
17. Eves, G. (1970), 'Joseph Hislop', *Recorded Sound*, No. 38, April, p. 606.
18. Bott, M. (1977), *The Record Collector*, XXIII, 9 & 10 June, p. 229.
19. The Glasgow Evening Times, 2 September 1930.
20. ibid.
21. The Glasgow Herald, 6 September 1930.
22. The Glasgow Herald, 8 September 1930.
23. Macqueen-Pope, W. and Murray, D.L. (1935), *Fortune's Favourites*, London, Hutchinson & Co. Ltd, p. 18.
24. Letter 18 December, EMI Archives.
25. Letter 19 December 1930, EMI Archives.
26. The Gramophone, May 1931, p. 587.
27. The Sunday Times, 9 September 1934.
28. Anecdote told to author by Mrs A.F.P. Hislop.
29. Photograph in Stockholms Tidning, 27 September 1934.
30. 'G.N.' in Gothenburg newspaper, 3 March 1936.
31. ibid.

Suplementary historical note:

First films made by opera singers: Mary Garden (1917); Enrico Caruso (1918); Giovanni Martinelli (1926); Tito Schipa (1929); Richard Tauber (1930); John McCormack (1930); Beniamino Gigli (1937).

13 Teaching in Sweden (1934–1947)

Immediately after he had finished *Mignon* in March 1936, Joseph announced to the press that he was about to retire from the stage and take up teaching.[1] This virtually marked the end of his career as a singer, but he had few regrets. After all, during the past ten years he had been one of the highest paid singers in the world.

A combination of factors led to Joseph's decision to retire, no doubt including his marital difficulties. His divorce and remarriage in 1940 certainly marked an emotional watershed. A deciding factor must also have been his relative lack of success in the ventures he had undertaken since 1930: *Frederica*, *The Loves of Robert Burns*, *Waltzes from Vienna* and latterly *Merrie England*. None gave full scope to his vocal abilities; none stretched his acting powers in the way that Grand Opera had done. The result was that, singing music without the fire of great emotion, acting in roles and plots weakly conceived and loosely executed, he looked and felt ill at ease. Many years later one of his most successful pupils, Birgit Nilsson, attributed his retirement to 'a poor technique and that was why he finished rather early.'[2] In fact he gave his last concert in the 1940s at the age of 58. Even in his nineties he could still sing a thrilling high C, as the baritone Donald Maxwell has testified.[3]

An important development for opera in Sweden took place in July 1934 when Joseph welcomed to Brottkärr an acknowledged rising young star of the operatic stage, the tenor Jussi Björling. (With him came a distinguished accompanist, Styrbjörn Lindedal, director of the Stora Teater in Gothenburg.) Since first arriving in Stockholm in 1928, Björling had been taken in hand by John Forsell, director of the Royal Swedish Opera. However Forsell, a baritone, was unable to show Björling how to sing higher than top B flat acceptably. Björn Forsell, the director's son who was a friend of Björling's, suggested he consult Joseph.[4]

Björling accordingly travelled across Sweden to Joseph's house at Brottkärr where Joseph explained how the voice should feel, probably along these lines:

> Think of your body, lungs and stomach as a triangle. When you inhale, without exaggerated support, loosen up your throat, lift up your head, relax the lower jaw, don't *squeeze* the vocal chords, just let the air flow. Don't press violently. Then you will form 'the silver thread', (the ping). You could sing a high C in a different way but, without doing what I have explained to you, it will be an ugly sound.[5]

Joseph demonstrated how to do it. Björling tried to sing a high C. Joseph went mad. 'Just imitate me.' 'I can't understand how you do it,' complained Björling. 'Just *imitate* me,' said Joseph producing an effortless high C. To his great relief, Jussi was soon able to sing even a high D.[6] Joseph was delighted and invited Björling to stay with him at Brottkärr the following summer. To teach Jussi was 'like sprinkling water on a piece of blotting paper': everything was absorbed at once. Always very concerned to perfect his art he learnt as much from a single lesson as a mediocre singer from six months of instruction.[7]

Along with Jussi came another pupil, Bernt Anderberg. Both had been instructed to practise some Italian vocal exercises and were sent to a small wooden house in the garden at Brottkärr to do so. After an hour or so Joseph returned to hear the result. Jussi sat deeply engrossed in a crime thriller while his companion was still exercising religiously. Jussi, however, could repeat the exercises note for note. He had learnt them just by listening to the other student![8]

The young tenor would be up with the lark (on one memorable occasion at three in the morning), his voice warm and shining as he sang standing on a huge rock in the garden looking out to sea. 'Look at the beast', Joseph would mutter, 'I have to work very hard to keep my voice in shape while he, with no practice, sings like a god.'[9] The following May Björling wrote to Joseph. 'I want to thank you for your great kindness to me last summer and for what I learnt from you in the difficult art of singing. It has been very useful to me and I realise more and more that it is the only right way.'[10]

There were other students at Brottkärr who came by train from Gothenburg. Alice Lindedal, for example. Michelle Flint Bøgebjerg and Knut Mörk also crossed over from Denmark. Others, such as the soprano Brita Hertzberg and the tenor Einar Beyron, came from the Royal Opera in Stockholm, sweeping by in a white convertible with the roof down. Both were beautifully dressed, Beyron driving with white gloves. When they passed by a murmur would go up among the astonished residents of Brottkärr.[11]

At the beginning of April 1936 the British press revealed that 'Mr Joseph Hislop, the well-known opera singer, has been appointed teacher of singing at the Royal Academy of Music in Stockholm, on condition that he

With Jussi Björling and Bernt Anderberg, 1934

renounces his British nationality.'[12] By June Joseph had taken up this post as well as another in the opera school of the Royal Swedish Opera, teaching some 16 hours a week. He now established himself in a spacious Stockholm flat containing a studio with excellent acoustics and good natural lighting ideal both for his teaching and his favourite relaxation, oil-painting.

He also began to take private singing pupils, one of the first being Sweden's best-loved and best-selling crooner, the baritone Sven-Olof Sandberg (affectionately known as 'SOS'). In his autobiography 'Från vintergatan mot aftonsjärnan' (From the Milky Way to the Evening Star) Sandberg recalled:

The Music Academy engaged Joseph on a ten-year contract as senior teacher in the Solo Song class. Being a clever businessman he added many benefits to his contract, including one clause which gave him several afternoons off each week for private teaching.[13]

After having been a professional singer for several years, I realized that I needed some expert guidance in the art of singing. I tried a number of different teachers with very poor results and was almost ready to give up when, in the Swedish newspaper *Svenska Dagbladet*, I happened to come across a small ad announcing: Joseph Hislop will accept a limited number of pupils. Interviews today at the Strand Hotel between 10.00am and noon.[14] At 9.55am I knocked on the door leading to the ballroom which included a grand piano and which Hislop had taken over to receive prospective students. I was the first to arrive.

Hislop asked me to sing a short piece and his secretary/accompanist began to play. I don't remember what I sang but I had chosen a moderately difficult piece. Hislop listened. When I had finished he thought hard for some time before saying anything. I was anxiously waiting for his judgement. Finally, rather hesitatingly, it came: 'Mr Sandberg, I know that you are famous, but please don't be offended by what I have to tell you. Your voice is like a large pile of manure. But on the top of that dungheap can be seen a beautiful but tiny flower. I believe we could make that flower grow but please consider carefully. It will be very hard work for us both.'

I was a bit stunned to say the least but I decided to accept the challenge. 'Well then, see you Monday at 2.00pm', said Hislop. 'Västmannagatan No. 99, 4th floor. My fee is 20 Kr a forty-five minute lesson and please call me Joseph.' I thanked him and, a little bewildered, left. And that was the beginning of everything.

The first lesson didn't work out very well. Eventually Joseph thumped his fist on the piano. 'There's something wrong here,' he said, 'we will have to go to Dr Arnoldsson and have a look at your throat.' That did not sound too good. We quickly arranged an appointment.

The doctor pushed a mirror down my throat and then gave his verdict: 'There are knots on the vocal chords. You have forced your voice too much', he said, 'the vocal chords are not closing properly and a lot of air is leaking and therefore full resonance cannot be achieved.'[15] 'What can be done about it?' I asked. 'There are two choices', replied the doctor. 'Either we operate or you will have to be quiet and not speak a word for six months. The first could change the nature of the voice, the second gives us a small chance of healing. The decision is yours.'

Joseph decided. His reply came without hesitation. 'You'll not say a word. You'll have to whisper and write messages down. However I don't think we'll have to wait six months before we can start some limited vocal work. Dr Arnoldsson will have to check you again in a few months.

I drove Joseph back home to Västmannagatan before I continued home. 'You can say all you need to say today', Joseph advised me. ' From tomorrow you won't say a word. And I'll give you a few more pieces of advice which Arnoldsson did not mention. You will have to take long walks, get out into the woods and breathe the fresh air in deeply. Eat grilled beef and boiled potatoes. Avoid butter, fat and vegetables. Eat vitamins instead. Exercise the whole body until you work up a bit of sweat. But don't over-exercise and for God's sake stop smoking.'[16]

In April 1937 Joseph finally took Swedish citizenship. The month had not, however, been without its lighter moments. A well-known musical dictionary had made an error in Joseph's date of birth[17] and so, much to his astonishment, on his 53 birthday almost 300 telegrams arrived from all over the world, masses of flowers and a lot of presents congratulating him on being 50 years old! Goodwill messages also came from some of the key figures in his long career, Count Hans von Stedingk, Nils Grevillius, Madame von Skilondz and the students of the Music Academy also paid their tribute.

An unforgettable moment came in October 1937 when Joseph sang his final four evenings at the Royal Opera. His farewell to this beloved stage which had plucked him from obscurity. *La traviata* came first on 12 October. Next morning Joseph received a note from Jussi Björling. 'You sang like a god yesterday. You delighted the ear and the eye, you were just wonderful. The papers think that you were finer 20 years ago, but I believe you are today more impressive than ever! Joseph, it was a marvellous night.'[18] A day later came a contract from Björling's lawyer, witnessing an agreement. Björling would pay Joseph Kr 30 for each lesson studying operatic roles to prepare for his planned American tour. Björling would also pay him Kr 500 for each opera role in the original language which he had completed studying.'[19] In retrospect, Joseph's technical contribution to Björling's preparation for his American debut in Chicago on 15 December as Rodolfo in *La bohème* paralleled the vocal coaching given by Joseph's old tutor, Tullio Voghera, formerly Caruso's accompanist.

The following year (1938) brought fresh hope to Sven-Olof Sandberg. Towards the spring his vocal chords healed and he was able to start having lessons. 'But don't think for a moment that I could start speaking again! I had to try to revive the throat muscles with light humming exercises.'[20]

Within a year Joseph was promoted to a 'senior teacher' with a 20-hour teaching load. As well as his work for the Conservatoire and the Opera School, he continued to teach privately, his great reputation attracting an increasing number of students to his studio. Sven-Olof Sandberg recalled that 'on his grand piano he kept a signed photograph of Puccini which was inscribed "To my ideal Rodolfo, Joseph Hislop".' This was the photograph given to Joseph by the composer the morning after his May 1920 debut at Covent Garden.[21]

Studies, if a little incomprehensible at first, progressed for Sandberg.

At the same time Joseph tried to explain to me the anatomical mysteries of the singing voice. He regarded the Italian *bel canto* method as being the only acceptable one.[22]

He had mastered the difficult art of economizing the breath for long and beautiful phrases. Once, when he was really furious with me during a lesson because I had wasted too much warm air, he sang 'Ack värmland du sköna" three times right through, without once taking a breath. I actually expected him to turn blue but all he did was take a deep breath to restore the oxygen balance.[23]

Joseph was an outstanding teacher but I did not understand a thing. I neither heard nor felt the mistakes I made. It was impossible to get close to my voice by demonstration, by good advice or by appealing to my musical ear. I had to be forced to sing correctly.

Joseph tried everything to awaken the vocal awareness of all his students. He was a master of impersonation and sometimes called all of us together and parodied our efforts showing us how we performed and then how it should be done.[24]

After these sessions he dismissed us and, loading his painting equipment onto his bicycle, he would ride out to Haga Park to paint away some of his anger and frustration.

However, at long last there were some signs of progress. But very, very slowly. Not like *My Fair Lady*. With Joseph standing beside me I could sing a fine high B, (an incredible high note for a baritone. Some tenors can never reach it), but no sooner did I get home to my own piano than I was grateful to reach a lowly F sharp.[25]

Just before the beginning of the war Joseph seriously considered the invitation he had received in 1931 to take up the post of Artistic Director in Melbourne (Australia), to be a moving force in a national opera scheme.[26] Fortunately for him he did not accept or he would have been cut off from his home and family in Sweden when hostilities began.

Meanwhile Sven-Olof Sandberg continued to make steady progress.

A few years passed. I would probably not have been able to stand my hot-tempered teacher had it not been for his wife Nancy (known as 'Snippie'). She was calm, intelligent and had a sense of humour. She could blow away with a smile all the frustrations one sometimes felt after a disastrous lesson. They complemented each other well, Joseph's explosions of fiery temper were needed to awaken the dormant instincts among us students as, sooner or later, a stage was reached where it was impossible to get results the gentle way.

At long last the day came when Joseph decided that it would be a good idea to show his friend Harald André, the director of the Royal Opera House, what we had achieved.[27] . . . André thought that I was reasonably good and suggested that they make preparations for my debut.

Joseph was pleased but he was very firm and said that there was to be no debut until I had ten leading baritone parts under my belt, both vocally and dramatically. In addition he insisted that I had my own costumes, wigs and so forth, he aimed at an international career for me, particularly as I was no longer a youngster. He added that after a successful debut there would be very little time for in-depth study.

Joseph knew what he was talking about. After that I said goodbye to André and got a pat on the back. He wished me luck and wanted me back when I felt ready.

All this happened in the autumn of 1939. My lessons continued but were now more devoted to arias, recitatives and acting than on vocalization. Joseph took me to the Royal Academy of Music and introduced me to his accompanist Vivan Wennberg with whom I studied some new parts including the father in *La traviata*, Wolfram in *Tannhäuser* and Tonio in *Pagliacci*.[28]

On New Year's Eve, 1939, I had a call from the director, Mr Stangenberg. He said, 'We have to do something now and there is no point waiting. We have put you down for a debut in *La traviata* on 11 January 1940. You start rehearsing on 2 January at 11.00am.'[29]

Joseph and Nancy, who were celebrating New Year with us, heard about the telephone call. I told them what had been said. 'You're out of your mind', was Joseph's reaction. 'It's far too early. You have to give yourself time to prepare thoroughly. You need guidance. And you must have ten parts up your sleeve if your debut is a success.'

I was in two minds myself but my wife Gun stood up and announced 'It's only reasonable that Sven should take this opportunity.' A heated argument followed in which I took no part. It ended with Gun giving Joseph a hard slap in the face. I think this was the only time in Joseph's life that he was slapped in the face without retaliating. He shook his head and gave in to her.[30]

Of the night of my operatic debut and of the performance itself I have very little recollection. . . . Joseph and Nancy came round to my dressing-room and told me that I had been a success.[31] . . . [All the papers] very kind and enthusiastic . . . welcom[ing] me to the Royal Opera which had long needed a lyric baritone. . . . I was a very happy opera singer.[32]

The year 1940 also marked the end of a long and acrimonious struggle to secure a divorce between Joseph and Karin who had been the mother to his children, a sheet-anchor during the stormy years of building a career, his inspiration and support and his greatest 'fan'. She had carefully kept every memento of every concert and operatic engagement, hoarding cuttings, programmes and photographs and making sure that every great artist Joseph ever performed with had signed her autograph album. Now all those carefree years at Brottkärr in the bosom of the Asklund family were over, and instead Joseph and Nancy faced Stockholm high society as man and wife.

With Joseph's help Nancy grew to love the city and set about learning the language. Joseph devoted his leisure time to painting and golf. Karin remained in Gothenburg on the west coast and from time to time sent the children to stay with their father in his flat in the capital, making the best of a situation that was little to her liking.

There were always new challenges for Joseph in his teaching and, like Dr Gillis Bratt before him, when developing a young singer he was not slow to show the iron fist when required.

Sven-Olof Sandberg remembered:

Joseph shouted and cursed. At times he was close to physically attacking me. Many times I felt so discouraged that I sat down on the stairs outside his studio and wept. On some of these days I didn't have to sit alone for very long. Shortly afterwards out would come a young farmer's daughter. She would sit beside me and our tears mingled. Today she doesn't have to cry on the singing teacher's staircase for she is Birgit Nilsson and her name is a glittering star on the stage of world opera.[33]

The young Birgit Nilsson was making rapid progress. She wrote gratefully to Joseph in January 1943 from her home in the south of Sweden:

I hope you will not be offended by this tiny parcel. My father is so anxious to show his great appreciation for all the good teaching you have given me.

The parcel is really very small but perhaps I can bring something else another time. My father tried hard to get hold of a goose but has been unsuccessful in spite of the fact that Skåne is the homeland of the goose. But if we do find one we shall send it to you straight away.

I have been singing in various churches over Christmas and have received great recognition. I am so happy and grateful. When most of the Christmas celebrations were over, I was taken into hospital to have my appendix removed.

I was recently discharged from the hospital and am not feeling too good at the moment. I don't think I can travel up in time for the 15th but will stay here a few more days. My parents are very grateful to you. We all send our kindest regards to you and Mrs Hislop.[34]

Faced with her strong but breathy voice Joseph had set about reducing the volume, focusing the sound into a 'silver thread', the ping in the voice. In all Birgit Nilsson spent some three years with Joseph at the Royal Academy.

At the height of her career Nilsson recalled those days at the Academy.

At 23 I auditioned at the Royal Academy in Stockholm and came out top. It was the happiest day of my life. The night before I went to Stockholm for the audition I milked ten cows and I had to do weeding in the fields. It was hard work and I hated it.

My first teacher at the Academy was a famous Scots tenor [Joseph]. He thought I knew what a good impression I had made, so he tried to put me down under the floor. It was very easy to do that. He said 'It doesn't matter if you have the best voice in the world if you have no brain, because it's really not for a farmer to become a singer.'

I went home crying the first day. . . . I had him for three years. My voice became smaller and smaller. He had the right idea, so does everyone, but the way to get there, that's the difficulty.

I had an incredibly big wooden voice, full of air. The voice didn't project. It was incredibly big in my head and to people close by but you have to have a voice which projects. So he wanted to take off all this unnecessary sound. He said 'Oh, listen to Birgit. Now the ship is leaving the harbour.' He tried to get a concentrated tone, but he put the work in the wrong place. He didn't put you to work on the support or the resonance.

He put the work directly on the vocal chords. I felt it was wrong. I got very tired and I was very unhappy. Finally the director of the Academy said 'You are going to ruin Birgit's voice.'[35]

Joseph's hostility was deliberately hypercritical. He used hostility and sarcasm to break down the complacency often felt by students who had been accepted for the Academy. Coming from a simple farming background, he probably understood that Birgit Nilsson needed to appreciate the enormity of the task in front of her. She would have to learn at least two foreign languages and in the process acquire a broad liberal education. Of Nilsson, Joseph remarked that 'she had no top notes when she began to sing. But she worked hard and purposefully, her voice is splendid. As a dramatic interpreter of Wagner she is the greatest in the world.'[36]

Many of Joseph's former students kept in contact with him. Jussi Björling was known to have rung him up from a telephone box before a recital and, floating a high C over the phone, asked 'How does that sound?'[37]

The methods used by Joseph were developed from those of Dr Bratt who, as a throat specialist, placed primary importance on forming the sound first in the vocal chords. 'My experience as a singer and teacher has convinced me that all vowels begin in the larynx and only the finer shades are formed in the mouth.'[38]

In addition, Joseph believed that 'the tone is carried on the breath into the head resonators, supported by the diaphragm, but without exaggerated muscular pressure. Resonance is of all importance, even when singing a dark coloured tone, be it forte or piano, a *silver thread* of resonance in the middle of the tone should lead and govern.'[39] The resonance should be that of the G string.'[40]

References

1. Berlingske Tidende, 24 March 1936.
2. Hines, J. (1983), 'Birgit Nilsson', *Great Singers on Great Singing*, Gollancz, p. 195.
3. Letter to author 1988, NLS.
4. Ladberg, B.T. (Jan 6th 1974), Röster om Jussi Björling samtalar med människor som kände honom. (Swedish Radio interview with Björn Forsell).
5. Joseph Hislop's vocal pedagogy as summarized to author by Joseph Hislop jnr.
6. Jussi Björling's saga (Dec 26th/27th 1977), Swedish TV documentary in two parts produced by Jan Sederholm and Thomas Olofsson.
7. Hislop, J. (1960), *En engelsk röst, En minnesbok*, Hagman, B. (ed.), Stockholm, Bonniers, p. 98.
8. Anecdote told to author by Joseph Hislop jnr.
9. ibid.
10. Letter (Stockholm) 24 May 1935, NLS.
11. Anecdote told to author by Joseph Hislop jnr.
12. The Glasgow Herald, 2 April 1930.
13. Sandberg, S.O. (1970), Från vintergatan mot aftonstjärnan, Stockholm, Sveriges Radio förlag, p. 175.
14. ibid. p. 173.
15. ibid. p. 176.
16. ibid. p. 177.
17. Svenska Dagbladet, 6 April 1937.
18. Letter 13 October 1937, NLS.
19. Letter 14 October 1937, NLS.
20. Sandberg op. cit. p. 179.
21. ibid. p. 175.
22. ibid. p. 179.
23. ibid. p. 175.
24. ibid. p. 180.
25. ibid. p. 181.

26. Stockholms Tidning, 5 December 1931.
27. Sandberg op. cit. p. 181.
28. ibid. p. 182.
29. ibid. p. 183.
30. ibid. p. 184.
31. ibid. p. 173.
32. ibid. p. 189.
33. ibid. p. 180.
34. Letter 11 June 1943, NLS.
35. Hines op. cit. p. 195.
36. Stockholms Tidning, 2 April 1964.
37. ibid.
38. Hislop, J. (undated), Introduction to the Hislops' Method of Teaching, NLS.
39. ibid.
40. The San Francisco Bulletin, 27 September 1921.

14　Teaching in the UK and retirement (1944–1977)

Joseph celebrated his sixtieth birthday in 1944. Two years later rumours circulated in the Swedish press that he was leaving Sweden to take up an advisory post at Covent Garden.[1] Sir David Webster, Director at Covent Garden, and Norman Tucker, Director of the Sadler's Wells Opera Company, went over to Stockholm to see Joseph during the spring of 1946. They listened to some of his pupils, both private and those at the Academy. Joseph explained to the Swedish press that Covent Garden was planning a new National Opera and in connection with this, an Opera School. He had been offered the post of director with some teaching responsibilities.[2]

In December Joseph was entertained to a farewell party at the Royal Swedish Academy of Music. This gave his students an opportunity to thank him. In the New Year Joseph was to take up his duties, with responsibility for the training of young students and of qualified singers. He would also be available for advice and comment as one of Covent Garden's Artistic Directors. The plan was to create a totally English opera, sung in English. In addition he was to be an Artistic Director at Sadler's Wells.[3] Joseph took up these posts in 1948 working in close liaison with Ivor Griffiths, a distinguished throat specialist consulted by both Covent Garden and Sadler's Wells.

One of Joseph's early successes was the tenor Charles Craig. The late Dennis Arundell noted that 'at Joseph Hislop's suggestion, Sir Thomas Beecham and I had "discovered" him in 1951 in the Covent Garden chorus'.[4] As a result Sir Thomas sponsored Craig for two years of vocal training after an initial period under Joseph. Subsequently he became a principal tenor with the Carl Rosa, Sadler's Wells and The Royal Opera House.

There was the famous story of when Joseph came back to London from Sweden in 1947:

> He was walking down Bond Street and in the distance he recognised a little short, dumpy Welsh tenor by the name of Parry Jones. Parry was a fine singer and had a great British career but never an international one. Probably there

190

was, not animosity, but not any love lost. Now Parry walked up to Joe and said 'Hello, Joe. Long time no see.' And Joe answered, spinning out a long high note 'Yes, Parry – long time no C–e–e–e–e !'[5]

Nevertheless, the two venerable tenors had to work together at the Royal Opera House, as Lord Harewood recalled:

> Joseph used to come to the auditions we held at Covent Garden and which, from about 1954, I ran in the sense of sifting the singers who could sing on stage and of informing them of our decisions. Joseph Hislop and Parry Jones were our 'experts' . . . but they by no means always agreed. I recall Joseph as on the whole a rather constructive and even charitable judge of what a singer could do and the stage of development he or she had reached.'[6]

The Cinzano Scholarship Competition, Royal Opera House, Covent Garden, 1964: Sir David Webster, immediately behind him Joan Ingpen (casting director) and Lord Harewood. Two rows behind Joseph Hislop is Donald Pilley, winner in 1962, (the first year of the competition), and a pupil of Hislop. Standing behind Pilley is Count Alberto Cinzano. The Cinzano Scholarship offered six months at La Scala, Milan. In 1964 the winner was Gwenyth Annear.

Another well-known singer who auditioned before Joseph was the bass Ian Wallace whom Joseph afterwards invited for a drink. Wallace described the encounter as follows:

> In the pub he smiled at me, and said, 'You have a good voice, and you act well, but it's that', he held his hands six inches apart, 'instead of that'. He increased the distance to a foot. 'But I'm sure that can be put right.' He was, of course, referring to the fact that in a house the size of Covent Garden a voice had to be fairly large to carry, and that mine was still comparatively small.[7]

Leonard Hancock, at that time a member of the Covent Garden staff, remembers that it 'was then a young company consisting largely of home-grown singers. Many of them went to him for lessons in vocal technique. At Sadler's Wells he occupied a similar position. He did not work on specific productions at either Covent Garden or Sadler's Wells. His brief was more in the nature of general observation of the singers and the actual technical teaching of some of them, particularly the young ones, and advice to the management about them.'[8]

His main function at Sadler's Wells was to advise on auditions. It did not take him long to make up his mind. When the late Amy Shuard auditioned, the first phrase of 'Ritorna Vincitor' (*Aida*) was sufficient for his stage whisper, 'Engage her'.[9]

'He was sort of omnipresent', recalled the opera administrator Peter Hemmings, then working at Sadler's Wells, 'sidling into the back of the stalls during rehearsals. He attended many auditions which were organized by my great friend Tom Hammond and by Leonard Hancock who was then head of the music staff.'[10]

One of Joseph's many protegés was the tenor Alberto Remedios, a cheery Liverpool-born former welder, who studied twice a week for three years with Joseph in the mid-60s whilst a member of Sadler's Wells.

Watching the young tenor in Joseph's music room were the photographs of Joseph and other great singers, among them the one, taken in 1914, of himself and Caruso outside Pagani's restaurant in London.[11]

Whenever Remedios had sung well and pleased the Maestro, Joseph would bring out the the crystal given to him by the King of Sweden and offer him a dram of whisky. 'It was always a pleasure to work with him because he knew everything about singing. Alright, maybe 15, 20 minutes of the lesson was reminiscing, but it was worth it. "You're a natural singer", he told me, "just keep being natural all your life".'[12]

Joseph took good care to accompany his students to important auditions. 'I went for my audition with Sir George Solti at Covent Garden', said Remedios.

> One of my arias to finish with was 'Salut demeure, chaste et pure'. Now, I sang it like Joseph told me to do, with a beautiful mezzo forte top C. Solti came bounding down from where he was sitting in the stalls. He said, 'I don't

want to hear a top C like that. I want to hear it full voice. Go away and come back and sing it to me. Give me the works.'

I went offstage and Joseph the maestro is standing there. He said. 'You're coming with me, Alberto, you don't have to sing for him any more. It was wonderful, your audition. Forget him.'

I argued. 'Look, I need the job, Maestro. I need it.' His reply was. 'Do you want to go back and *bawl* a top C at him? I've told you, it's not nice in that aria.' I pleaded 'Let me just do the last bit, I'll just see what happens.' He muttered. 'You're mad, you're *mad*. I'll let you do it but you're a very naughty boy!'

So I went back. 'I'm ready, Maestro', I called to Solti. So I sang 'Saluet demeure' and I ripped it out. I didn't like the sound of the note but Solti congratulated me. 'That's how I want to hear it.' And I got the job.[13]

Remedios concludes 'Joseph Hislop was one of the true Greats in the Golden Age of Singing. He mustn't be lost, he must be remembered. Always.'[14]

Another of the young singers Joseph took under his wing was the Australian Elizabeth Fretwell.

> After auditioning for Sadler's Wells in 1955 and being accepted as a principal soprano I was advised by Norman Tucker to contact Joseph Hislop. At that time he was vocal consultant at Sadler's Wells, giving valuable advice as to casting. I have always been grateful to him as he would never allow me to sing roles that would harm my voice in any way, the reason so many young singers today have short careers.
>
> Before going to England I sang as a mezzo-cum-dramatic-soprano but he saw the possibilities of my being able to sing the *spinto* repertoire and began by preparing me for the role of Violetta in *La traviata*. He made my voice lighter in texture but greatly improved the carrying power, and also added three notes to the top of my range.
>
> During lessons he had a habit of going outside the studio to listen and if he didn't like any of our notes he would whistle loudly which meant 'Stop and repeat again!' Although in his seventies he was able to demonstrate a vocal point making it easier to understand. I sang many roles with Peter Glossop and we really enjoyed going to our lessons together.[15]

After Joseph had finished developing Elizabeth Fretwell's voice Norman Tucker wrote to him: 'I must thank you and congratulate you for what you have done for Betty Fretwell. She has come off marvellously well. It is very satisfying to have produced something like this between us. The hardest part, consolidation, lies ahead but I am sure she can do it. She seems to know how to work.'[16]

In 1949 Joseph had been made an honorary Professor at the Royal Academy of Music in Stockholm.[17] In London more regular teaching work again came his way in three years later when he was appointed a Professor at the Guildhall School of Music and Drama. In this capacity he taught a number

Teaching the Australian soprano Elizabeth Fretwell, London

of fine young British singers: the baritone Peter Glossop, Joyce Blackham and William McAlpine the tenor, who revealed in later years that 'I shall always be grateful to him, for putting my name right at the top, thus paving the way for my international career.'[18]

As a teacher Joseph did not mince his words and understood his own worth very clearly 'I remember him as a caustic Scot', John Gardner reminisced. 'One story lingers in my memory. William Dickie, the Scottish baritone, sang for him on one occasion. Joe's verdict was "I'll tell you two things. One, you can't sing. Two, it'll cost you two guineas to be told it." '[19]

Arthur Reckless, a colleague at the Guildhall School recalled that

> Joseph became a very popular and colourful teacher largely due to his vast operatic experience on the Continent and undoubtedly due to the wide acclaim accorded him as a *Maestro* while resident in Sweden. The knowledge that the famous Swedish tenor Jussi Björling was one of his proud successes focused a veritable spotlight on the window-dressing brought to the Guildhall School of Music and Drama in the mid-fifties. He was an enormous asset to the staff and his dignified presence was felt and indeed appreciated by everyone.
>
> Always immaculately dressed, he assumed the gentlemanly poise of a distinguished diplomat. Joseph was of a genial disposition, positive in outlook

and blest with that tinge of conceit which established him a true and likeable Scot.[20]

One of the students accepted by Joseph was the tenor Donald Pilley.

I was a very raw Exonian and a bricklayer by trade. I came up to London in 1959 and started with Joe. He had heard me sing and probably thought there was something there he could work on. I would lay bricks all day, knock off work at five o'clock, have a wash in the site toilets, change into a suit and go along to his house at Westbourne Terrace for my half-hour lesson.

In the music room of his house there was a fine Jacobean desk with two drawers. Joe would amble across to the desk and open the drawer nearest to me. It would be full, absolutely full of five pound notes and shilling pieces. 'Stick it in there, Donald', he would say. He was a true Scotsman. He always insisted on being paid, not in pounds but guineas.

I had many things in common with Joe. I had, like him, been a chorister (at Exeter Cathedral). In my ignorance one day I was talking about acoustics and I said 'What are the acoustics like at Covent Garden, Maestro, I hear they're bad?' 'Donald', he said, 'there are no bad acoustics, only bad singers.'

You always knew exactly where you stood with Joseph in lessons. You either sang well or badly. He didn't mince his words.[21]

Arthur Reckless remembered that in assessing the potential of any would-be tenor he would invariably apply his favourite yardstick, the opening phrase of Don Ottavio's aria in Mozart's *Don Giovanni*, 'Dalla sua pace'. There was hope for a singer approaching the upper G with apparent ease.[22]

Assisting and supporting Joseph in his teaching were, of course, his accompanists. Donald Pilley recalls that 'from 1947 to 1968 Joseph had four main pianists who accompanied at his lessons; Geoffrey Vince, Peter Wright, Keith Bonnington and Ronnie Smythe. They played interminable numbers from Lütgen, Concone, 'Roma è bella' and all the 'Arie antiche' that were ever written. I know for a fact that Ronnie Smythe played them all by memory and even in his sleep (and I'm sure that on many occasions when I was singing them he wished he were asleep).[23]

Although a professional to his fingertips, Joseph had a wry sense of humour. Donald Pilley remembers that 'A baritone at the Guildhall School of Music was having lessons. He was singing 'Eri tu' from *Un Ballo in Maschera*.

He was just about to sing the big G natural at the end when all of a sudden Joseph said 'My boy, I sincerely hope you are taking your *teacher's* diploma?'

Once a famous baritone at Covent Garden phoned up Joseph and said 'Maestro, I've been contracted to sing *Tannhäuser* at Covent Garden and I'm a little perturbed about it.' Through the years the voice had probably diminished just a little.

Joe told him to come for a singing lesson and he phoned up Keith Bonnington who was a very fine pianist. 'Do you know *Tannhäuser*, Keith?'

Teaching at home, London *c.* 1955

Keith answered 'Well, no'. 'Get a score out of the library. Come along. I've got a well-known singer coming.' So Keith turned up at two o'clock and was sitting there when in came the famous baritone. Joe said 'Right. We'll start with the aria "O Star of Eve".'

The baritone sang the aria. Joe got out of his chair and went to Keith and put his arms around him saying 'My son, you can take the afternoon off. This is far worse than I ever expected.'[24]

Joseph made it his business to spread his knowledge and expertise as widely as possible. He made a number of radio broadcasts on the lives of eminent singers whom he had known (including Titta Ruffo and Toti Dal Monte) and took part in a radio discussion on *Science and the Singer*.[25] He also delivered papers on the thorny topic 'Are there British voices of

International Opera Standard? If not, why not?' and in 1959 to the Association of English Singers and Teachers gave 'Some Thoughts on Singing' in which he insisted that there was little wrong with the basic material of British voices which properly conducted opera schools and permanent opera houses could not cure – views which had been put forward many years before by Sir Thomas Beecham.[26]

The tenor Kenneth Ormston, who studied with Joseph at the Guildhall, was particularly struck by his 'stay down' technique in singing a top C. It had a psychological effect which helped the physical achievement because one had to 'think down' as one rose in the vocal range. This was one reason why his top notes were so powerful, so resonant and yet so mild (never raucous). 'He used to stand and press down with his hands as he went up to his top notes. Even in his sixties he could still demonstrate how to sing a top C.'[27]

On vocal production Joseph had strong views. Vocal exercises were of no use whatever if they consisted of 'physical jerks' for the voice – running up and down scales and singing printed exercises. If these exercises were not directed by the mind and the ear, 'always on the alert for even quality and beautiful colour', and not advised and directed by a real teacher of experience, then the student could go on singing them for years with anything but good results. How often had he heard from adjacent rooms, immature voices yelling away at top notes under the impression, an erroneous one, that they would surely develop stamina and power, when all they did was lose quality and tire their voices. If they continued long enough in that way, they would eventually ruin them.[28]

At his spacious home in Westbourne Terrace, Joseph taught privately to a host of eager young singers. Associated with him in this work was his wife Nancy, who was later to teach at the Royal Northern College.

Even though domiciled in London, Joseph kept up a close association with Jussi Björling; 'we met every time he was in London for recitals, and we often discussed the art of singing.'[29]

Donald Pilley had a chance introduction to Jussi Björling:

> In 1960 I went for a lesson. I used to lay bricks in the daytime to pay for my singing lesson in the evenings and with fear and trembling I went along to the elegant vestibule in the music room at Westbourne Terrace. I was sitting there one evening at about half past five. I heard this voice. 'Fantastic'. He was better than me and I was jealous. Out came Joseph 'Come in, Donald, there's somebody you might like to meet.' I walked in and there the great man was seated, Jussi Björling, singing 'I dream of Jeannie with the light brown hair'.[30]

Joseph continues the story of his last association with Jussi Björling (who was to suffer a heart attack in the wings and died six months later). In March 1960 at Covent Garden, during an orchestra rehearsal for his guest appearances in *La bohème* he sat with Jussi in his dressing-room during one of the intervals. Joseph noticed that Jussi's voice sometimes seemed to lose its former great freedom in the highest notes. He suggested how to resolve this niggling problem. Jussi's mastery returned 'on the night of the performance his high C revealed itself, a flower of perfection'.[31]

As a musical personality Joseph nevertheless was not free from prejudice or temperament. Ellis Keeler, a professor at the Guildhall School of Music and Drama, adds this illuminating personal note about Joseph. 'He had no great appreciation of English song and on one occasion at a meeting of the Association of English Singers and Teachers, when English song was under discussion, he stunned the members present by walking out, saying "There aren't any".'[32] Against this one has to place the fact that Joseph's concert repertoire included almost 100 English vocal compositions (folksongs as well as art-songs) which he had almost invariably included in his performances. The composer Cyril Scott wrote to him on one occasion 'I want to thank you for singing my songs as you do so often. Also I should so much like to ask you to come here one evening or afternoon at your convenience. It would give me great pleasure to meet you.'[33]

Teaching duties sometimes permitted Joseph to lecture more specifically on his own career and on the singers he had worked with. In April 1959

Hislop with Björling and President Kokkinen of Finland, at a Björling concert in London in the 1950s

Joseph gave a talk to the Edinburgh Gramophone Society (President Sir Compton Mackenzie), its script being largely that delivered earlier in the year to the Association of English Singers and Teachers. The autobiographical passages in it were later recorded on the Rococco label and printed as an article in the journal *78 rpm* (February 1969 No. 4).

'The musical illustrations Joseph used were special pressings produced for him by HMV on 78 rpm shellac. At the time the 78 rpm record was a thing of the past', remembered Nicholas Curry, who was present at Film House in Edinburgh's Randolph Crescent to hear Joseph. 'The dubbing of 78s onto LPs was limited to bestselling artists such as Caruso, Gigli and so forth, the deluge of historical re-issues having only begun.'[34]

One of the singers Joseph used to illustrate his talk was Titta Ruffo whose voice and technique he so greatly admired after their performance together in 1920. Joseph repeated the following anecdote because it reinforced his own views on the voice:

> A young bass called Mattania was singing a small part in an opera with Titta Ruffo and had been forcing some of his high notes. At the fall of the curtain the great Ruffo put his hands on the shoulders of the young man, saying 'Senti ragazzo, always remember the words of the great Battistini "Never ask of your voice more than your voice can give".' This good advice the young singer Mattania never forgot.[35]

As they got older both Joseph and Nancy continued to have a strong yen for Scotland. They enjoyed holidaying there, to paint and play golf. Joseph made a sentimental journey in 1959 to take part in the first reunion dinner of the ex-Choristers of St Mary's Episcopal Cathedral, being its oldest and most distinguished member. Of the 783 boys who had been members of the Choir since it began in 1880, as many as 94 were present at the dinner in the Royal British Hotel in Princes Street. When Joseph entered the room a great cheer went up. The celebration was punctuated by many speeches, reliving old times, remembering with particular affection Dr Thomas Collinson, the fearsome 'Collie'.[36]

Joseph's eightieth birthday was marked in London with a special reception given by the Swedish ambassador in London, Gunnar Hägglöf, at the Swedish embassy.[37] Then he travelled to Venice with Nancy to celebrate the occasion by staying beside the Grand Canal in the palazzo where Wagner had written part of *Tristan und Isolde*.[38] While in Venice Joseph and Nancy had dinner with his pupil, the tenor and former bricklayer Donald Pilley, who was studying at La Scala (Milan) as winner of the Count Cinzano Scholarship.[39] Pilley recalls the meeting. 'I was in Venice in 1964. Joe came out and had his 80th birthday. He invited me out to dinner with Nancy. We had a lovely meal but I finished up footing the bill.'[40] Nevertheless, before an audience at the La Fenice opera house (that included Joseph and Nancy) Pilley went on to win the international Verdi Competition singing 'Che gelida manina' as Joseph had done in the same theatre in 1923 (but this time without the Claque!)

Although Joseph was 80 he could still be a formidable character. One of his students at the time, Grahame McIntosh, a baritone who sang at Covent Garden for ten years before going out to the Sydney Opera House, recalls one typical incident.

> I went to his house for my lesson one day to find him walking up and down the studio obviously just cooling down from a rage. Though a very old man at this time he still walked a lot and went regularly on the London tube trains. I used to see him frequently in the winter striding past Covent Garden stage door at quite a pace with his overcoat almost down to his ankles.
>
> However, this particular day he had been angered by a young man who had pushed in front of him and sat down. Joseph said, 'Excuse me, I think you are extremely rude. My nephew is coming over from Sweden shortly and if he had been with me this morning he would have knocked your block off.' Then as an afterthought he added, 'In fact by the look of you, I could do it myself.' The young man left the train soon after and when Joseph opened his paper, still in a violent rage, he glanced at the page and there before him was a picture of a boxing-match.[41]

Away from the daily grind of teaching, almost every summer Joseph and Nancy spent a few weeks with his daughter Elsa just outside Gothenburg. On one occasion Joseph went to Lerum to visit the Danish marine artist Axel Lind and his wife Eva. Joseph would set up his easel next to Lind's and enjoy many hours of putting paint to canvas.

His wife Nancy had not, however, been in good health for a number of years. This led to their deciding to leave London and move north to Scotland. Joseph retired from full-time teaching in 1969 but continued to teach privately. James Robertson, his former colleague at Sadler's Wells and now director of The London Opera Centre, wrote to him. 'News has come to me that you have retired to your native country. I want, therefore, to congratulate you on a magnificent life's work for opera, both as a singer in the international world and, since then, as a teacher.'[42]

Joseph and Nancy moved into a farmhouse at Berryside, near New Gilston, in the fertile East Neuk of Fife with their two King Charles spaniels. Nancy had connections with Cupar on her mother's side and for Joseph, the golf courses of Lundin Links and St Andrews proved a great attraction. Now, instead of striding past Covent Garden every day, he was able to take daily walks in the countryside. 'We love it here and the people are so friendly', he enthused.[43]

Having arranged for their former home at Westbourne Terrace to be converted to flats, Joseph and Nancy lived at Berryside financed by the modest rents which they shared with a business partner in London. Joseph also received a small teacher's pension from the Swedish government and the income from regular singing students, some of whom would come to stay in the caravan near the house.

Joseph had had a sunroom added to the house with a patio door leading straight into the garden. This became a favourite retreat. But Berryside was a working farm; there was always activity – a tractor trundling through the yard or the car of the *grieve* (farm-manager) passing by. Nancy knew all the farmworkers by name and looked after Joseph attentively.

The older he got the more he lived with his memories. Visitors who came to the house would insist on hearing his recordings; after each record they would applaud as if he were on stage. However, Joseph would never allow certain of them to be played because he felt the performance was flawed. One of them, 'The Flower Song' from *Carmen*, he damned from the first note which he considered to have been too 'covered', not open enough. He judged himself no less severely than he judged his own pupils.[44]

In the sunset of his life Joseph nurtured yet one more singer of international standing, the Scottish baritone Donald Maxwell. As Maxwell recalled: 'I first met the Hislops in 1969. It was thanks to George Donald, who not only came to Joseph for singing lessons but also worked for him as an accompanist, who took me through to Berryside when I was still studying Geography at Edinburgh University. Joseph advised me to "stick to Geography" on that occasion, which I did, teaching for five years.[45]

Acting as accompanist on many occasions was George Donald, today the pianist and anchor-man of the review group 'Scotland the What?' He also received lessons from Joseph. His strongest recollection of the Hislop method was the need to 'release' the voice when moving, for example, from a high note at the end of one phrase to a low note at the beginning of the next. This was done by relaxing the vocal mechanism.[46]

When Gothenburg celebrated its 350th anniversary in 1971, Joseph and Nancy were invited as guests of honour by the President of Gothenburg Town Council, Captain Hans Hansson, on behalf of the City of Gothenburg to attend a performance of *Aida* in the giant Scandinavium.

The Scandinavium had been built as a result of a skilful compromise between Left and Right-wing local political parties. The Left wanted an ice-hockey arena, the Right demanded a concert hall. The Scandinavium, seating between 12 and 15 thousand, and capable of staging both ice-hockey and cultural events, was the outcome.

Aida was sung by Joseph's former student Birgit Nilsson, and he and Nancy were guests of honour. At the celebratory dinner after the opera Claes Jacobsson, a baritone at the Stora Teatern, was asked to sing the traditional 'schnapps song'. Joseph was in a mood of great elation and in the middle of Jacobsson's performance he capped it with a magnificent final high C. Birgit Nilsson commented admiringly, 'Ah, that's Hislop'.[47]

Joseph was also scheduled to play an exhibition golf match for Swedish Television with his old friends Birger Sörvik (aged 92) and Bruno Zachrisson (aged 82), the son of his old photoprocess boss Waldemar Zachrisson. Jack Nicklaus and a group of other international pros were coming to Gothenburg to play golf for the first time in Sweden, the idea of the match with this antique triumvirate being to show how golf could keep you mobile and healthy even into advanced old age.[48] Regretfully, it was cancelled at the last minute.

Meanwhile Donald Maxwell persisted with his lessons. 'I next went back in about 1971 to go over *The Messiah* solos with him. I was rather keen to make an impression in 'The trumpet shall sound' but all my efforts only served to elicit the dry comment, "You're awfully fond of that bloody trumpet!"'[49]

Grampian Television decided to do a two-part feature on Joseph in January 1973 around Burns Day in the series 'Thompson at Teatime'. In the first part he was interviewed at his Berryside home by the presenter Ron Thompson, and, in the second, introduced in the Aberdeen studio where he was even persuaded to sing 'My love, she's but a lassie yet' accompanied on the piano by George Donald. This was the first time he'd ever sung on television. 'Of course, the voice we heard was not the voice that thrilled the world so long ago', wrote *The Sunday Post* (28 January 1973). 'Yet, it was strangely moving. And what viewers did not see was that the men behind the scenes, the cameramen, lighting engineers and producer, all stood with unashamed tears in their eyes, listening to the grand old man of opera singing his last song to the biggest audience he's ever had.'

Later that year, as a complete surprise, Joseph and Nancy were flown to Sweden to be the 'mystery guests' in a television programme, 'På Parkett' (In the Stalls), featuring his former pupil, the baritone Sven-Olof Sandberg, along the lines of 'This is Your Life'.[50]

From time to time Joseph still went to the opera. Peter Hemmings, at that time administrative director of Scottish Opera, recalls that he came to a couple of performances in Edinburgh. 'I remember his coming backstage. Subsequently he came to one of the opening performances of the Theatre Royal in Glasgow and we also saw him when we gave "midi" performances in Perth and Kirkcaldy.'[51]

His Polish barber in nearby St Andrews, Michael Zamora, was a passionate devotee of Robert Burns. Accordingly Joseph and Nancy were invited to the annual Burns Celebration where he was even persuaded to sing. In January 1974 they were both honoured guests for The Scottish Night at the Byre Theatre and then, in 1976, he attended the Burns Supper of the club at which the Scottish composer and Professor of Music at St Andrews University, Cedric Thorpe Davie, proposed 'The Immortal Memory'.[52]

Although the prestigious Swedish institution, The Friends of the

Hislop in old age, *c.* 1975

Drottningholm Opera, wanted to invite Joseph over to Sweden for a celebration in his honour, he turned them down as he now found flying
uncomfortable and not a little frightening. He attended the St Andrews
Burns supper instead.

As well as being interested in the songs of Burns and the collections of Marjorie Kennedy-Fraser, Joseph had always been on excellent terms with the greatest Scots music hall star, Sir Harry Lauder. A curious connection with Sir Harry Secombe also came to light through his singing-teacher, Manlio Di Veroli, who had accompanied Joseph and whose songs Joseph sang many times. Secombe recalled that Di Veroli 'frequently mentioned Joseph Hislop and always with admiration and respect for his voice, holding him up to me as a classic example of the "bel canto" singer.'[53]

In about 1974 Donald Maxwell started going regularly to Berryside.

> I'll never forget driving up to the farmhouse and hearing him busily practising the day's scales, for he warmed up his voice rigorously even though over 90 and once produced an amazing top C at that age to the chagrin of the tenor who was trying to make it.
>
> His lessons at that time were not dwelling on his past but very much businesslike and practical. Only once do I remember things going wrong when I was yelling out my exercises *con tutta forza* and he kept saying 'louder'. He then excused himself, put another battery in his hearing-aid and pronounced himself satisfied when I'd all but deafened him in the next exercise.
>
> In 1976 I decided to go full time into singing and he was kind enough to send an introductory letter to Scottish Opera which I'm sure did much, as Sir Alexander Gibson had fond memories of him from the late 1940s and early 1950s in London.
>
> My strongest memory is of sitting in Berryside on a summer's day looking over to Largo Law and discussing Scots songs. I'm sure that his recordings of 'Bonnie Mary of Argyle' and 'Macgregor's Gathering', with their vivid diction and unique sense of style, will remain unmatched as evidence of one of the greatest tenor voices to come from Britain.
>
> My last memory of him was about a couple of months before he died. We were sitting listening to the re-releases of some of his records. He was by then rather frail but typically, for a tenor, he smiled approvingly at his top note.[54]

Towards the end he would go to the extension, sitting for long periods, teaching from his chair, even in the last year managing the occasional high C. A favourite view was from the top of the hill at Berryside, a windswept, dramatic landscape, very cold in winter yet peaceful and strangely beautiful. The view over the Firth of Forth was breathtaking. Gradually he took to his bed, to all appearances completely at peace with himself and the world.

About two days before he died his pianist and pupil George Donald went to see him. He was weak, without much energy. It was as if his body was telling him 'I've had enough'. 'Ah, George', he said quietly, 'it's hopeless now.'[55] When his time came he slipped slowly into unconsciousness and died peacefully at home in his sleep on 6 May 1977.

His funeral took place on 10 May at Kirkcaldy Crematorium, a simple, modest ceremony. 'I had the honour of singing "Panis Angelicus" at his funeral service', recalls Donald Maxwell, 'and remember racing to

Kirkcaldy Crematorium after the hearse, reviving memories of his driving (which was, I believe, highly erratic).'[56] After his death Nancy could not bear to listen to any of his recordings.

In all Joseph Hislop had three separate careers: photoprocess engraver, singer and teacher, excelling at all three. Had he not been an exceptional craftsman he would not have been sent to London for advanced training, nor would he have been recommended to Waldemar Zachrisson to teach his Swedish tradesmen the latest three-colour reproduction techniques. It was his restless quest for excellence in everything he did that made him an international star.

What of his position in the world rankings of operatic tenors? To some extent the facts speak for themselves. His special place as principal tenor at Stockholm and his appearances at Covent Garden, in which he was paired with some of the most renowned singers of the century, both testify to the prominent position he occupied during the years of his prime. The tribute of Puccini to 'my ideal Rodolfo' must carry weight, and the appreciation of his fellow artists Tauber and McCormack are worth remembering also, as are Caruso's solicitous enquiries as to 'how young Hislop did'.

His recordings, all too few in number, are generally fine in quality. The veteran critic Herman Klein declared that Hislop's studio recording of *Faust's* 'Cavatina' was the finest he had heard since what he called 'the palmy days of Edward Lloyd', and from him that was a compliment indeed.[57]

David Bicknell, EMI's manager of international artists for many years, recalled that 'in the 1920s, when Hislop was in good voice, he was the equal of the best lyric tenors of his time'.[58] That he is still valued is confirmed in the pages of Michael Scott's *The Record of Singing* where his vigour, cleanness and 'high degree of competence' are specially commended.[59] In *The Grand Tradition* John Steane writes (as he does in the Foreword to this book) of the personal affection Hislop's voice inspires on records.[60] In *Opera on Record* Lord Harewood describes his recording of 'Pourquoi me réveiller?' from *Werther* as 'a fine souvenir of a distinguished artist'.[61]

Hislop was also, as the late Dame Eva Turner recalled, 'a superb recitalist and an excellent professor of voice.'[62] His memory remains a treasured and honoured one among many pupils and friends, and in Sweden particularly his name is still one to be conjured with.

Indeed, memory of him crops up in some unlikely places. The Scottish bass Ian Wallace remembers a conversation with the veteran singer Augusto Beuf while singing in *Don Giovanni* at Parma not long after the Second World War. Beuf asked whether Wallace was English. 'Inglese, lei?' 'No', Wallace replied, 'scozzese'. The Italian's response to this was a further question. 'Ah, cognosce 'Eeslop?' To which Wallace replied that yes, he did know Hislop a little. Beuf nodded and added some words which might have brought a glow of pride to the old man's cheeks could he have heard them. 'Ah, 'Eeslop. 'E was a great-a tenor – Era un gran' tenore.'[63]

References

1. Dagens Nyheter, 26 August 1946.
2. Aftonbladet, 11 December 1947.
3. ibid.
4. Arundell, D. (1978), *The Story of Sadler's Wells*, London, David and Charles, p. 240.
5. Pilley, D., from My Ideal Rodolfo, BBC.
6. Letter to author, 30 July 1986, NLS.
7. Letter to author, 10 December 1985, NLS.
8. Letter to author, 18 December 1985, NLS.
9. Letter to author, 10 December 1985, NLS.
10. Letter to author, 23 November 1987, NLS.
11. Interview recorded by author at Theatre Royal, Glasgow, 22 March 1989, NLS.
12. ibid.
13. ibid.
14. ibid.
15. Letter to author, 1 September 1987.
16. Letter 11 February (undated) (in private possession).
17. Svenska Dagbladet, 12 February 1949.
18. Letter to author (undated) 1986, NLS.
19. Letter to author, 29 June 1986, NLS.
20. Letter to author (Reminiscences of Joseph Hislop), 24 September 1983, NLS.
21. Pilley op. cit.
22. Reckless op. cit.
23. Pilley op. cit.
24. ibid.
25. Transcribed from a telediphone recording, 30 November 1955, NLS.
26. NLS, Acc. 10304.
27. Ormston, K. *My Ideal Rodolfo*, BBC Radio 3, 12 July 1989.
28. Some Thoughts on Singing, NLS.
29. Hislop, J. (1960), En engelsk röst, En minnesbok, Hagman (ed.), Stockholm, p. 98.
30. Pilley op. cit.
31. Hislop op. cit.
32. Letter to author, 27 September 1983, NLS.
33. Letter in private possession (undated)
34. Letter to author, 22 December 1986, NLS.
35. Hislop, J. '*Titta Ruffo*', BBC Radio 3, 15 July 1956.
36. Unidentified Scottish newspaper, 1958, NLS.
37. The Scotsman, 1 April 1964.
38. Göteborgs-Posten, 5 April 1964.
39. Opera, December 1963, p. 802.

40. Pilley op. cit.
41. Letter to author, 15 May 1986, NLS.
42. Letter to Joseph Hislop (in private possession).
43. Unidentified Fife newspaper, December 1967, NLS.
44. Account given separately by George Donald and Joseph Hislop jnr to author.
45. Letter to author (undated) 1988, NLS.
46. Account given to author by George Donald.
47. Account given to author by Joseph Hislop jnr.
48. Göteborgs-Posten, 30 August 1971.
49. Maxwell op. cit.
50. Göteborgs-Posten, 4 April 1974.
51. Letter to author, 23 November 1987, NLS.
52. Menu of 100th annual celebration of St Andrews Burns Club, 24 January 1976, NLS.
53. A Recollection of Manlio Di Veroli, July 1988, NLS.
54. Maxwell op. cit.
55. Account given to author by George Donald.
56. Maxwell op. cit.
57. The Gramophone, November 1927.
58. Letter to author, 4 June 1988, NLS.
59. Scott, M. (1979), *The Record of Singing*, Vol. 2: 1914 to 1925, London, Duckworth, p. 275.
60. Steane, J.B. (1974), *The Grand Tradition*, London, Duckworth, p. 275.
61. Harewood, Lord.(1979), *Opera on Record*, London, Hutchinson, p. 504.
62. Letter to author, 27 July 1986, NLS.
63. Letter to author, 27 July 1986, NLS.

Appendix 1
Stage roles 1914–1937: debuts and frequency

Work	Composer	Role	Debut	Frequency
Merrie England	German	Raleigh	1934	c. 376
Frederica	Lehár	Goethe	1930	c. 118
La bohème	Puccini	Rodolfo	1917	81
Tosca	Puccini	Cavaradossi	1917	62
Faust	Gounod	Faust	1914	41
Madama Butterfly	Puccini	Pinkerton	1914	34
Rigoletto	Verdi	Duke	1917	31
Lucia	Donizetti	Edgardo	1920	28
Lakmé	Delibes	Gerald	1916	26
Manon	Massenet	des Grieux	1916	25
Wienervalsen	after Strauss	J. Strauss jnr.	1932	c. 24
Mignon	Thomas	Wilhelm	1936	c. 24
Aida	Verdi	Radames	1916	20
Mefistofeles	Boito	Faust	1915	16
La traviata	Verdi	Alfredo	1918	16
Roméo et Juliette	Gounod	Roméo	1916	15
Pagliacci	Leoncavallo	Canio	1918	15
Carmen	Bizet	José	1928	13
Werther	Massenet	Werther	1926	9
Manon Lescaut	Puccini	des Grieux	1929	9
Marouf	Rabaud	Muezzin	1915	7
Les Pêcheurs de Perles	Bizet	Nadir	1918	7
Violantha	Korngold	Alfonso	1918	6
Louise	Charpentier	Julien	1923	6
Cavalleria Rusticana	Mascagni	Turridu	1917	3
Falstaff	Verdi	Fenton	1925	3
Gianni Schicchi	Puccini	Rinuccio	1925	2
Les Huguenots	Meyerbeer	Raoul	1916	2
Gillet på Solhaug	Stenhammar	1st servant	1914	2

To summarize, Hislop gave some 921 performances of opera and operetta from his relatively small repertoire of 29 (although the fact that he was required to sing many of them in two language versions should be taken into account). This makes an average of 46 performances per annum between 1914 and 1934. Between 1914 and 1941 Hislop also gave around 390 concerts.

Appendix 2
Opera house debuts (as the leading tenor)

Date			House/Company	Opera	Total Appearances (in any role)
1914	Sep	12	Royal Opera, Stockholm	Faust	285
1919	Apr	26	Opéra Comique, Oslo	Rigoletto	2
1920	Jan	15	San Carlo, Naples	Lucia	30
	May	14	Covent Garden, London	La bohème	25
	Nov	20	Auditorium, Chicago	Tosca	15
1921	Jan	24	Manhattan, New York	Tosca	3
1922	Mar	17	Stora, Gothenburg	Tosca	20
	Dec	30	La Fenice, Venice	La bohème	3
1923	Feb	7	Regio, Turin	Lucia	19
	Mar	11	La Scala, Milan	Lucia	4
1925	Feb	12	La Monnaie, Brussels	La bohème	21
	Mar	14	Théâtre Royale, Liege	Tosca	5
	Apr	4	Théâtre Royale, Antwerp	Tosca	4
	Jul	1	Colón, Buenos Aires	Falstaff	13
1926	Mar	26	Opéra-Comique, Paris	La bohème	9
1927	Feb	10	Líceo, Barcelona	La bohème	3
	Apr	1	Theatre Royal, Copenhagen	La bohème	5
1929	Apr	21	Empire, Edinburgh	La bohème	3
1930	Feb	17	Finnish Opera, Helsinki	La bohème	17
	Mar	18	National Opera, Riga	Tosca	5
1933	Jan	27	Estonian Opera, Tallinn	Tosca	3

Appendix 3
Concert repertoire

Opera

Aria	*Work*	*Composer*	*First performed*
I love you	Eugene Onegin	Tchaikovsky	1911
Siegmund's Spring Song	Die Walküre	Wagner	1913
Prize Song	Die Meistersinger	Wagner	1913
Narration	Lohengrin	Wagner	1913
O Paradiso	L'Africana	Meyerbeer	1913
Bianca al par di neve	Les Huguenots	Meyerbeer	1913
Flower Song	Carmen	Bizet	1913
O merveille! (with Åke Wallgren)	Faust	Gounod	1916
Dai campi	Mefistofele	Boito	1916
Solo, profugo, reietto (with Åke Wallgren)	Martha	Flotow	1916
La donna è mobile	Rigoletto	Verdi	1916
Au fond du temple (with Åke Wallgren)	Les Pêcheurs de Perles	Bizet	1916
E lucevan le stelle	Tosca	Puccini	1916
Adoucis la rigeur	Masaniello	Auber	1917
Magische Töne	Die Königin von Saba	Goldmark	1919
Le Rêve	Manon	Massenet	1919
Che gelida manina	La bohème	Puccini	1919
Ah, lève-toi, soleil	Roméo et Juliette	Gounod	1919
E lucevan le stelle	Tosca	Puccini	1919
Celeste Aida	Aida	Verdi	1919
Vesti la giubba	Pagliacci	Leoncavallo	1920

(all the above sung in Swedish)

M'appari	Martha	Flotow	1920
Lamento di Federico	L'Arlesiana	Cilea	1921
Salut, demeure	Faust	Gounod	1921
Una furtiva lagrima	L'Elisir d'Amore	Donizetti	1922
Recondita armonia	Tosca	Puccini	1922
Tombe degli avi miei	Lucia di Lammermoor	Donizetti	1922
Pourquoi me réveiller?	Werther	Massenet	1922

Aria	Work	Composer	First performed
Dido's Lament	Dido and Aeneas	Purcell	1926
O Mimi, tu più non torni (with John C. Thomas)	La bohème	Puccini	1923
O soave fanciulla (with Ada Sari)	La bohème	Puccini	1923
Questa o Quella	Rigoletto	Verdi	1923
O where has fled?	Eugene Onegin	Tchaikovsky	1923
Ma se m'e forza perderti	Un Ballo in Maschera	Verdi	1924
Cielo e mar	La Gioconda	Ponchielli	1924
O quanti occhi fissi? (duet)	Madama Butterfly	Puccini	1924
Ch'ella mi creda . . .	La Fanciulla del West	Puccini	1924
Cherry Duet (Tutto tace) (with Evelyn Scotney)	L'Amico Fritz	Mascagni	1924
Ah, Fuyez, douce image	Manon	Massenet	1926
Aubade	Le Roi d'Ys	Lalo	1926
Comme un petit oiseau	Suzanne	Paladilhe	1926
Un dì all'azzurro spazio	Andrea Chénier	Giordano	1927
Nessun dorma	Turandot	Puccini	1927
Aldrig jag hennes (Donna non vidi mai)	Manon Lescaut	Puccini	1930
Ack, Manon (Ah Manon mi tradisce)	Manon Lescaut	Puccini	1930
Dal labbro il canto	Falstaff	Verdi	1931
Dalla sua pace	Don Giovanni	Mozart	1932
O Souverain, O Juge, O Père	Le Cid	Massenet	1933
Silent Worship	Ptolemy	Handel	1934
Where'er you walk	Semele	Handel	1935

Operetta and Light Opera

Then you'll remember me (The Bohemian Girl)	The Bohemian Girl	Balfe	1919
O Maiden, my Maiden	Frederica	Lehár	1931
O Mädchen (sung in German in Norway)	Frederica	Lehár	1931
Wonderful	Frederica	Lehár	1931
Wayside Rose	Frederica	Lehár	1931

Oratorio

Obadiah	Elijah	Mendelssohn	1913
Angels waft her to the skies	Jephtha	Handel	1926
Tenor part	Messiah	Handel	1926

Aria	Work	Composer	First performed
Onaway, awake, beloved (BBC broadcast)	Hiawatha's Wedding	Coleridge-Taylor	1932
Tenor Solo	Pied Piper of Hamelin	Parry	1936

Songs

Song	Composer	First performed

Scottish (in some cases the composer is unknown)

Song	Composer	First performed
2 Scots songs		1919
Bonnie Mary of Argyle	Nelson	1921
The Island Herdmaid	Kennedy-Fraser arr.	1921
Heart of Fire-Love	Kennedy-Fraser arr.	1921
Annie Laurie	Lady John Scott	1921
My love is like a red, red rose		1921
Of a' the airts	Marshall	1921
The Bagpipe Man	McKinney	1921
Auld Lang Syne		1921
MacGregor's Gathering	Lee	1921
Hundred Pipers		1921
Hey, Johnnie Cope		1921
My love, she's but a lassie yet	Short arr.	1922
An Eriskay love lilt	Kennedy-Fraser arr.	1922
Herding Song	Lawson arr.	1922
Kishmul's Galley	Kennedy-Fraser arr.	1922
Auld Joe Nicholson	Short arr.	1922
Wilt thou be my dearie?	Kennedy-Fraser arr.	1922
Afton Water	Hume	1922
To Mary in Heaven	Short arr.	1923
Corn Rigs	Short arr.	1923
The Lea Rig	Short arr.	1923
Bonnie wee thing	Short arr.	1923
Dark Lochnagar		1923
My Wife's a winsome thing		1923
O my love's bonny		1923
The Land o' the Leal	Lady Nairne	1925
Gae bring tae me a pint o' wine		1925
An Island Sheiling Song	Kennedy-Fraser arr.	1926
Lord Randal	Scott arr.	1927
Mary	Richardson	1928
Bonnie Wee Thing	Scott arr.	1928
Corn Rigs	Scott arr.	1928
Ye Banks and Braes		1931
Bonnie George Campbell	Keel	1932
Isle of my Heart	Kennedy-Fraser arr.	1935
The Laird of Cockpen	Lady Nairne	1935

Song	Composer	First performed
Song to the Seals	Kennedy-Fraser arr.	1941
Annie Laurie	Lady Scott/Lehmann arr.	1942

English

Romance	d'Hardelot	1916
Sea Fever	Ireland	1919
Ask not one least word	Granville Bantock	1919
Love went a-riding	Bridge, Frank	1919
I hear you calling me	Marshall	1919
Looking back	Scott, Cyril	1919
Life and Death	Coleridge-Taylor	1920
Invictus	Huhn	1920
O Mistress Mine	Quilter	1921
Eleanore	Coleridge-Taylor	1921
Come you, Mary	Craxton	1921
Thank God for a Garden	del Riego	1921
Ave Maria	Kahn	1921
Votre Voix	Pringle	1921
Passing by	Purcell/Cochrane	1921
Song of the Palanquin Bearers	Shaw	1922
Thine am I	Somerville	1922
Cargoes	Dobson	1922
An Uncouth Love-Song	Walford Davies	1922
Windy Nights	Stanford	1922
At the mid hour of night	Cowen	1922
The Letter	Walthew	1922
Go not, happy day	Bridge, Frank	1922
Charity	Hagemann	1922
The Great Awakening	Kramer	1922
My Lovely Celia	Lane Wilson arr.	1922
Ah, Moon of my Delight	Lehmann	1922
Down in the Forest	Ronald, Landon	1922
Where the Bee Sucks	Arne	1922
A Pastoral	Lane Wilson arr.	1922
Love's Quarrel	Scott, Cyril	1922
For You Alone	Geehl	1923
A Wayside Flower	d'Hardelot	1923
Tears of Joy	Kahn	1923
The Cloths of Heaven	Dunhill	1923
If I such wondrous music knew	Di Veroli	1923
To Mary	White	1923
Isobel	Bridge, Frank	1923
Go, lovely Rose	Quilter	1923
Lovely kind and kindly loving	Holst	1923
Throb of the passionate day	Löhr	1923
Russian Snow-Song	Löhr	1923
In Summertime on Bredon	Peel	1924
Pastoral	Lane Wilson arr.	1924

Song	Composer	First performed
Lighted lamps	Di Veroli	1924
Five Eyes	Armstrong Gibbs	1924
And so I made a Villanelle	Scott	1924
The Unforeseen	Scott	1924
Sigh no more, ladies	Aiken	1924
Willow Tree	Kahn	1926
Come buy	Buzzi-Peccia	1926
A Spirit Flower	Campbell Tipton	1926
I heard you singing	Coates	1927
In the Silver Moonbeams	Scott	1927
Toll Gate House	Rowley	1927
Birds' songs at evening	Coates	1927
A Birthday	Manson, W.	1927
Nightfall at Sea	Phillips	1927
Sweet Phyllis	Strickland	1928
Trees	Heyman	1928
Songs my mother taught me	Dvořák	1930
A Widow Bird	Granville Bantock	1931
Mary had a little Lamb	Hughes arr.	1931
Mary, Mary, quite contrary	Hughes arr	1931
Doctor Foster	Hughes arr.	1931
There was a Crooked Man	Hughes arr.	1931
The Queen of Hearts	Hughes arr.	1931
I am disquieted	Parker	1931
The Dew upon the Lily	German	1931
Lonesome Moonlight	Strickland	1931
The Star	Rogers	1931
Down in the Forest	Ronald, Landon	1931
Strew on her roses	Ronald, Landon	1931
A Pair well matched	Ronald, Landon	1931
Just for To-day	Seaver	1931
When Dawn breaks through	Haydn Wood	1931
A Song down the Valley	Haydn Wood	1931
Piggesnie	Warlock	1931
Goin' Home (arr. from New World Symphony by W. A. Fisher)	Dvořák	1931
Were you there?	Burleigh arr.	1931
Nobody Knows	Burleigh arr.	1931
The Cornish Witch	Murray	1933
South Winds	Kahn	1933
Annabel Lee	Di Veroli	1933
The River and the Leaf	Di Veroli	1934
Always	Smith	1935
When dull care	Lane Wilson arr.	1941
On Wenlock Edge	Vaughan Williams	1941
The little damozel	Novello	1941
Captain Stratton's Fancy	Warlock	1941
Mary of Allendale	Lane Wilson arr.	1942
The pretty creature	Lane Wilson arr.	1942

Song	Composer	First performed
Smilin' through	Penn	1942

Irish

Macushla	MacMurrough	1920
The Snowy Breasted Pearl	Robinson arr.	1920
The Fairy Tree	O'Brien	1931
The Kerry Dance	Molloy	1935
Eily Aroon	Barratt	1941
Open the door softly	Hughes arr.	1941
Kitty, my love	Hughes arr.	1941

Swedish

Drömmen	Hallén	1911
Trollsjön	Söderman	1911
Jungfrun under lind	Peterson-Berger	1913
Skogen sofver	Alfvén	1913
Alla mina drömmar	Sjögren	1913
Die geheimnisvolle Flöte	Sjögren	1913
Chanson de Fortunio	Sjögren	1913
Vårjubel	Körling, F.	1913
Hymn	Olsson	1913
Värmlandsvisan	Alfvén arr.	1913
Hemlängtan	Josephson	1913
Serenad	Wideén	1914
Sverige	Stenhammar	1916
Chinesisches Trinklied	Sigurd v Koch	1919
Du ser på mig	Sjögren	1919
Jag längtar dig	Alfvén	1919
Rondeau	Rangström	1922
Trösta	Håkanson	1922
Du sover blott	Lundvik	1922
Mens jeg venter	Grieg	1922
Du är melodien	Wiklund	1924
Silkeskö	Wiklund	1924
Söndag	Järnefelt	1924
Melodi	Rangström	1927
Ditt namn jag	Peterson-Berger	1928
Tonen	Eriksson	1928
Som stjärnorna	Peterson-Berger	1928
Två visor (folkton)	Peterson-Berger	1928
Lina	Järnefelt	1929
Som ett silversmycke	Jonsson	1929
Land, du välsignade!	Althén	1930
Ibland myrten och jasminer	Peterson-Berger	1932
En positivvisa	Stenhammar	1932
Og jeg vil drage	Sjögren	1932
Kung Heimer och Aslög	Söderman	1933

Song	Composer	First performed
Danish		
Thorstens sang	Heise	1913
Mai	Bechgaard	1913
Norwegian		
Tak for dit Råd	Grieg	1919
En Drom	Grieg	1919
En Svane	Grieg	1921
Bække	Jordan	1922
Magnis Sång	Ulfrstad	1922
En Fuglevise	Grieg	1928
Spillemænd	Grieg	1928
Ragnhild	Greig	1928
Ved sjøen	Kjerulf	1928
Verdens gang (Lauf der Welt)	Grieg	1929
Fra Monte Pincio	Grieg	1932
I love thee (Jeg elsker dig)	Grieg	1934
Finnish		
Morning Song	Melartin	1913
Den första kyssen	Sibelius	1913
Mademoiselle Rococo	Melartin	1928
Som glödande kolet	Merikanto	1930
En flicka sjunger där	Sibelius	1932
Kuin hiipuva hiillos (in Finnish)	Merikanto	1933
Was it a dream? (Var det en dröm?)	Sibelius	1933
Det var i vårens	Kilpinen	1933
Vårmelodi	Kilpinen	1933
Mitt sagoland	Kilpinen	1935
Danslek	Kilpinen	1935
German		
Ich denke dein	Schumann	1913
Unterm Fenster (duet)	Schumann	1913
Der Lenz ist gekommen	Hildbach	1916
Pavillon aus Porzellan	Mahler (Lied von der Erde)	1917
Breit über mein Haupt . . .	Strauss, R.	1919
Heimkehr	Strauss, R.	1919
Impatience (Ungeduld)	Schubert	1923
Meine Liebe ist grün	Brahms	1924
Cäcilie	Strauss, R.	1924
Adelaide	Beethoven	1926

Song	Composer	First performed
Die Mainacht	Brahms	1926
Minnelied	Brahms	1926
Der Doppelgänger	Schubert	1926
Ständchen	Strauss, R.	1926
Frühlingsglaube	Schubert	1926
Firenze	Lange-Müller	1928
Der Tod, das ist die kühle Nacht	Brahms	1928
Meine Liebe ist grün	Brahms	1928
Du bist die Ruh	Schubert	1931
To-morrow (Ungeduld)	Strauss, R.	1931
The Lover's Pledge (Heimliche Auforderung)	Strauss, R.	1931
Night (Die Nacht)	Strauss, R.	1931
All Souls' Day (Allerseelen)	Strauss, R.	1931

French

Aime-moi	Bemberg	1921
J'ai pleuré en rêve	Hue	1926
D'une Prison	Hahn	1926
O Lord Most Holy (Panis Angelicus)	Franck	1927
The Grey House (from *Fortunio*)	Messager	1931
Carnival	Fourdrain	1931
Le Papillon	Fourdrain	1931
Chanson Norvégienne	Fourdrain	1931

Italian

Goodbye	Tosti	1916
La Danza	Rossini	1924
Nel cor non più mi sento	Paisiello	1926
Amate	Tosti	1926
L'alba separa dalla luce . . .	Tosti	1926
Ideale	Tosti	1926
Fiocca la Neve	Cimara	1926
Stornellatrice	Respighi	1930
Venetian Vision	Brogi	1931
Girometta	Sibella	1931
Vaghissima sembianza	Donaudy	1931
O del mio amato	Donaudy	1931
Land ever calm and peaceful	Donaudy	1931
Quando io ti vedrò	Donaudy	1931
Stizzoso	Pergolesi	1932
Marechiare	Tosti	1932
Nebbie	Respighi	1932
Mattinata	Leoncavallo	1933
Serenade Française	Leoncavallo	1934
'A vucchella	Tosti	1934

Song	*Composer*	*First performed*
Spanish		
Ayes: Tres coplas	Rodrigo, M.	1933
Serenita esta la noche	Rodrigo, M.	1933
Russian		
Love and Memory	Borovsky	1921
At Night	Rachmaninoff	1921
The Dreary Steppe	Grechaninoff	1924
The Clock	Sakhnovsky	1924
To the Children	Rachmaninoff	1927
The Sea	Borodin	1927
Spring Waters	Rachmaninoff	1927
The Rose enslaves the Nightingale	Rimsky-Korsakoff	1933

To summarize, as far as can be established: Joseph Hislop had a total repertoire of some 254 songs and arias which he performed throughout his career on the concert platform. This could be broken down as follows: material in English (92), Scots (37), Swedish (33), German (23), Italian (20), Norwegian (13), Finnish (11), Russian (8), French (8), Irish songs (7) and Danish (2). A typical Hislop concert, as given in Washington, USA, in 1921 consisted of Italian arias, English songs, French, Swedish and Norwegian classics, Scottish ballads and songs of the Hebrides.

Appendix 4
Discography

Compiled by Alan Kelly, Boris Semeonoff and Michael Turnbull, with acknowledgements to the earlier work of M.F. Bott and Björn Englund, including the following:

Bott, M.F.(1977), *The Record Collector*, **23**, (9 & 10), June, 230–7.
Bott, M.F.(1979), *The Record Collector*, **25**, (1 & 2), March, 41–2.
Englund, Björn (1970), 'Joseph Hislop's Swedish Recordings', *Talking Machine Review*, **4**, 109–10.
Mason, D.H. and Bott, M.F. (1969), 'Joseph Hislop: A Discography', *78 rpm*, **4**, February.

The layout of the discography is in chronological order of performance and as follows:
Reference number; title and composer etc., followed by matrix and take number(s); single-side number; double-side number, where applicable.
'Take' numbers indicate successive renderings of the same title, usually (but not always) at the same session. Published takes indicated by italic type. A letter (eg. -1A) indicates a separate simultaneous recording on another machine. Bb, BR, BE, BS, 0B, 2B – 10" issues; prefixes Cc, CR, CE, CS, 2B, 2EA – 12" issues.
Suffixes to Zonophone and Swedish groups: e, ab, ae – 10" issues; af – 12" issues.

Single-side numbers were used as catalogue numbers until the introduction, around 1923, of double-sided 'celebrity' records, but continued in use and appeared on labels until around 1933.
The Zonophone records were issued only in double-sided form and have a dark green label; some late pressings carry the HMV 'dog' trademark in gold outline. A few still later pressings have a light green label.
The Gramophone Company's Swedish series are green label, with the wording GRAMOPHONE CONCERT RECORD.
The single-sided HMV discs, later coupled in the DA (10") and DB (12") series, are Red Label.
From 1929 onwards 'popular' material by Hislop was issued in the cheaper Plum label B (10") and C (12") series, but operatic and other more 'serious' titles continued to be given Red Label 'celebrity' status.

ACOUSTIC RECORDING PROCESS

1914 January 17. GC Stockholm (piano) [1]

1. For you alone (Geehl)   6108ab

1914 June 18. GC Zonophone. Hayes, Middlesex (piano)

2. Mid the fair throng (Questa o quella. *Rigoletto* – Verdi)   ae 17944e
   X-3-42204   1387

3. Woman is fickle (La donna è mobile. *Rigoletto* – Verdi)   ae 17945$^{1}/_{2}$e
   X-3-42205   1387   [3]

4. Queen of the Earth (Pinsuto)   af 8008f   Z-042071   A154

5. Good-bye (Tosti)   af 8009f   Z-042070   A154

6. Heavenly Aida (Celeste Aida. *Aida* – Verdi)   af 8010f   [6]

7. All hail thou dwelling (Salut, demeure. *Faust* – Gounod)   af 8011f
   Z-042073   A156

1914 November 7. GC Stockholm (orchestra)

8. Din kära röst mig når (*Because* – d'Hardelot, tr G. Bratt)   6191ae
   2-282649

9. Gud vet vem som kysser dig nu (I wonder who's kissing her now? – Howard/
   Swedish words by Hislop)   6192ae   2-282650

1914 November 9. GC Stockholm (piano)

10. Serenad: Tallarnas barr (Widéen)   6239ae   [10]

11. Violer (*Salut d'amour* – Elgar) (with violin obbligato)   6240ae   2-282814

1916 September. Pathé Frères. Stockholm. Tullio Voghera (piano)

12. Kom äter (*Tradimento* – Bonincontro)   90584   S3258   R11004

13. Öfver skog, öfver äng (Dai campi. *Mefistofele* – Boito)   90586   S3259
    R11005   [13]

14. O Lola (*Cavalleria Rusticana* – Mascagni)   90587   S3258   R11004

15. Ack som (La donna è mobile. *Rigoletto* – Verdi)   90588   S3259   R11005

1921 August 15. GC Hayes (orch – Spencer Clay)

16. Bonnie Mary of Argyle (Nelson)   Bb397   (-1 -2 -3)

17. Addio alla madre (*Cavalleria Rusticana* – Mascagni)   Cc398   (*-1* -2)
    2-052200   DB522

18. Come into the garden, Maude (Balfe)   Bb399   (-1)

1921 August 16. GC Hayes (orch – Spencer Clay)

19. Bonnie Mary of Argyle (Nelson/Jeffreys)   Bb397   (-4 -5)

20. Lend me your aid (Inspirez-moi. *Reine de Saba* – Gounod)   Cc400   (-1)

1922 May 17. GC Hayes (piano – Spencer Clay)

21. Herding Song (Songs of the North: 2nd Collection – arr. Lawson)
     Bb1350   (*-1* -2 -3)   5-2565   DA444

22. O, my love's bonnie (arr. Short)   Bb1351   (*-1* -2)   5-2566   DA443

23. Afton Water (Hume/words by Robert Burns)   Bb1352   (-1 *-2*)
     5-2567   DA443

24. Charity (Richard Hageman)   Bb1353   (-1 -2 -3)

1922 May 18. GC Hayes (orch – George Byng)

25. Che gelida manina (*La bohème* – Puccini)   Cc1357   (-1 -2)

26. La donna è mobile (*Rigoletto* – Verdi)   Bb1358   (-1 -2)

27. An Eriskay love lilt (Songs of the Hebrides – arr. Kennedy-Fraser)
     Bb1359   (*-1* -2)   5-2568   DA444

1922 June 1. GC Hayes (orch – George Byng)

28. Che gelida manina (*La bohème* – Puccini)   Cc1357   (-3 *-4*)   2-052232
     DB522

29. Morning was gleaming (Prize Song: *Die Meistersinger* – Wagner)   Cc1414
     (-1 -2)

30. In distant lands (Grail Song: *Lohengrin* – Wagner)   Cc1415   (-1)

1922 October 11. GC Hayes (orch – Spencer Clay)

31. Morning was gleaming (Prize Song: *Die Meistersinger* – Wagner)   Cc1414
     (-3 -4)   02976   DB681

32. In distant lands (Grail Song: *Lohengrin* – Wagner)   Cc1415   (-2 -3 -4)

1922 October 12. GC Hayes (orch/piano – Spencer Clay)

33. Che gelida manina (*La bohème* – Puccini)   Cc1357   (-5 -6 -7)

34. La donna è mobile (*Rigoletto* – Verdi)   Bb1358   (-3 -4 *-5*)   7-52221

35. My lovely Celia (G Monro/arr. Lane Wilson, piano – Spencer Clay)
     Bb1957   (-1 -2)   5-2631

36. Thank God for a garden (Del Riego) (piano – Spencer Clay)   Bb1958
     (-1 -2)

1922 November 6. GC Hayes (orch – Spencer Clay)

37. Che gelida manina (*La bohème* – Puccini)   Cc1357   (-8 -9 -*10*)
2-052232X   DB522

38. Morning was gleaming (Prize Song: *Die Meistersinger* – Wagner)
Cc1414   (-5 -6)

39. In distant lands (Grail Song: *Lohengrin* – Wagner)   Cc1415   (-5 -*6*)
02976   DB681

40. Thank God for a garden (Del Riego) (piano – Spencer Clay)   Bb1958
(-3 -4 -5)   5-2632 (not issued)

1923 November 21. GC Hayes (orch – Julius Harrison)

41. Tombe degl'avi miei (*Lucia di Lammermoor* – Donizetti)   Cc3872
(-*1* -2)   2-052248   DB695

42. Fra poco a me ricovero (*Lucia di Lammermoor* – Donizetti)   Cc3873
(-*1* -2)   2-052249   DB695

43. Ella mi fu rapita (*Rigoletto* – Verdi)   Bb3874   (-1 -*2*)   7-52252   DA226

1923 November 22. GC Hayes (orch – George Byng)

44. Parmi veder le lagrime (*Rigoletto* – Verdi)   Bb3880   (-*1* -2)   7-52253
DA226

45. Tu che a Dio spiegasti l'ali (*Lucia di Lammermoor* – Donizetti)   Bb3881
(-1 -2)

46. I love thee (Grieg Op. 5 No. 3)   Bb3882   (-1 -2)

47. Simonetta – Serenade (Rumbold) with guitar/cello/mandolin/vln/tuba/
piano   Cc3883   (-1 -2)

1923 December 20. GC Hayes (orch – Julius Harrison)

48. Dovunque al mondo (*Madama Butterfly* – Puccini) with Dinh Gilly (baritone) and William Parnis (tenor)   Cc4006   (-*1* -2 -3)   2-054140   DB743

49. Amore o grillo (*Madama Butterfly* – Puccini) with Dinh Gilly (baritone)
Cc4007   (-*1*)   2-054141   DB743

50. I love thee (Greig Op. 5 No. 3: piano – J.M. Beck)   Bb4010   (-1 -2 -3)

1924 February 19. GC Hayes (piano – Clarence Raybould)

51. Corn Rigs (arr. Short/words by Robert Burns)   Bb4222   (-1 -2 -*3*)
5-2913   DA588

52. My love, she's but a lassie (arr. Short/words by Robert Burns)   Bb4223
(-1 -*2*)   5-2914   DA588

53. Bonnie wee thing (Fox/words by Robert Burns)   Bb4224   (-1 -2 -3 -4)
5-2915

1924 December 15. GC Hayes (orch – Julius Harrison)

54. Ma se m'e forza perderti (*Un Ballo in Maschera* – Verdi)   Cc5478   (*-1* -2)
2-052268   DB822

55. Ah, non credevi tu (*Mignon* – Thomas)   Cc5479   (*-1* -2)   2-052269
DB822

56. Vesti la giubba (*Pagliacci* – Leoncavallo)   Bb5480   (-1)

ELECTRIC RECORDING PROCESS

1925 October 19. GC Hayes (piano – Percy Kahn)

57. Bonnie wee thing (Fox/words by Robert Burns)   Bb7004   (-1 *-2*)
6-2327   DA749

58. Sigh no more, ladies (Aitken)   Bb7005   (-1)   6-2340

59. Spring time (Aitken)   Bb7006   (-1)

60. The MacGregor's Gathering (Lee/words by Sir Walter Scott)   Bb7007
(-1 *-2*)   6-2328   DA749

1925 December 14. GC Hayes (orch – Julius Harrison)

61. Le Rêve (*Manon* – Massenet) with Selma d'Arco (soprano)   Cc7508
(-1 -2 -3)   [61]

62. Ah, fuyez, douce image (*Manon* – Massenet)   Cc7509   (-1 -2 -3)

1926 May 13. GC Small Queen's Hall (orch – George Byng)

63. O Mimi, tu più non torni (*La bohème* – Puccini) with Apollo Granforte
(bar)   CR370   (-1 -1A *-2* -2A)   2-054157   DB939   [63]

64. Solenne in quest'ora (*La Forza del Destino* – Verdi) with Apollo Granforte
(bar)   CR371   (-1 *1A* -2 -2A)   2-054158   DB939

1926 May 25. GC Hayes (orch – George Byng)

65. Le Rêve (*Manon* – Massenet) with Selma d'Arco (soprano)   Cc7508
(-4 -5)

66. Ah, fuyez, douce image (*Manon* – Massenet)   Cc7509   (-4 -5)

1926 May 28. GC Hayes (orch – George Byng)

67. Pourquoi me réveiller? (*Werther* – Massenet)   Cc8467   (*-1* -2)   2-032101
DB944

68. Addio alla madre (*Cavalleria Rusticana.* – Mascagni)   Cc8468   (-1)

1926 June 2. GC Hayes (piano – Percy Kahn)

69. Afton Water (Hume/words by Robert Burns)   Bb8483   (-1 -2)

70. An Eriskay love lilt (Songs of the Hebrides arr. Kennedy-Fraser)
Bb8484   (-1)   6-2549   DA789

71. Herding Song (Songs of the North: 2nd Collection – arr. Lawson)
Bb8485   (*-1* -2 -3)   6-2550   DA789

1926 June 9. GC Hayes (orch – George Byng)

72. Le Rêve (*Manon* – Massenet) with Selma d'Arco (soprano)   Cc7508
(-6 -7)

73. Ah, fuyez, douce image (*Manon* – Massenet)   Cc7509   (-6)

74. Salut, demeure (*Faust* – Gounod) (violin – Marjorie Hayward)   Cc8518
(*-1*)   2-032102   DB944

1926 September 17. GC Small Queen's Hall (piano – Kahn/vln – Hayward/ cello – Nifosi)

75. At Dawning (Cadman)   Bb9218   (-1 *-1A* -2 -2A)   6-2621   DA819   [75]

76. I heard you singing (Eric Coates)   Bb9219   (-1 -2 -2A -3 *-3A*)   6-2622
DA818

77. For you alone (Geehl)   Bb9220   (-1 -1A -2 *-2A*)   6-2623   DA819

78. Nightfall at sea (Montague Phillips)   Bb9221   (*-1* -1A -2 -2A)   6-2624
DA818

79. So we'll go no more a-roving (M.V. White)   Bb9222   (-1A)

1926 October 4. GC Small Queen's Hall (orch – Byng)

80. A dream garden (Montague Phillips)   Bb9289   (-1)

1927 June 14 . GC Small Queen's Hall (piano – Kahn/vln – Hayward/cello – Cedric Sharpe)

81. (a) When the swallows homeward fly (Wenn die Schwalben – Abt) (b) Let
us forget (M. V. White)   Bb10940   (-1 *-2*)   6-2817   DA887

82. Bird songs at eventide (Eric Coates)   Bb10941   (*-1* -2)   6-2818   DA887

83. Mens jeg venter (Grieg Op. 60 No. 3) (in Norwegian with piano only)
Bb10942   (-1 *-2*)   7-82212   DA890

84. En Svane (Grieg Op. 25 No. 2) (in Norwegian with piano only)
Bb10943   (-1 *-2*)   7-82213   DA890

85. (a) Bœkken (Jordan) (b) Vesle blomme enge blomme (Castberg) (piano)
Bb10944   (-1 *-2*)   7-82214   DA889

86. Evigt dig till Hjärtat Trycka (Sjögren) (piano)   Bb10945   (-1 *-2*)   7-82215
DA889

1927 June 17. GC Kingsway Hall (orch – Piero Coppola)   [87]

87. Afton Water (Hume/words by Robert Burns)   CR1379   (-1 *-1A* -2 -
2A)   2-02222   DB1058

88. Bonnie Mary of Argyle (Nelson)   CR1380   (-1 *-2*)   2-02233   DB1058

1927 June 20. GC Small Queen's Hall (orch – Piero Coppola)

89. E il sol dell'anima (*Rigoletto* – Verdi) with Lotte Schöne (soprano)
Cc10964   (-1 -2)   2-054179   DB1127

1927 June 22. GC Small Queen's Hall (piano – Kahn/vln – Hayward/cello – Sharpe)

90. Mary (Scots ballad arr. Richardson)   Bb10965   (-1 -2 -3 -4 -5)   6-2848
DA901

91. My love is like a red, red rose (words by Robert Burns)   Bb10966   (-1 -2)
6-2849   DA901

1928 June 22. Faust (Gounod) Royal Opera House, Covent Garden. GC (Royal Opera Orch – Eugene Goossens/recorded during a public performance)

92. Rien! En vain j'interroge – Act 1 (with Royal Opera Chorus)   CR2097
(-1 -1A)   [92]

93. Paresseuse fille – Act 1 (with Chorus)   CR2098   (-1 -1A)

94. Duo: Faust/Mephistopheles pt. 1 Act 1 – Mais ce Dieu (with
Chaliapin)   CR2099   (-1 -1A)

95. Duo: Faust/Mephistopheles – pt. 2 Act 1 (with Chaliapin)   CR2100
(-1 -1A)

96. Duo: Faust/Mephistopheles pt. 3 – Eh bien, que t'en semble? Act 1 (with
Chaliapin)   CR2101   (-1 -1A)

97. Nous nous retrouverons Act 1 (with Laugier/Chaliapin/Chorus)
CR2104   (-1A)   2-034047   DB1189

98. Salut, demeure chaste et pure Act 2   CR2106   (-1)   2-032143   DB1189 [98]

99. Vous qui faites l'endormie Act IV (with Chaliapin)   CR2109   (-1)   [99]

1928 September 26. GC. Konserthuset, Stockholm (orch – Nils Grevillius)

100. Jungfrun under lind (Peterson-Berger)   BS2994   (-1 -2)   7-82246
DA1006

101. Sondag (Järnefelt)   BS2995   (-1 1T1 -2)   7-82247   DA1007   [101]

102. Du sover blott (Lundvik)   BS2996   (-1 -2)   7-82248   DA1007

103. Tonen (Eriksson)   BS2997   (-1 -2)

104. Mademoiselle Rococo (Melartin)   BS2998   (-1 -2)   7-82249   DA1006

105. Melodi (Rangström) acc. Adolf Wiklund (piano)   BS2999   (-1 -2 -3)
7-82250 (not issued)

106. Brita-Lills vaggvisa (Emile Stiebel) acc. A. Wiklund (piano)   BS3000
(-1)   [106]

1928 December 4. GC Small Queen's Hall (piano – Kahn)

107. Goodbye (Tosti) Cc15402 (-1 *-2*) 2-02296 (not issued)

108. A song remembered (Eric Coates) Bb15403 (-1 -2)

109. Corn Rigs (arr. Short/words by Robert Burns) Bb15404 (*-1* -2) 7-2267 DA1020

110. My love, she's but a lassie (arr. Short/words by Robert Burns) Bb15405 (-1 *-2* -3) 7-2268 DA1020

1928 December 6. GC Small Queen's Hall (orch – Byng)

111. Lonesome moonlight (Strickland) Bb15418 (-1 -1A -2 -2A -3) 7-2269 (not issued)

112. Little lady of the moon (Eric Coates) Bb15419 (-1 -1A -2 -2A) 7-2270 (not issued)

113. To the children (Rachmaninoff Op. 26 No. 7) Bb15420 (-1A -2 *-2A*) 7-2271 B3154

114. A song remembered (Eric Coates) Bb15421 (-1A *-2*) 7-2266 (not issued)

1928 December 10. GC Small Queen's Hall (orch – John Barbirolli)

115. Che gelida manina (*La bohème* – Puccini) Cc15428 (-1 -1A *-2* -2A) 2-052392 DB1230

116. Addio alla madre (*Cavalleria Rusticana* – Mascagni) Cc15429 (-1A -2 -2A *-3* -3A) 2-052393 DB1230

1928 December 14. GC Small Queen's Hall (orch – Horace Sheppard)

117. A night idyll (Loughborough) Bb15454 (-1)

118. Lord Randall (Scots Border ballad arr. Cyril Scott) C15455 (-1 -2)

119. Annie Laurie (Lady John Scott) Cc15456 (-1 -2)

1929 February 14. GC Small Queen's Hall (orch – Byng)

120. A night idyll (Loughborough) Bb15454 (-3 -4 -5)

121. Lonesome moonlight (Strickland) Bb15418 (-4 -5 -6)

122. Little lady of the moon (Eric Coates) Bb15419 (-3 -4 -5)

123. Annie Laurie (Lady John Scott) Cc15456 (-3 -3A)

1929 February 18. GC Small Queen's Hall (piano – Percy Kahn/violin – Brosa/cello – Pini)

124. I kiss your hand, Madame (Erwin) Bb15904 (-1 -2 -3)

125. Lord Randall (Scots Border ballad arr. Cyril Scott) Cc15905 (-1 -2 -3)

1929 May 6. GC Small Queen's Hall (orch – Byng)

126. Lonesome moonlight (Strickland) Bb15418 (-7A -8 -8A -9)

1929 May 6. GC Small Queen's Hall (orch – Barbirolli)

127. The Grey House (*Fortunio* – Messager) Bb16849 (*-1* -2 -2A) 7-2504
B3154

128. Goin' home (Dvořák – after *New World Symphony*) Bb16850 (-1 -2)

1929 May 7. GC Small Queen's Hall (piano – Kahn)

129. I kiss your hand, Madame (Erwin) Bb15904 (-4A -5 -5A)

130. Serenade (Toselli) (vln – Brosa/cello – Pini) Bb16854 (-1 -1A -2 -2A)
7-2506 (not issued)

131. Annie Laurie (Lady John Scott) Cc16855 (-1A -2 -2A -3 -3A)

1929 May 15. GC Small Queen's Hall (orch – Barbirolli)

132. Of a' the airts (arr. Ross/words by Robert Burns) Bb16895 (-1 *-2*)
7-2469 B3155

133. Turn ye to me (words by John Wilson arr. Gibilaro) Bb16896 (*-1* -2 -3)
7-2508 B3155

134. Roses and women (Grothe) Bb16897 (-1 -2) 7-2509

135. Lonesome moonlight (Strickland) Bb15418 (-10 -11) 7-2505

1929 July 10. GC Small Queen's Hall (orch – Barbirolli)

136. E lucevan le stelle (*Tosca* – Puccini) BR2439 (-1 *-2*) 30-940
DA1063

137. Recondita armonia (*Tosca* – Puccini) BR2440 (-1 *-2*) 30-941
DA1063

138. Vesti la giubba (*Pagliacci* – Leoncavallo) BR2441 (-1 -2 *-2A*) 30-942
DA1062

139. No, Pagliaccio non son (*Pagliacci* – Leoncavallo) BR2442 (*-1*) 30-943
DA1062

1929 July 12. GC Large Queen's Hall (orch – Barbirolli)

140. Morning was gleaming (Prize Song: *Die Meistersinger* – Wagner) CR2443
(-1 -1A -2A) 32-731 DB1351

141. In distant lands (Grail Song: *Lohengrin* – Wagner) CR2444 (-1 -2 *-2A*)
32-732 DB1351

142. La fleur (*Carmen* – Bizet) CR2445 (-1 -2 -2A) 32-733 [142]

1929 November 1. GC Kingsway Hall (orch – Leslie Heward)

(The Loves of Robert Burns – pot pourri in 4 parts – arr. Heward)

143. Spoken Introduction/Loch Lomond Bb17837 (*-1* -1A) 30-1928
B3264 Part 1

144. Ye banks and braes/Bonnie Mary of Argyle (Nelson) Bb17838 (-1A -2
-2A -3 *-3A*) 30-1929 B3264   Part 2

145. Annie Laurie (Lady John Scott) Bb17839 (*-1* -1A -2 -2A) 30-1930
B3265   Part 3

146. Afton Water 17840 (-1 -2 *-2A*) 30-1931 B3264   Part 4

[Note: Other songs recorded on the soundtrack of the film by The British &
Dominions Film Corporation (using the Western Electric Sound system) are: Annie
Laurie (Reel 1), Auld Lang Syne (R2/R3/R10), Comin thro' the rye (R3/R4), O a'
the airts (R4), Green grow the rushes O – with chorus (R4), Rantin', rovin' Robin
(R4), Bonnie Wee Thing (R4), Sweet Afton (R6/R7/R10) and The silver tassie (R7).
The words of two of the songs are not by Burns: those of 'Bonnie Mary of Argyle'
are by Charles Jefferys; words and music of 'Annie Laurie' by Lady John Scott.]

**1929 December 12. GC Stockholm hotel (orch – Nils Grevillius & Royal
Opera House Chorus)**

147. Ack, Manon (Ah, Manon mi tradisce: *Manon Lescaut* – Puccini) with Greta
Söderman (soprano) BE2075 (-1 -2 *-3*) 30-2212 DA1083 [147]

148. Blander alla (Tra voi belle: *Manon Lescaut* – Puccini) with Theodor
Andrésen (tenor) and chorus BE2076 (-1 -2 -3) 30-2214 DA1084

149. Forlät mig (Guardate, pazzo son: *Manon Lescaut* – Puccini) with Josef
Herou (bass), Sven Herdenberg (bass) and chorus BE2077 (-1 *-2*)
30-2215 DA1084

150. Aldrig jag hennes (Donna non vidi mai: *Manon Lescaut* – Puccini) BE2078
(-1 *-2*) 30-2213 DA1083

151. Du, du, min äskling (Tu, tu, amore: *Manon Lescaut* – Puccini) with Greta
Söderman (soprano) CE2079 (-1 -2 -3) 32-1094 DB1394

152. Ack kärleken (*O tentatrice: Manon Lescaut* – Puccini) with Greta Söderman
(soprano) CE2080 (-1) 32-1095 DB1394

1930 September 22. GC Kingsway Hall (orch – Jacques Heuvel)

153. Wonderful (*Frederica* Act I – Lehár) Bb19750 (-1) 30-4542 B3589

154. Wayside Rose (*Frederica* Act I – Lehár) Bb19751 (-1 *-2*) 30-4543
B3589

155. A heart as pure as gold (*Frederica* Act 3 – Lehár) Bb19752 (-1 *-2* -3)
30-4544 B3590

156. O Maiden, my maiden (*Frederica* Act 2 – Lehár) Bb19753 (-1 *-2*) 30-
4545 B3590

1931 January 29. GC Small Queen's Hall (piano – Sir Landon Ronald)

157. Strew on her roses (Ronald)   OB273   (*-1* -2)   30-5766   B3817

158. A pair well matched (Ronald)   OB274   (*-1* -2 -3)   30-5767   B3816

159. It is a beauteous evening (Ronald)   OB281   (-1)   [159]

1931 February 2. GC Kingsway Hall (orch – Lawrance Collingwood)

160. The Lea Rig (Blamphin arr. Gibilaro)   OB447   (*-1* -2)   30-5935   B3771

161. My mother (Marsden arr. Gibilaro)   OB448   (*-1* -2)   30-5965   B3774

162. When the Dawn breaks through (Haydn Wood arr. Gibilaro)   OB449
      (-1 -2)

1931 February 9. GC Small Queen's Hall (piano – Landon Ronald)

163. When I am dead (Ronald)   OB299   (-1 *-2*)   30-5768   B3816

164. Down in the forest (Ronald)   OB300   (*-1* -2)   30-5769   B3817

1931 February 13. GC Small Queen's Hall (orch – Lawrance Collingwood)

165. Land o' the leal (Lady Nairne arr. Gibilaro)   OB310   (-1 *-2*)   30-5936
      B3771

166. Bonnie banks o' Loch Lomond (old Scots song arr. Gibilaro)   OB311
      (-1 *-2*)   30-5966   B3774

167. Ye banks and braes (arr. Gibilaro/words by Robert Burns)   OB312
      (*-1* -2)   30-6186   B3832

168. O sing to me the old Scotch songs (Leeson)   OB313   (*-1* -2)   30-6187
      B3832

1932 December 12. GC Abbey Road (orch – Clifford Greenwood)

169. Jessie, the flower of Dunblane (Smith)   OB4361   (*-1* -2)   B4413

170. The Island Herdmaid (Songs of the Hebrides – arr. Kennedy-Fraser)
      OB4362   (-1 *-2*)   B8042

171. Annie Laurie (Lady John Scott)   OB4363   (-1 *-2*)   B4413

172. Rose Marie (*Rose Marie* – Friml)   OB4364   (*-1* -2)   30-10746   B4404

1933 March 8. GC Abbey Road (orch – Clifford Greenwood)

173. Ah, Moon of my delight (In a Persian Garden – Liza Lehmann)   2B6467
      (-1)

174. The Indian love call (*Rose Marie* – Friml)   OB6468   (-1)   30-10747
      B4404

175. Angels guard thee (Berceuse de Jocelyn – Godard)   2B6469   (-1 -2)

176. An Island Sheiling Song (Songs of the Hebrides – arr. Kennedy-Fraser)
OB6470   (-1 *-2*)   B8042

1933 December 7. GC Abbey Road (orch – C. Greenwood)

177. Ye banks and braes (arr. Gibilaro/words by Robert Burns)   OB5824   (-1 -2)

1935 February 26. HMV Abbey Road (orch – C. Greenwood)

178. For love alone (Siever – Thayer)   2EA794   (*-1* -2)   C2729

179. The English Rose (*Merrie England* – Sir Edward German)   2EA795
(-1 *-2*)   C2729

180. Talk on Rococo R5283   (later published in *78 rpm*, No. 4, April 1970)

MICROGROOVE RE-ISSUES

(numbers refer to preceding entries in this Appendix)

Golden Age of Opera EJ 452	96	
Famous British Tenors EMI HQM	155	

Faust Harvest 1002 (excerpts with Chaliapin)	
OASI 580-D	63
Rococo 5283	43, 44, 48, 49, 57, 74 (or 98), 63, 64, 139, 147, 148, 149, 150 and talk by Hislop (reprinted in *78 rpm* No. 4 1970)
Singers in Sweden – Rubini GV 33	102
Joseph Hislop – Rubini GV 43	8, 9, 12, 13, 14, 15, 83, 84, 85, 86, 115, 116, 136, 137, 138, 139
Joseph Hislop – Rubini RS 308	11, 21, 27, 48, 37, 49, 61, 62, 75, 76, 77, 78, 89, 90, 91, 132, 133, 143, 144, 145, 146, 147, 148, 149, 150, 151, 152
Joseph Hislop – Rubini RDA 010	2, 3, 39, 41, 42, 43, 44, 51, 52, 54, 55, 57, 60, 67, 70, 71, 72?, 74, 87, 88, 113, 127, 143, 158, 161, 163, 169, 170, 171, 176
Royal Opera House, Covent Garden, Historic Recordings of Actual Performances EMI RLS 742	97, 98, 99
The Art of Chaliapin Melodiya D028551-52	99

Röster från Stockholmsoperan
under 100 år.
EMI   C 153 – 35350/8   51 Singing Lesson (see LB 8164 below)

Record of Singing Vol. 2
EMI RLS 743   4

The Grand Seasons Vol. 2
Pearl GEMM 259/10   48, 49

LOCATIONS OF EXISTING HISLOP RECORDED MATERIAL

Swedish National Archive of Recorded Sound and Moving Images (ALB)

1938 December 9   *Med gåvor och gengåvor*
                   O paradiso (*L'Africana* – Meyerbeer) with Lehár potpourri

1947 November 7   *Musikkrönika: En dag på musikhögskolan*
                   Singing lesson with Joseph Hislop
                       (Sveriges Radio LB 8164 – also Röster från Stock-
                       holmsoperan under 100 år. Side 13 Band 1)

1960 January 24   *Joseph Hislop: vandringsår och operadebut*
                   interview with Per Lindfors

1960 February 14   *Joseph Hislop: runt världens operascener*
                   interview with Per Lindfors

1972 August 8   *Carusos Kronprins*
                   interview with Ulf Börge Berg

National Sound Archive (The British Library)

c. 1950   Singing lesson (T3942W & R/T3943W & R/T3944W & R)
1970 April 14   Singing lesson – BBC Radio 4 (P 515 W)

Scottish Film Archive (Scottish Film Council. Glasgow)

Black & White 16 mm Silent Positive films (6).
Various subjects (domestic/travel) and dates (late 1920s/early 1930s)

National Film Archive (British Film Institute)

The Loves of Robert Burns (1930). British & Dominion Films dir. H. Wilcox.

Grampian Television Archive

Thompson at Teatime (c. 1970), interview with Hislop
Joseph Hislop (North Tonight) 29 Aug 1990, unveiling of house-plaque

Radio Features (in English)

Joseph Hislop. Music Weekly BBC Radio 3, John Steane, 15 April 1984
The Art of Joseph Hislop. WNYC (USA), The Opera Box, Jim Svedja, 15 April 1988
Joseph Hislop. BBC Radio Scotland – Tuesday Review, Michael Turnbull, 11 April 1989
My Ideal Rodolfo. BBC Radio 3, John Steane, 12 July 1989

Notes to Discography

1. Test recording for the Gramophone Company Ltd (GC).
3. An unissued take was given the matrix number *ae 17945e* (the $\frac{1}{2}$ was later superseded by -1, -2 etc)
6. The master is noted as 'broken'. Intended to be coupled with 7 on A 156; replaced by Song of Triumph (Anderson) sung by Peter Dawson.
10. Noted as 'broken'.
13. The same title, with matrix 90585 is noted as 'rejected'.
61. Hislop sang *Tosca* and *Manon* with Selma d'Arco in 1925 at Liège and Antwerp. She was the wife of his manager, Sidney Hecht.
63. Hislop sang Rodolfo to Apollo Granforte's Marcello in *La bohème* at the Liceo, Barcelona in February 1927.
75. See the anecdote reported by the *Stockholm Tidning* (March 31st 1933)
87. Piero Coppola conducted Hislop in *Rigoletto* in Oslo in April 1919.
92. The version of *Faust* used at Covent Garden during this recording was divided into four (not five) Acts, with two scenes in Act I.
99. Not included in earlier discographies; take numbers unknown. A slightly shortened version of the scene, with Hislop singing one word – 'Marguerite'.
101. The take number – 1T1 indicates a dubbing.
106. Written by Hislop's friend, the bass Emile Stiebel.
142. Broadcast in *Carusos Kronprins*. Berg, Ulf Börje, 1972, Arkivit för ljud och bild, Stockholm (ALB).
147. According to Hislop recorded in a Drottninggatan hotel in Stockholm on Thursday 12 December as the theatre technicians were on strike. The ALB in Stockholm thinks it more likely that the recordings took place in the Konserthuset between 6 and 19 December.
159. The recording sheet notes: 'For Mr Gaisberg and Mr Hislop'.

Select Bibliography

Åstrand, H. (ed.) (1975–78), *Sohlmans Musiklexikon* (5 vols), 2nd edition Stockholm: Solhmans Förlag.

Blyth, A. (1976), 'Harold Holt Limited' in *Gala Centenary Concert* programme, Royal Albert Hall, 1 July.

Bott, M.F. (1977), 'Joseph Hislop', *The Record Collector*, **XXIII**, (9 & 10), June.

Bott, M.F. (1979), 'Addendum', *The Record Collector*, **XXV**, (1 & 2), March.

Bott, M.F. (1980), 'Riccardo Martin', *The Record Collector*, **XXVI**, (1 & 2), May, 6-40.

Bott, M.F. (1984), 'Joseph Hislop – A Centenary Tribute', *Opera*, July, 730–4.

Caamaño, R. (1969), *La Historia del Teatro Colón 1908–1968*, Buenos Aires: Editorial Cinetea.

Dalla Libera, S., *Il Teatro La Fenice – Cronologia degli Spettacoli*, Archivo Storico Musicale, Teatro La Fenice (unpublished typescript).

Davis, R. (1966), *Opera in Chicago 1850–1965*, New York: Appleton-Century.

Dennis, J. (1974), 'Alfred Piccaver', *The Record Collector*, **XXII**, (5, 6 & 7), November, 101–27.

Gishford, A. (ed.) (1972), *Grand Opera*, London: Weidenfeld & Nicolson.

Gualerzi, G. (1987), 'Spain, land of tenors' Part 1, *Opera*, **38**, (11), November; Part 2, *Opera*, **38**, (12), December.

Hagman, B. (1973), 'Sweden – by Appointment, Supplier of Great Singers to the World', *Tradition and Progress in Swedish Music* (special edition of *Musikrevy*), 13–6.

Harewood, Lord. (1979) 'Werther' – *Opera on Record*, London: Hutchinson, 504.

Harvey, H. (1950) 'Dinh Gilly', *The Record Collector*, **V**, (7), July 147–54.

Hay, Robert. (1973), 'Talking with Joseph Hislop', *Scots Magazine*, May, 173–8.

Hetherington, J. (1967), *Melba*, London: Faber & Faber.

Holdridge, L.F. (1975), 'Charles Hackett', *The Record Collector*, **XXII**, (8 & 9), February, 174–202.

Hurst, P.G. (1946), *The Golden Age Recorded*, Henfield (pub. privately).

Jackson, S. (1972) *Caruso*, London: W.H. Allen.

Jaffa, Max (1991), *A Life on the Fiddle*, Hodder & Stoughton, 111–13.

Law, R. (1979), 'Die Meistersinger von Nürnberg, *Opera on Record*, London: Hutchinson, 385.

Morgan, C.I. (1979), 'John Charles Thomas', *The Record Collector*, **XXV**, (1 & 2), March, 5–14.

Osborne, R. (1979), 'Rigoletto', *Opera on Record*, London: Hutchinson, 219.

Roscioni, C.M. (1987), *Il Teatro di San Carlo – La Cronologia 1737–1987*, Guida Editori.

Rosenthal, H. (1958), *Two Centuries of Opera at Covent Garden*, London: Putnam & Co.

Rosenthal, H. (1974), 'Opera in Stockholm' from *Edinburgh International Festival Official Programme*, 12, 20 (notable for the omission of Hislop).

Sachs, H. (1974), *Music in Fascist Italy*, London: Weidenfeld & Nicolson.

Sällström, A. (1977), *Opera på Stockholmsoperan*, Stockholm: Norstedt.

Short, G. (arr.), *Songs of the Scots*, Edinburgh: Methven, Simpson Ltd, Vol. 1 (1923), Vol. 2 (1925), Vol. 3 (1928).

Simpson, H. (1972), *Singers to Remember*, London: The Oakwood Press.

Steane, J.B. (1974), *The Grand Tradition*, London: Duckworth, 250, 257, 588–9.

Strömbeck, K.G. and Sune Hofsten, (1974), *Kungliga Teatern, Repertoar 1773–1973*, Stockholm: Operan.

Thompson, R. (1975), *Book of the Braemar Gathering*, Arbroath: Herald Press, 207.

Thompson, R. (1975), *Never a Dull Moment*, David Winter & Son, 144 ff.

Turnbull, M.T.R.B. (1987), *Edinburgh Portraits*, John Donald, 35–7.

Turnbull, M.T.R.B. (1990), 'Joseph Hislop (1884–1977): A Cultural Ambassador', *Review of Scottish Culture*, No. 6, 21–6.

Valdivielso, A.C.S. (1986), *Miguel Fleta – memoria de una voz*, Madrid: Albia.

Vose, J. (1982), *The Lancashire Caruso*, Blackpool: United Writers Publication.

Sources Consulted

Libraries and Archives

Australia

Mitchell Librarian, State Library of New South Wales
Mortlock Library of South Australiana, Adelaide
Music Librarian, State Library of Queensland

Belgium

Archives, Théâtre Royal de la Monnaie, Bruxelles
Bibliothèque Publique, Liège
Bibliothèque Royale Albert 1er, Bruxelles

Canada

Calgary Public Library, Calgary
Central Library, Montreal
Hamilton Public Library Board, Hamilton
Legislative Library of Manitoba, Winnipeg
Metropolitan Toronto Reference Library, Toronto

Denmark

Professor Tage Kaarsted, Historiographer Royal, Copenhagen
Royal Library, Copenhagen
Theatre Royal Library, Copenhagen

Eire

Dublin Public Library, Dublin

England

Avon County Library, Bristol
Brighton Reference Library, Brighton
Cambridge University Library, Cambridge

Central Library, Doncaster
Central Library, Leeds
Central Library, Newcastle upon Tyne
County Library, Nottingham
Central Library, Oxford
Central Library, Portsmouth
Central Library, Torquay
City Librarian, Brown, Picton & Hornby Libraries, Liverpool
County Library, Carlisle
County Library, Middlesbrough
Director of Education & Arts, Bolton
District Central Library, Blackpool
Douglas Public Library, Douglas, Isle of Man
Gonville & Caius College Library, Cambridge
East Area Library, Bournemouth
Local History Library, Taunton
National Film Archive, British Film Institute London
Reference Library, Birmingham
SE Divisional Library, Worthing, West Sussex
Sheffield City Libraries, Sheffield
Social Sciences Library, Central Library, Manchester

Estonia

Estonian Theatre and Music Museum, Tallinn

Finland

Turku University Library

France

Bibliothèque et Musée de l'Opéra, Paris
Bibliothèque Nationale, Paris

Germany

Deutsche Staatsoper, Berlin
Europa-Center, Berlin
Landesarchiv, Berlin
Stadtarchiv, Stuttgart

Italy

Archivio Storico Musicale, Teatro La Fenice, Venice
Ufficio Stampa, Teatro alla Scala, Milano

Latvia

State Library of the Latvian SSR, Riga

New Zealand

Auckland Public Library, Auckland
Canterbury Public Library, Christchurch
City of Dunedin Public Library, Dunedin
Invercargill Public Library, Invercargill
National Library of New Zealand, Wellington
Timaru Public Library, Timaru
Wanganui City Council Library, Wanganui
Wellington Public Library, Wellington

Northern Ireland

Belfast Public Libraries, Belfast

Norway

Den Norske Opera, Oslo
Royal University Library, Oslo

Scotland

Archivist, Heriot-Watt University
Borders Regional Library, Selkirk
Central Library, Aberdeen
Central Library, Dundee
Curator, Scottish Film Archive
Director, Filmhouse, Edinburgh
District Librarian, Midlothian District Council
District Library, Stirling
Edinburgh District Libraries, Edinburgh
Librarian, Scottish Television, Glasgow
Library, D C Thomson & Co, Dundee
Library, Royal Scottish Academy of Music & Drama, Glasgow
Mitchell Library, Glasgow
Music Library, University of Edinburgh
National Library of Scotland
Scottish Music Information Centre, Glasgow

South Africa

Centre for SA Music Research, Pretoria
City Library, Cape Town
City Library, Durban
Johannesburg Public Library, Johannesburg
Natal Society Library, Pietermaritzburg, Natal

Spain

Biblioteca i Museu, Institut del Teatre, Barcelona
Institut Municipal D'Historia de Barcelona, Barcelona

Sweden

Ahlén & Åkerlunds Forlag, Stockholm
Archivist, Swedish Royal Opera
Biblioteket, Musikmuseet, Stockholm
Curator, Teaterhistoriska Museet, Gothenburg
Drottningholms Teatermuseum, Stockholm
Göteborgs-Posten, Gothenburg
Gothenburg University Library
Landsarkivet, Gothenburg
Royal Library, Stockholm
Stadsbiblioteket, Gothenburg
Stora Teatern, Gothenburg
Svenska Dagbladet, Stockholm
Sveriges Riksradio AB, Stockholm
Uppsala University Library
Vice Chancellor, Kungl. Slottet, Stockholm

United States

Archives, War Memorial Opera House, San Francisco
Boston Public Library, Boston
Carnegie Library of Pittsburg, Pittsburg
Chicago Lyric Opera, Chicago
Chicago Public Library, Chicago
City of Saint Paul Public Library, Saint Paul
Denver Public Library, Denver
Iowa State Historical Department, Iowa City
Kansas City Public Library, Kansas City
Los Angeles Public Library, Los Angeles
Martin Luther King Memorial Library, Washington
Milwaukee Public Library, Milwaukee
Salt Lake City Library, Salt Lake City
Springfield City Library, Springfield
University of Washington Libraries, Seattle

Wales

Aberconwy Area Library, Llandudno
Central Library, Cardiff
Clywd Central Library
West Glamorgan Library, Swansea

Zimbabwe

National Archives of Zimbabwe, Harare

TRANSLATIONS

I am indebted to the following: Evi Carmichael, Gudrun Giffen, Joseph and Agnete Hislop, Johanna McDonald, Frank Nicholson, Ziegfrids Sapietis, Birte Tange, Andrew Thackrey, Barbara Turnbull, the late Ulf Torson Westman

SPECIALIST SOURCES

Chorister Training: C. Robert Kidd, W. G. Lugton, Dr Dennis Townhill

Cinematography: Murray Callen, L. P. Williams, Freddie Young OBE

General Background: Cyril Baxter, George and Isabelle Donald, Joseph and Agnete Hislop, Eunice Standish-Taylor

Opera History: Bertil Hagman, Bettine McLaughlan, Rodney Milnes, the late Harold Rosenthal, Harvey Sachs, Stanley Sadie, John Steane

Opera Performance: Elizabeth Abercrombie, Nigel Douglas, Norman Feasey, Elizabeth Fleming, Elizabeth Fretwell, John Gardner, Sir Alexander Gibson, Leonard Hancock, the Earl of Harewood, Peter Hemmings, Professor Roy Henderson, the late Max Jaffa OBE, William McAlpine, the late Canon Sydney MacEwan, Donald Maxwell, Gerald Moore, Kenneth Ormston, Professor Robin Orr, the late Sir Peter Pears, Donald Pilley, Arthur Reckless, Alberto Remedios, James Robertson CBE, Sir Harry Secombe, Professor Henri Temianka, Sir John Tooley, the late Dame Eva Turner, Ian Wallace

Performance and Recordings: The late David Bicknell, George Burr, Roderick Fairley, Charles Jahant, Alan Kelly, Grahame McIntosh, Dr Boris Semeonoff, Richard Telfer, Dr T. Michael Turnbull, Norman White

Photo-Engraving: Gustaf Bondeson, Rupert Cannon, John Philipson, George Whitham

A selection of Hislop recordings has been reissued on compact disc: GEMM CD 9956 is available on the Pearl label from Pavilion Records Limited, Sparrows' Green, Wadhurst, East Sussex TN5 6SJ. Telephone: 089 278 3591. Pavilion Records are distributed in North America by Koch International.

Index

Aborigines (Australia) 141

Adriatic (liner) 111

Agate, James (critic) 172

Åkerlund, Erik (Swedish publisher) 8

Albers, Henri (French baritone) 82

Albert, Dr (Munich inventor) 9

Alda, Frances (1883–1952) New Zealand soprano 54, 77, 103, 112, 113, 139

Alfvén, Hugo (1872–1960) Swedish composer 18, 19

Allin, Norman (1884–1973) English bass 69

Althén, Ragnar (Swedish composer) 36

d'Alvarez, Marguerite (1886–1953) English contralto 70

Amundsen, Signe (1899–) Norwegian soprano 95, 154

Anderberg, Bernt (Hislop pupil) 181, 182 (photo)

André, Harald (1879–1975) Swedish producer 31, 80, 96, 185

Andrésen, Ivar (1896–1940) Norwegian bass 11, 59

Ansseau, Fernand (1890–1972) Belgian tenor 58, 86

d'Aranyi, Jelly (1895–1966) Hungarian/British violinist 134

Arbo, Jens (critic) 38, 122

D'Arco, Selma (Italian soprano) 71, 72, 73, 75

Arnold, Matthew (1822–88) English poet 173

Arnoldsson, Dr (Swedish throat-specialist) 183

Arrau, Claudio (1904–1991) Chilean pianist 113

Arundell, Dennis (1898–1988) English composer and actor 190

Asklund,
  Olof (Hislop's father-in-law) 13
  Mrs (Hislop's mother-in-law) 10, 13, 25
  Karin (Hislop's first wife) 10, 25, 26, 27, 29 (photo), 30, 32, 36, 40, 42, 50, 68, 70, 73, 75, 77, 78, 83, 105, 111, 115, 138, 141, 143, 148, 177, 186

Association of English Singers and Teachers (Britain) 197, 199

Aussenac, Marie (Portuguese pianist) 149

Austral, Florence (1894–1968) Australian soprano 115, 137, 155

Backhaus, Wilhelm (1884–1969) Austrian pianist 115, 117 (photo), 134, 137, 139

Baillie, Isobel (1895–1983) Scottish soprano 114

Baird, Martha (pianist) 115

Baklanoff, Georges (1882–1938) Russian baritone 52, 55, 56

Balfour, Margaret (English contralto) 118

Barbirolli, John (1899–1970) English conductor 51, 58, 62, 90, 92, 122, 123

Barnett, Maughan (New Zealand organist) 142

Baroni, Giuseppe (Italian conductor) 63

Barsova, Valeria (1892–1967) Russian soprano 106, 107

Battaille, Louis-Charles (critic) 82

Battistini, Mattia (1856–1928) Italian baritone 199

Bavagnoli, Gaetano (1879–1933) Italian conductor 50

Baxter, Harold (friend of Hislop's) 8, 9, 10, 12, 28

Beecham, Sir Thomas (1879–1961) conductor and impresario 43, 44, 49, 50, 51, 58, 65, 149, 190, 197

Beck, William (American baritone) 38

Berg, Natanael (1879–1957) Swedish composer 19

Berkeley, Capt. Reginald (film scriptwriter) 168

Bel canto 13, 61, 184

Benson, Mona (mezzo-contralto) 91

Berling, Mrs Wilhelm Carl (Ingeborg Suneson) (Swedish soprano) 31, 130

Berlitz School (Milan) 39

Bérat, Louise (mezzo) 50

Bernhardt, Sarah (1844–1923) French actress 23, 157

Beuf, Augusto (1894–1969) Italian baritone (later bass) 205, 206

Beyron, Einar (1901–79) Swedish tenor 181

Bicknell, David (International Classical manager EMI) 59, 205

Bilde, Tage (1886–) Swedish conductor and critic 11

Björling
    Jussi (1907–60) Swedish tenor 31, 69, 96, 180, 181, 182 (photo), 184, 188, 194, 197, 198 (photo)
    Sigurd (1907–83) Swedish baritone 96

Blackham, Joyce (English soprano) 194

Blackwood, William (journalist) 118

Blois, Eustace (1879–1933) (Director, Covent Garden) 88

Bøgebjerg, Michelle Flint (Danish soprano) 181

Bohème, La (Puccini) projected Herbert Wilcox film 166, 169

Bolt Court (School of Photo-engraving & Lithography) 5, 8

Bonci, Alessandro (1870–1940) Italian tenor 52, 83

Bonini, Signora (Pensione, Milan) 39, 73

Bonnington, Keith (accompanist) 195

Borghi-Zerni, Ayres (Italian soprano) 41

Borgioli, Dino (1891–1960) Italian tenor 75, 76, 77

Bosse, Harriet (actress – last wife of August Strindberg) 22

Brain, Aubrey (English horn-player) 119

Branzell, Karin (1891–1974) Swedish mezzo 19, 25, 32

Bratt, Dr Gillis (1870–1925) Swedish throat-specialist and teacher 11, 12, 13, 14 (photo), 15, 19, 22, 25, 26, 59, 61, 65, 186

Bratza, Milan (Serbian violinist) 114, 134, 136, 137

British and Dominions Film Corporation 165

Brothier, Yvonne (1880–1967) French soprano 80

Brown, J. Aitken (Scots versifier) 132

Brunskill, Muriel (1899–1980) English contralto 66, 68, 69, 114, 119, 139

Brusubarda, G. (critic) 107

Buckman, Rosina (1880–1948) New Zealand soprano 50, 136

Burke, Thomas (1890–1969) English tenor 51, 58, 59

Burns, Robert (1759–96) Scottish poet 121, 166, 204

Burt, Marjorie 119

Butt, Dame Clara (1873–1936) English contralto 7, 114, 116, 117 (photo), 137, 149

Byng, George (English conductor) 62, 67, 82, 122

Cadell, Jean (1884–1967) Scottish actress 168

Cahier, Mme Charles (1870–1951) American contralto 31

Calvé, Emma (1858–1942) French soprano 127

Caruso, Enrico (1873–1921) Italian tenor – greatest of the century 7, 22, 23, 24 (photo), 31, 39, 40, 45, 49, 52, 54, 56, 57, 58, 59, 77, 80, 111, 112, 131, 132, 133, 155, 184, 192, 199, 205

Caskett, James (critic) 62

Chaliapin, Feodor (1873–1938)
Russian bass and actor viii, 87, 88, 89,
112, 113, 122, 139, 143, 166
Chamlee, Mario (1892–1966) American tenor 54, 59
Chaplin, Charlie (1889–1977) English comic actor 72
Choir (St Mary's Cathedral, Edinburgh) 4
Cilla, Luigi (1885–) Italian tenor 50
Cimini, Paolo (Italian conductor) 76
Cinzano, Count Alberto (competition sponsor) 191 (photo)
Cirulis, J. (critic) 106
Claeson, Jean (cabaret-singer) 21
Claque
Venice 63
Barcelona 84
Claque, Master Chief of
Milan 78
Buenos Aires 78
Claussen, Julia (1879–1941) Swedish contralto 19
Clay, Spencer (American accompanist) 35, 36, 58, 62, 71, 92, 112, 113, 131, 133, 152
Clément, Edmond (1867–1928) French tenor 72
Cliff, Laddie (operetta producer) 170
Cline, Leonard (critic) 130
Coates, Albert (1882–1953) Anglo-Russian conductor 36, 38, 43, 50, 108, 112
Collingwood, Lawrance (1887–) English conductor 124
Collinson, Thomas H. (1858–1928) Edinburgh choirmaster 4, 7, 132, 138, 199
Coltbridge School (Edinburgh) 3
Coolidge, Calvin (1872–1929) American Vice President 128
Coppola, Piero (1888–1971) Italian conductor 38, 85, 120
Cortot, Alfred (1877–1962) Swiss pianist 54, 127
Crabtree, C.M. (critic) 118, 124, 174
Craig, Charles (1919–) English tenor 190
Craxton, Harold (1885–1971) English accompanist 112

Crimi, Giulio (1885–1939) Italian tenor 54, 59
Crucikshank, Enid (English contralto) 174
Curry, Nicholas (discophile) 199
Curzon, Clifford (1907–82) English pianist 119

Dahlström, Fru (Swedish accompanist) 14
Dal Monte, Toti (1892–1976) Italian soprano ix, 64, 196
Dalla Rizza, Gilda (1892–1975) Italian soprano 50, 51, 83
Dalman, Gösta (1884–1963) Swedish ship-broker 36
Dane, Marjorie (English soprano) 136
Dannebrog, Knight of (Denmark) 85
Darlington, W.A. (critic) 177
David, Léon (1867–1962) French tenor 72
Davie, Cedric Thorpe (1913–83) Scottish composer 202
Davies,
Ben (1858–1943) Welsh tenor 9
Tudor (1892–1958) Welsh tenor 65, 69
Dawson, Peter (1882–1961) Australian bass-baritone 139, 148
Defrère, Desiré (1888—1964) Belgian baritone 73
De Luca, Giuseppe (1876–1950) Italian baritone 54, 76, 77
De Reske, Jean (1850–1925) Polish tenor 114
Di Veroli, Manlio (1888–1960) Italian composer and accompanist 115, 204
Dickie, William (1914–) Scottish baritone 194
Didur, Adamo (1874–1946) Polish bass 75
Divorce (1940) 186
Don Giovanni (Mozart) *Dalla sua pace* as tenor voice-test 195
Don Quixote (Cervantes) Herbert Wilcox film with Chaliapin 166
Donald, George (pupil and accompanist) 201, 202, 204
Dorfmann, Ania (Viennese pianist) 156
Dowden, Bishop John (St Mary's Cathedral, Edinburgh) 3

Drottningholm Opera, Friends of (Sweden) 202, 203

Dryden, John (1631–1700) English poet 173

Dua, Ottavo (1882–1952) one-eyed Italian buffo tenor 76, 77

Dux Engraving Company (Glasgow) 5

Edinburgh Gramophone Society 199

Edström, Anna (1884–1940) Swedish soprano 38, 85

Edvina, Louise (1880–1948) French-Canadian soprano 70

Edwardes, Felix (theatre producer) 172

Eisteddfod (Swansea) 119

Ellinger, Désirée (English soprano) 50

Elstree (Boreham Wood film studios) 166

Empire Theatre (Edinburgh) 91

Encores, protest at number of 134, 157

Enwall, Helmer (1889–1974) Swedish concert manager 94

Equity, British 96

Erhardt, Otto (producer) 96

Evans, Greek (American baritone) 102

Eves, Grenville (English actor and opera historian) 93, 170

Farrar, Geraldine (1882–1967) American soprano 100, 112

Fear, Arthur (baritone) 123

Ferdinand, (1863–1914) Archduke of Austria 25

Fielding, Harold (violinist) 156

Flagstad, Kirsten (1895–1962) Norwegian soprano 11, 59

Fleta, Miguel (1893–1938) Spanish tenor 83, 106

Fokine, Mikail (1880–1942) Russian/American dancer and choreographer 38

Formichi, Cesare (1883–1949) Italian baritone 69, 70, 75

Forsell,
    John (1868–1941) Swedish baritone, opera house director and teacher 19, 32, 69, 85, 95, 180
    Björn (1915–1975) Swedish baritone 180

Fossati, Signor (Master Chief of Claque, Milan) 78

Franci, Benvenuto (1891–) Italian baritone 41

Fraser Passmore, Nancy (soprano) Hislop's second wife 176, 176 (photo) 177, 185, 186, 197, 199, 200, 202, 205

Fretwell, Elizabeth (1922–) Australian soprano 193, 194 (photo)

Friedman, Ignaz (1882–1948) Polish pianist 114

Fumigalli Riva, Zita (1893–) Italian soprano 63

Gaisberg, Fred (Gramophone Co. manager) 21, 23, 24, 172

Galeffi, Carlo (1882–1961) Italian baritone 59

Gall, Yvonne (1885–) French soprano 55

Galli-Curci, Amelita (1882–1963) Italian soprano vii, ix, 54, 55 (photo), 56, 59, 71, 112, 115, 117 (photo), 136, 139

Gandhi, Mohandas (1869–1948) Indian leader 149

Garden, Mary (1874–1967) Scottish soprano and manager ix, 43, 52, 56, 96

Gardner, John (1917–) English composer/coach/conductor 194

Gatti-Casazza, Giulio (1869–1940) Italian impresario 57, 80, 87

Gautier-Wennegren, Marguerite (Swedish soprano) 25

Geikie, Ramsay (pianist) 132, 133

Gentle, Alice (1888–1958) American mezzo 99, 101, 102, 103

German, Sir Edward (1862–1936) English composer 177

German Stage Society 87

Ghione, Franco (Italian conductor) 64

Gibson, Sir Alexander (1926–) Scottish conductor, co-founder of Scottish Opera 204

Gigli, Beniamino (1890–1957) Italian tenor 39, 42, 54, 57, 58, 76, 77, 94, 106, 112, 159, 199

Gilly, Dinh (1877–1940) French/Algerian baritone viii, 43, 50, 66, 67, 68, 70

Glossop, Peter (1928–) English baritone 193, 194

Gluck, Marie (soprano) 157, 158, 159
Goossens, Eugene III (1893–1962)
  English conductor 88, 89, 114, 136
Goodman, Isidor (South African
  pianist) 149, 150, 151
Granforte, Apollo (Italian baritone) 82,
  83
Gray, Eve (actress) 168
Greenfield, Edward (critic) 93
Greenwood, Clifford (English conduc-
  tor) 174
Grevillius,
  Ragnar (music critic) 9
  Nils (1893–1970) Swedish conduc-
    tor 22 (photo), 23, 24, 38, 93, 95,
    121, 178, 184
Grieg, Edvard (1843–1907) Norwegian
  composer 140
Griffith, Hubert (critic) 172
Griffiths, Dr Ivor (throat specialist) 190
Guerrieri, Fulgenzio (Italian conduc-
  tor) 100
Gustav III (1746–92) assassination at
  Royal Opera House 71, 115
Gustav V (1858–1950) from 1907 King
  of Sweden 20
Gustav Adolf (Prince of Sweden) 85

Hackett, Charles (1899–1942) Ameri-
  can tenor 57, 65, 73, 118
Hadath, Gunby (poet) 118
Haggard, Sir Henry Rider (1856–1925)
  English novelist 144
Hägglöf, Gunnar (Swedish ambassa-
  dor) 199
Hallén, Andreas (1846–1925) Swedish
  composer 13
Hambourg, Mark (1879–1960)
  Russian pianist 148
Hammerstein, Mrs Oscar (American
  theatre-owner and impresario) 54,
  56
Hammond, Tom (répétiteur and
  translator) 192
Hancock, Leonard (1923–) English
  conductor and répétiteur 192
Handel's Messiah 4, 118
Hansson, Capt. Hans (President,
  Gothenburg Town Council) 201
Hare, Robertson (1891–1979) English
  comic actor 166

Harewood, Lord (1923–) English
  festival director and critic 83, 191
  (photo), 205
Harrison, Julius (1885–1963) English
  conductor 67, 68, 71
Harrold, Orville (1878–1933) Ameri-
  can tenor 54, 58
Hasselbacksfesten (Stockholm restau-
  rant celebration) 28
Haye, Reginald de la (Scottish conduc-
  tor) 24
Hayes, Middlesex (Gramophone Co.
  factory and recording theatre) 21, 23
Hayward, Marjorie (1885–1953)
  English violinist 119, 120
Hecht, Sidney (Hislop's American
  manager) 73, 76, 80, 118
Hedmont, Charles (1857–1940)
  American heldentenor 91
Heifetz, Jascha (1901–) Russian/
  American violinist 120
Heinze, Prof. Sir Bernard (1894–1982)
  Australian conductor 105
Hemmings, Peter (opera company
  manager) 192, 202
Hempel, Frieda (1885–1955) German
  soprano 116, 117 (photo), 137
Henderson, Roy (1899–) Scottish
  baritone and teacher 139
Herold, Vilhelm (1865–1937) Danish
  tenor 8
Hertzberg-Beyron, Brita (1901–76)
  Swedish soprano 181
Hess, Dame Myra (1890–1956)
  English pianist 114
Heuvel, Jacques (conductor) 170
Heward, Leslie (1897–1943) English
  conductor 166
Hidalgo, Elvira de (1882–) Spanish
  soprano 68
Higgins, Henry (1852–1928) Chairman
  of the Grand Opera Syndicate, Covent
  Garden 57, 58

HISLOP, Joseph

  ACTING

    acting, lack of satisfactory – 1915
      Faust (Stockholm) 28, 29
    acting, indifferent – 1930 Goethe
      (London) 172

action, soberness of – 1925 Rodolfo (Liège) 72

actor, excellent – 1927 Rodolfo (Barcelona) 84

actor, natural film – 1930 Robert Burns (London) 169

affectation, free from – 1927 (Edinburgh) 139

amorist, not the wicked – 1924 Duke of Mantua (London) 69

appearance, awkward – 1914 Pinkerton (Stockholm) 25

arrogance – 1921 (Edward Ziegler, New York) 57

aristocratic – 1924 Duke of Mantua (London) 68

artifice, absence of dramatic – 1931 Radames (Helsinki) 107

artistry, refined – 1925 Cavaradossi (Liège) 71

clumsiness on stage – 1915 Faust (Stockholm) 29

comedy, touches of – 1927 Rodolfo (Copenhagen) 85

convincing – 1923 Rodolfo (London) 66

convincing – 1925 Alfredo (Buenos Aires) 76

costumed elegantly – 1925 Roméo (Buenos Aires) 76

costumes, richness of – 1925 des Grieux (Liège) 72

deportment, easy and natural – 1920 Rodolfo (London) 44

dignity – 1925 Roméo (Buenos Aires) 76

distinction, actor of – 1921 Rodolfo (Milwaukee) 103

elegant Frenchman – 1930 Alfredo (Riga) 107

eyes, glowing – 1927 Don José (Melbourne) 105

eyes, striking – 1929 Canio (Edinburgh) 92

expressive actor – 1927 Melbourne 141

gesture,
 eloquent – 1929 Canio (Edinburgh) 92
 simplicity of – 1925 Rodolfo (Liège) 72

gestures of hands – 1929 Canio (Edinburgh) 92

grace, easy – 1927 (Timaru NZ) 143

histrionic ability – 1921 Rodolfo (Montreal) 104

humour, droll – 1925 Rodolfo (Antwerp) 72

intelligence
 1921 Rodolfo (Los Angeles) 102
 1923 Edgardo (Turin) 63
 1933 Faust (Helsinki) 108

intelligence, highly-developed – 1921 Cavaradossi (Denver) 102

intelligence, marked – 1924 (Glasgow) 128

intelligence, outstanding – 1921 Rodolfo (Los Angeles) 102

intelligence, marked – 1920 (Glasgow) 128

interpretation, lacklustre – 1928 Faust (London) 89

lived role – 1925 des Grieux (Liège) 72

lives role – 1925 Cavaradossi (Liège) 71

lyrical, passionately – 1924 Alfredo (London) 70

manly – 1930 Duke of Mantua (Helsinki) 106

masculine, youthful – 1920 Cavaradossi (Chicago) 52

mechanical and wooden, little bit – 1923 Edgardo (Turin) 63

movement, dramatic – 1921 Rodolfo (Kansas City) 103

naturalness – 1925 Cavaradossi (Liège) 71

passionate, politely – 1921 New York 56

physique
 lean, thin-featured – 1920 Rodolfo (Chicago) 52
 thin and bony – 1926 Rodolfo (Paris) 82
 weight and height 67

power – 1927 Rodolfo (Copenhagen) 85

power, dramatic – 1923 Rodolfo (Manchester) 67

prepossessing – 1921 Cavaradossi (New York) 56

presence, stage
    1921 Rodolfo (Montreal) 104
    1925 Roméo (Buenos Aires) 76
    1929 Canio (Edinburgh) 92
prompter
    (Karin Hislop) – 1920 Pinkerton
    (London) 50
    use of condemned – 1925 Rodolfo
    (Antwerp) 72
refinement, lack of – 1921 Rodolfo
    (Edward Zcigler) 57
realism
    1920 Rodolfo (London) 45
    1920 Rodolfo (Chicago) 52
    1921 Rodolfo (San Francisco) 100
    1923 Rodolfo (London) 66
    1930 Rodolfo (Riga) 107
realistic dramatically – 1925 Roméo
    (Buenos Aires) 76
romantic – 1920 Cavaradossi
    (Chicago) 52
simplicity – 1933 Radames (Hel-
    sinki) 107
simplicity of gesture – 1925 Rodolfo
    (Liège) 72
sincerity, real – 1925 Rodolfo (Liège)
    72
skill – 1921 Rodolfo (New York) 56
taste – 1933 Faust (Helsinki) 108
traditional Paris Opera interpretation
    – 1933 Faust (Helsinki) 108
traditional operatic style – 1936
    Wilhelm Meister (Gothenburg)
    178
traditional, costume not – 1920
    Rodolfo (Chicago) 52
underplaying
    1927 Copenhagen 85
    1933 Don José (Helsinki) 107
understanding of character – 1925
    Roméo (Buenos Aires) 76
understanding, depth of – 1925
    Rodolfo (Liège) 72
virility – 1930 Cavaradossi (Helsinki)
    106
wooden, little bit too – 1923
    Edgardo (Turin) 63

VOICE

altissimo, final A sung in – 1927
    Adelaide 141

art, admirable – 1921 Pinkerton
    (Chicago) 54
articulation
    clearness of – 1924 (Glasgow) 128
    exceptionally good –
    1923 (The Gramophone) 62
attack, swiftly certain in – 1920
    Cavaradossi (Chicago) 52
attack, untidiness of attack – 1923
    Perth 133
baritonal in lower notes – 1931
    Cavaradossi (Tallinn) 108
baritone, no hint of the – 1920
    (Edinburgh) 128
beautiful
    1924 Duke of Mantua (London)
    68
    1923 Edgardo (Turin) 64
    1927 Cavaradossi (London) 86
beauty
    1920 Pinkerton (London) 50
    joyous vocal – 1920 Duke of
    Mantua (Chicago) 53
    exceptional – 1920 (Edinburgh)
    131
    quite exceptional – 1922 (Edin-
    burgh) 131
bel canto, training in – 1933
    Cavaradossi (Taillinn) 108
breath, command of admirable –
    1921 (Boston) 128
charm
    poignant lyric – 1920 Rodolfo
    (Chicago) 52
    uncommon – 1921 Cavaradossi
    (Seattle) 99
chest-voice at half volume – 1925 des
    Grieux (Liège) 72
clear – 1924 Alfredo (London) 70
clear, crystal – 1933 Rodolfo (Hel-
    sinki) 107
climaxes, saving greatest intensity for
    – 1927 (Copenhagen) 84
cold, a little – 1934 Edinburgh 159
colour, full of – 1929 Rodolfo
    (Edinburgh) 92
colouring, darkened – 1931 (Perth,
    Australia) 152
compass, wide
    1927 Rodolfo (Barcelona) 84
    1930 Duke of Mantua (Riga) 107

diction
    excellent – 1921 (Boston) 129
    clear – 1922 (Perth) 133
    not too clear – 1933 (The Gramo-
        phone) 174
darker Rimbaud shade – 1930
    Cavaradossi (Riga) 106
discretion in use of voice – 1921
    Rodolfo (Los Angeles) 102
dramatic rather than lyric – 1930
    Don José (Riga) 107
dramatic singer – 1927 (Durban) 144
dramatic singing – 1925 Rodolfo
    (Brussels) 71
dynamics
    great variation of – 1931 Rodolfo
        (Helsinki) 107
    highly expressive – 1925 Rodolfo
        (Brussels) 71
ease through compass – 1920
    Rodolfo (London) 49
easy way of soaring – 1924 Duke of
    Mantua (London) 68
effort, absence of – 1927 (Timaru
    NZ) 143
equality, perfect thro' entire scale –
    1921 Rodolfo (Montreal) 104
even thro' expressive range – 1920
    (Middlesborough) 127
even thro' registers – 1921 Detroit
    129
evenness of quality thro' range –
    1925 Cavaradossi (Liège) 71
expression, command of sympathetic
    – 1920 Rodolfo (London) 44
expressive –
    1923 Rodolfo (London) 16
    1925 Rodolfo (Antwerp) 72
expressiveness – 1922 (London) 113
exaggeration – 1930 Goethe
    (Glasgow) 170
    tendency to – 1931 (The Gramo-
        phone) 124
falsetto, too much – 1933 Roméo
    (Helsinki) 107
flexible – 1925 (Antwerp) 72
flexibility, amazing – 1932
    (Kilmarnock) 155
force
    use of much – 1926 Werther (Paris)
    82

use of deplored – 1927 (Christchurch
    NZ) 142
forced, never – 1925 Rodolfo (Liège)
    72
freshness – 1920 (Dublin) 127
free
    1923 Edgardo (Turin) 64
    1924 Alfredo (London) 70
    1925 Cavaradossi (Liège) 71
full-bodied – 1921 (New York)
    56
full-throated – 1921 (Springfield
    USA) 129
fullness, easy – 1929 Rodolfo
    (Edinburgh) 92
hard, rather than sensuous – 1924
    (Glasgow) 115
head voice
    delicacy of – 1922 Dundee 133
    skilful use of – 1931 (Perth,
        Australia) 152
    control of – 1932 (Dublin) 155
high, role too – 1931 Roméo (Hel-
    sinki) 107
high B with ease – 1922 (Edinburgh)
    132
high C, brilliant – Faust (Tallinn)
    1931
high notes a natural extension of
    middle register – 1922
    (Middlesborough) 134
    compressed – 1926 Werther
        (Paris) 82
    executed with ease – 1927 Rodolfo
        (Barcelona) 84
    strained for – 1931 Roméo
        (Helsinki) 107
honeyed – 1926 The Messiah
    (London) 118
interpretation, gradual building-up –
    1927 (Copenhagen) 85
intonation
    sure – 1921 (Boston) 128
    trifle under pitch – 1922 Birming-
        ham 134
    a little below pitch – 1922 Perth
        133
    not in tune – 1927 Cavaradossi
        (London) 86
    some lapses in – 1931 Rodolfo
        (Helsinki) 107

nearly semitone above – 1931
Cavaradossi (Tallinn) 108
Italian opera house, grand manner –
1924 Duke of Mantua (London) 68
Italian opera, tricks of – 1920
(Huddersfield) 127
Italian style – 1921 (Springfield
USA) 129
Italian style, standardised formulae
of – 1924 (London) 69
Italian tenors, not in usual style –
1923 Edgardo (Turin) 63
Italianate – 1922 (Stockholm) 61
legato – 1923 Edgardo (BBC Radio
3) 67
lyric – 1925 (Buenos Aires) 76
lyric tenor – 1930 Cavaradossi (Riga)
106
lyrical in a dramatic way – 1930
(Riga) 106
messa di voce – 1923 Edgardo
(recording) 67
mezza voce
fascinating – 1922 (Edinburgh)
132
not used enough – 1923 Edgardo
(Turin) 64
open-throated – 1925 Roméo
(Buenos Aires) 76
equals best tenors – 1925 Roméo
(Buenos Aires) 76
charming – 1926 Werther (Paris)
82
loveliest – 1926 Faust (The
Gramophone) 82
does not travel – 1927 (The
Gramophone) 121
charming – 1930 Alfredo (Riga)
107
warm – 1931 Cavaradossi
(Tallinn)
mezzo type of tenor – 1930 Don José
(Riga) 107
mezzo forte, more body in – 1920
Rodolfo (London) 45
modulation, skill in – 1919 (Oslo) 38
naturalness of execution – 1930
Cavaradossi (Riga) 106
open tone to F natural – 1926
Rodolfo (Paris) 80
passion – 1920 (Huddersfield) 127

phrasing
flawless – 1922 (Perth) 133
rare feeling for – 1927 Cavaradossi
(London) 86
sensitive clean-cut – 1920 Rodolfo
(Chicago) 52
placed
beautifully – 1922 (Edinburgh)
131
well – 1925 Rodolfo (Brussels) 71
portamento   1923 Edgardo (BBC
Radio 3) 67
power
1920 (Edinburgh) 128
abundant – 1920 Rodolfo (London) 45
great – 1920 (Middlesborough) 127
great – 1920 (Bolton) 127
splendid – 1920 Rodolfo (Chicago) 52
great – 1921 (Detroit) 130
unlimited – 1921 Rodolfo
(Milwaukee) 103
wonderful – 1921 Rodolfo (Toronto) 104
endless reserves of – 1927 (Adelaide) 141
plenty of – 1927 Cavaradossi
(London) 86
powerful – 1924 (Glasgow) 128
production,
ease of – 1921 Rodolfo
(Milwaukee) 103
perfect vocal – 1921 (Kansas City)
103
hard – 1926 Werther (Paris) 82
Puccini tenor – 1920 (Glasgow)
128
pure, lyrical type – 1923 Edgardo
(Milan) 64
pure tenor – 1920 Duke of Mantua
(Chicago) 53
purity, exquisite – 1921 (Detroit)
130
quality
beautiful – 1920 (Edinburgh) 128
good – 1920 Rodolfo (London) 44
lovely, smooth – 1920 Rodolofo
(London) 45
luscious – 1921 Rodolfo (Davenport) 103

sweetness and warmth in its –
1921 Rodolfo (San Francisco)
100
excellent – 1921 (Boston) 128
impressive in – 1921 Pinkerton
(New York) 56
liquid – 1922 (Dundee) 133
rich, creamy – 1922 (Edinburgh)
131
unforced – 1924 Duke of Mantua
(London) 69
perfect evenness – 1925
Cavaradossi (Liége) 71
pleasing and refined – 1925
(Buenos Aires) 75
first class – 1925 Roméo (Buenos
Aires)
pure velvet – 1926 (Edinburgh)
138
lyric – 1927 (Timaru NZ) 143
without effort – 1927 Cavaradossi
(London) 86
range
abundant – 1920 Rodolfo
(London) 45
large – 1921 (Detroit) 129
strong, flexible, grateful – 1922
(Glasgow) 131
ff to high B with ease – 1922
(Edinburgh) 132
wide – 1925 Rodolfo (Brussels)
71
marvellous compass – 1926
(Edinburgh) 138
wide – 1934 (Edinburgh) 159
register
upper (ring in) – 1912 (Uppsala)
15
higher (ringing tones in) – 1922
(Edinburgh) 131 upper
(unusually warm) – 1923 Edgardo
(Turin) 64
middle keeps quality – 1920
Rodolfo (London) 44
middle (sympathetic) – 1920
(Huddersfield) 127
middle (high notes a natural
extension) – 1923 (Birmingham)
134
(strength in middle tones) – 1923
(Birmingham) 134

middle (warm & golden) – 1923
(Birmingham) 134
middle (exceptional quality) –
1927 (Sydney) 140
middle (dryness) – 1930
Cavaradossi (Riga) 106
lower (sympathetic timbre) – 1920
(Leeds) 127
registers, even throughout – 1921
(Detroit) 129
resonance
exquisite – 1921 (Detroit) 130
powerful in higher notes – 1926
Rodolfo (Paris) 80
powerful – 1930 (Riga) 106
resonant – 1914 Faust (Stockholm) 25
resources, husbanding of – 1927
(Copenhagen) 85
restraint in voice – 1922 Stockholm
61
rich
1920 Duke of Mantua (Chicago)
53
1921 (Boston) 129
1929 Rodolfo (Edinburgh) 92
rich tenor tone – 1920 Roméo
(Chicago) 54
richest in upper register – 1930 Duke
of Mantua (Riga) 107
richness
1912 (Stockholm) 14
1920 Rodolfo (Chicago) 52
1922 (London) 113
richness in lower notes – 1922
Edinburgh 131
robust
1920 (Leeds) 127
1921 (Detroit) 129
1925 Cavaradossi (Liège) 71
1926 Rodolfo (Paris) 80
1933 (Leeds) 156
slurring, style of – 1934 Raleigh
(London) 177
smooth, finished vocalisation – 1921
Rodolfo (Toronto) 103
smoothness, effortless – 1929 (The
Gramophone) 93
soft, seamlessly – 1925 (Buenos
Aires) 76
sophistication – 1931 (The Gramophone) 124

sophisticated, too – 1923 (Glasgow) 134

sostenuto, soft – 1922 (Aberdeen) 132

spinto, a little – 1925 (Buenos Aires) 76

strain (high C with no effort) – 1932 (Dublin) 155

strength, ample – 1921 Rodolfo (Montreal) 104

strong – Edgardo 1923 (Turin) 64

style
 passionate – 1920 (Glasgow) 128
 general finish of – 1920 Pinkerton (London) 50
 good operatic – 1921 (Boston) 129
 perfection of – 1923 Rodolfo (London) 66
 outstanding sense of – 1923 Rodolfo (London) 66
 elegance of – 1925 Rodolfo (Liège) 72
 fine sense of – 1926 (London) 119
 aristocratic – 1926 (Opera on Record) 83

sweet – 1923 Edgardo (Milan) 64

sweetness, outstanding – 1920 Pinkerton (London) 50

sweetness – 1921 Rodolfo (Washington DC) 104

taste
 great – 1925 Rinuccio (Buenos Aires) 75
 sang with – 1925 Alfredo (Buenos Aires) 76

timbre
 warm – 1914 Faust (Stockholm) 25
 fine – 1920 Roméo (Chicago) 54
 thrilling vibrant – 1920 (Middlesborough) 127
 sympathetic middle register – 1920 (Huddersfield) 127
 appealing – 1921 Rodolfo (Montreal) 104
 a little baritonal – 1923 Edgardo (Turin) 64
 easy on the ear – 1926 Werther (Paris) 82
 pleases in all registers – 1927 Rodolfo (Barcelona) 84

warm – 1928 (Oslo) 122

lacks gentleness – 1930 Duke of Mantua (Riga) 107

dark – 1930 (Riga) 106

tone
 fine – 1926 (The Gramophone) 82
 vibrant – 1929 (The Gramophone) 93
 golden – 1929 (Copenhagen) 123

tones too deep in mouth – 1930 Duke of Mantua (Riga) 107

vibrant voice – 1921 Rodolfo (Toronto) 104

warm
 1921 Rodolfo (Montreal) 104
 1923 Edgardo (Turin) 64
 1925 Rodolfo (Antwerp) 72

RELATIONS WITH LEADING SINGERS who partnered Hislop

Alda, Frances 54, 77, 103, 112, 113, 139

Chaliapin, Feodor viii, 87, 88, 89, 112, 113, 122, 139

Galli-Curci, Amelita vii, ix, 54, 55 (photo), 56, 59, 71, 112, 115, 117 (photo), 136, 139

Melba, Dame Nellie viii, 7, 39, 51, 65, 66, 137, 139, 143, 149

Pagliacci, La Monnaie 1925 (accident with knife) 73

Pascova, Carmen 53

Raisa, Rosa 52, 53, 54, 56

Ruffo, Titta ix, 39, 52, 53, 111, 113, 196, 199

COMPARISONS with other singers

Caruso
 greater brilliance and vocal expansion 1916 des Grieux (Stockholm) 31
 Hislop criticized for copying 1919 (Copenhagen) 39
 famous 'sob' effect 1920 (Birmingham) 134
 richness of tone reminscent 1920 (Middlesborough) 133
 'Swedish Caruso' 1920 (Chicago) 52

successors to Caruso 1921
(London) 58
Gigli's opinion 58
Scotti's opinion 103
some of lighter Caruso roles 1921
(New York) 56
successor 1921 (Davenport) 103
'successor to Caruso' (billing)
1922 (Aberdeen) 132
more lyrical, less purely dramatic
1922 (Aberdeen) 133
lack of real passion 1922 (Glasgow) 131
not warmth and richness 1922
(Dundee) 132
passion more restrained 1922
(Aberdeen) 133
equal art, more of the intellectual
1922 (Dundee) 132
famous 'sob' effect 1923 (Birmingham) 134
acclaimed as a new Caruso 1923
(Birmingham) 134
reminds nostalgically 1926
Rodolfo (Paris) 80
lacks tremendous power of Caruso
1932 (Kilmarnock) 155
Chaliapin – 1928 (Oslo) 122, 143
Clément, Edmond – 1925 des
Grieux (Liège) 72
David, Léon – 1925 des Grieux
(Liège) 72
Fleta, Miguel – 1927 (Barcelona) 83;
1930 (Riga) 106
Gigli, Beniamino – 1920–21 (Na-
ples) 39, 42; 1925 (Buenos Aires)
76; 1930 (Riga) 106
Hackett, Charles – 1921 (New York)
57; 1925 Alfredo (Paris) 73
Lloyd, Edward – 1926 Werther
(recording) 82
McCormack, John – (1924) 115;
(1931) 172, 173, 174
McGuckin, Barton – 1934 (Crieff)
159
Martinelli, Giovanni – 1921 Rodolfo
(Toronto) 103
Mullings, Frank – 1922 (Glasgow)
131
Muratore, Lucien – 1920 Roméo
(Chicago) 54

Pertile, Aureliano – 1923 Edgardo
(Milan) 64
Reeves, Sims – 1922 (Aberdeen) 133
Schipa – 1921 (New York) 56; 1925
(The Gramophone) 121
Slezák, Leo – 1925 (The Gramo-
phone) 121; 1928 (Oslo) 122
Smirnoff, Dimitry – 1925
Cavaradossi (Liège) 72
Tauber, Richard – 1933 (Helsinki)
107; 1930 (London) 170
Thomas, John Charles – 1924
(London) 114

PERSONAL LIFE

vital statistics 27, 67
bronchitis 36, 41, 57
engagement (to Karin 1914) 26
marriage (to Karin 1915) 28
divorce (from Karin, 1940) 186
marriage (to Nancy 1940)
Hislop
Elsa (daughter) 32
Geraldine (daughter) 30, 68
Joseph Dewar (father) 3, 28
Dr. Stephen (brother) 13, 25, 131, 159
Mrs Mary (mother) 3, 31
Olof (Joseph jr) (son) 76,
William (brother) 7, 27
Hislop & Day (photo-engravers,
Edinburgh) 5
Hobson, Harold 89
Holt
Harold (agent) 73, 113, 115, 116,
117 (photo), 137, 154, 155
Paul (critic) 169
Horwa, Martha (soprano) 71
Hosking, Frederick (singing-teacher) 8
Howson, Al (Warner Bros executive) 165
Hybinette, Samuel (1876–1939)
Swedish surgeon and tenor 15, 65
Hyde, Walter (1875–1951) English
tenor 69

Ibbs & Tillett (concert agents) 154
Ibsen, Henrik (1828–1906) Norwegian
dramatist 21
Illingworth, Capt. (concert manager)
157
Ingpen, Joan (casting director) 191
(photo)

Ingrid – Princess of Sweden 85
Ivogün, Maria 1891–1988) Hungarian soprano 69
Izal, Franco (Italian tenor) 105

Jacobsson, Claes (Swedish baritone) 201
Jaffa, Max (1912–91) English violinist 157, 158
Jansson, Frederick (Swedish baritone) 18
Järnefelt, Armas (1869–1958) Finnish/ Swedish conductor and composer 25, 107
Javór, Maria (1889–) soprano 38
Jazz (Hislop's opinion of) 129, 140, 149
Jeritza, Maria (1887–1982) Czech soprano 59, 112
Johnson, Edward (1878–1959) Canadian tenor and manager 52, 58, 65
Jolson, Al (1886–1950) Russian/ American actor and singer 112
Jones, Parry (1891–1963) Welsh tenor 190, 191
Josephson, Prof. Carl David (1858– 1939) Swedish gynaecologist and patron of the arts 15

Kahn, Percy (accompanist) 114, 115, 116 (cartoon), 118, 119, 120, 137, 138, 139, 154, 156, 157
Kaiser (birthday of) 18
Kedroff Quartet (Russian vocalists) 138
Keeler, Ellis (professor of singing) 198
Keith, John (Edinburgh schoolmaster) 4, 132
Keltie, Madeleine (American soprano) 63, 69
Kennedy, Daisy (violinist) 123, 130
Kennedy, Lauri (1898–) Australian cellist 112
Kennedy-Fraser, Marjorie (1857– 1930) Scottish collector and arranger 113, 124, 204
Kesson, Dave (American director of film photography) 166
King/Queen
　　Belgium 84, 120
　　Denmark 85
　　Britain 65
　　Norway 43, 154
　　Sweden 61, 85, 192
Kingston
　　Claude (Australian tour manager) 105, 148, 149, 150, 151
　　Morgan (1881–1936) English tenor 54, 59, 103
Klein, Herman (critic) 82, 88, 92, 120, 122, 205
Körling, Sven (1879–1948) Swedish composer and organist 19
Kreisler, Fritz (1875–1962) Viennese violinist 54, 115, 116, 117 (photo), 137, 154
Kurz, Selma (1874–1933) Austrian soprano viii, 69, 70
Kusnetsova, Maria (1880–1966) Ukrainian soprano 35, 43, 44

Labbette, Dora (1898–1984) English soprano 115, 119, 133, 136
Laffitte, Frank (1901–) English pianist 112
Lamb, Paterson (accompanist) 132
Lamperti, Francesco (1811–92) Italian teacher of singing 13
Lang, Josef (1865–1946) Bohemian harpist 20
Långholmen prison (Stockholm) 29
Lankow, Edward (1883–1940) American bass 81
Lappas, Ulysses (1881–) Greek tenor 59, 75
Larsén-Todsen, Nanny (1884–1982) Swedish soprano 19, 34
Lauder, Sir Harry (1870–1950) Scottish comic actor and singer 137, 154, 156, 204
Laurenti, Mario (1890–1922) Italian baritone 100
Lauri-Volpi, Giacomo (1892–1979) Italian tenor 75, 76
Lauweryns, Georges (conductor) 81
Laval, Jane (1891–) French soprano 70
Lemba, Theodore (critic) 108
Lemming, Erik (1880–1930) Swedish Olympic javelin champion 13
Lett, Phyllis (English contralto) 114
Levine, Marks (concert agent) 146
Levitski (pianist) 148

Licette, Miriam (1892–1969) English soprano 51, 66, 67

Liljefors, Ruben (1865–1946) Swedish composer and conductor 19

Lima, Edna de (soprano) 66, 69

Limberg, G (Swedish conductor) 18

Lind
Axel (Danish painter) 200
Eva 200

Lindedal
Styrbjörn (1904–) Swedish conductor and opera house director 178, 180
Alice (Swedish soprano) 181

Lindi, Aroldo (1889–1944) Swedish/American tenor 75

Lindström, Magnus (Swedish tenor – discoverer of Hislop) 11, 12 (photo), 13

Ljungberg, Göta (1893–1955) Swedish soprano 11, 59, 86

Lloyd, Edward (1845–1927) English concert tenor 82, 205

Lo Giudice (Italian tenor) 75

Longone, Paolo (agent) 39, 40, 43, 52, 53, 56, 57, 58, 111

Loreley (paddle-steamer) 18

Loves of Robert Burns, The (film) 165, 166, 167 (photo), 168 (photo), 169

Lublin, Fru (accompanist) 13, 14

Lunn
John (Hislop's New Zealand uncle) 143
Kirkby (1873–1930) English mezzo 127, 133
Stephen (Hislop's uncle) 5

Lynn, Ralph (English comic actor) 166

Lyrico spinto 61, 84

McAlpine (1935–) Scottish tenor 194

MacBride, Florence (violinist) 138

McCallum, David (1897–72) Scottish violinist 155

McCormack, Count John (1884–1945) Irish tenor 7, 58, 77, 93, 111, 112, 113, 115, 130, 154, 155, 173, 174, 205

MacEwan, Canon Sydney (1909–1991) Scottish tenor 93

McGuckin, Barton (1852–1913) Irish tenor 159

McIntosh, Grahame (baritone) 200

Mackenzie, Sir Compton (1883–1972) critic and novelist 62, 82, 118, 173, 199

Marcato (critic) 118

Marconi Company (England) 51

Marinuzzi, Gino (1882–1945) Italian conductor 52, 56, 63

Mario, Queena (1896–1951) American soprano 73, 100, 102, 103, 104

Marshall, Eric (baritone) 114, 134

Martin, Riccardo (1874–1952) American tenor 49, 50, 52

Martinelli, Giovanni (1885–1969) Italian tenor 39, 54, 58, 59, 103, 113, 165

Mathewson, John (baritone) 138

Mattania (Italian bass) 199

Maudru, Pierre (critic) 80

Maxwell, Donald (1948–) Scottish baritone 201, 202, 204

Mayer Inc., Daniel (agents) 146

Melba, Dame Nellie (1861–1937) Australian soprano viii, 7, 39, 51, 65, 66, 137, 139, 143, 149

Menges, Isolde (1893–1976) English violinist 127, 133

Mentiplay, Catherine (Scottish contralto) 132

Merola, Gaetano (1881–1953) Italian conductor and manager 146

Mertens, Otto (Berlin agent) 86, 87

Methuen Simpson (concert agents) 154

Minghetti
Angelo (Italian tenor) 96
Lisa (violinist) 156

Miranda, Beatrice (Australian soprano) 66

Mitchell, Nancye (soprano) 159

Moiseiwitsch, Benno (1890–1963) Ukrainian pianist 123, 131, 136

Moldowsky, Sonia (Russian violinist) 159

Molin, Conny (1885–1943) Swedish baritone 19

Möller, Mr (Swedish photo-process engraver) 8

Moore, Gerald (1899–) English accompanist 124

Morini, Erica (violinist) 138

Mörk, Knut (Danish baritone) 181

Mountains of Mourne, The (film) 166, 168, 169
Mugnone, Leopoldo (1858–1941) Italian conductor 39, 40
Mullings, Frank (1881–1953) English tenor 131, 139
Mummery, Browning (tenor) 65, 70
Muratore, Lucien (1878–1954) French tenor 54, 56
Murray, Alan (composer in the audience) 155
Music (Hislop's views on) 129
Mussolini, Benito (1883–1945) Italian dictator 64, 65, 95
Muzio, Claudia (1889–1936) Italian soprano ix, 54, 75, 76, 77

Naylor, Robert (tenor) 172
Newton, A.J. (1872– *c.* 1930) principal, Bolt Court 7
Newton, Ivor (1892–) English accompanist 114, 156, 157
Newman, Ernest (critic) 45, 64, 69, 70
Nicastro, Oscar (Uruguayan cellist) 128
Nicis, Charles (Russian tenor) 105
Nicklaus, Jack (American golfer) 202
Niedzielski (pianist) 156
Nifosi, Alexander (cellist) 119
Nikisch, Mitja (1899–1936) Austrian pianist 133
Nilsson, Birgit (1922–) Swedish soprano 186, 187, 201
Nilsson, Christina (1843–1921) Swedish soprano 157
Norena, Eidé (1884–1968) Norwegian soprano 70
Novello, Ivor (1893–1951) English composer 125, 154
Nyblom, Sven (1868–1931) Swedish tenor and stage teacher 25, 27

Ogilvie, Helen (Scottish soprano) 123
Öhman, Carl Martin (1887–1967) Swedish tenor 68
Olsson, Otto (1879–1964) Swedish composer and organist 17, 119, 121
Orff-Solscher, Alice (German soprano) 105
Ormston, Kenneth (English tenor) 197
Ottein, Angeles (1895–1981) Spanish soprano 63, 101, 102

Paci, Leone (baritone) 75
Paderewski, Ignacy Jan (1860–1941) Polish pianist 23
Pagani's (London restaurant) 22, 23, 24, 192
Palet, José (1877–1946) Catalan tenor 100
Pålson-Wettergren, Gertrud (1897–91) Swedish soprano 59
Panizza, Ettore (1875–1967) Argentinian conductor 69
Pankhurst, Sylvia (1882–1960) suffragette 43
Pareto, Graziella (1888–) Italian soprano 51
Parnis, William (tenor) 68
Pascova, Carmen (mezzo) 53
Pasini, Laura (1894–1942) Italian soprano 75, 77
Passmore, Walter (Savoyard and Hislop's father-in-law) 177
Pavlova, Anna (1885–1931) Russian ballerina 51, 139, 149
Pears, Sir Peter (1910–86) English tenor 125, 159
Penn, Henri (accompanist) 152
Perelli, Lucy (soprano) 81
Pergament-Parmet, Simon (1897–1969) accompanist 124
Pertile, Aureliano (1885–1952) Italian tenor 58, 59, 64, 86
Peterson-Berger, Wilhelm (1867–1942) Swedish composer 15, 17
Pettersson, Pippi (Swedish opera manager) 69
Phoenix Restaurant (Gothenburg) 11
Phoenix Palats (Palace) Restaurant (Stockholm) 21
Piatigorski, Gregor (1903–76) Russian cellist 156
Piccaver, Alfred (1884–1958) English tenor 57, 58, 59, 69
Pilley, Donald (English tenor) 195,191 (photo), 199
Pinza, Ezio (1892–1957) Italian bass 64, 76, 77
Pitt, Percy (1870–1932) English conductor 51, 65, 66, 68
Polyglot opera 50, 65, 66, 67, 68, 80, 105
Powell, Lionel (agent) 113, 115, 116, 117 (photo), 137, 154

Pozemkowsky, Georges (Russian tenor) 35

Primrose, William (1903–82) Scottish viola-player 166

Printemps, Yvonne (1894–) French actress 51

Puccini, Giacomo (1858–1924) Italian composer 44

Prince of Wales, Edward (1894–1972) 77, 78

Princess
  Alice 144
  Helena Victoria 144
  Louise, Duchess of Argyll 117

Quensel, Isa (1905–81) Swedish soprano 174, 175 (photo)

Quinlan, Thomas (Irish impresario) 113, 127, 130

Radford, Robert (1874–1933) English bass 117

Raisa, Rosa (1893–1963) Polish soprano 52, 53, 54, 56

Rasmussen, Rudolf (1866–1946) Norwegian impresario 119

Raybould, Clarence (1886–1972) English conductor 114, 134

Reckless, Arthur (Professor of singing) 194, 195

Reeves, Sims (1818–1900) English tenor 133

Remedios, Alberto (English tenor) 192, 193

Richter, Carl (baritone) 85

Ricketts, Charles RA (stage designer) 91

Robertson, James (opera school director) 200

Ronald, Sir Landon (1873–1938) English composer 133, 172, 173

Rookery Nook (film) 166, 168

Roselle, Anna (1894–) Hungarian soprano 100, 102, 103

Rosenblatt, Cantor (tenor) 112

Rossetti, Christina (1830–94) English poet 174

Roth, Alfred (1870–1947) Swedish pianist 157, 158, 159

Rubens, Harold (pianist) 159

Ruffo, Titta (1877–1953) Italian baritone ix, 39, 52, 53, 111, 113, 196, 199

Rumford, Kennerley (1870–1957) English baritone 149

Rummel, Walter (1887–1953) German pianist 137, 138

Russell, Arthur (concert manager) 137

Ruthström, Julius (1877–1944) Swedish violinist 10

Rydberg, Richard (Copenhagen agent) 86, 86

St Mary's Episcopal Cathedral (Edinburgh) 3, 4

Sandberg, S-O. (1905–74) Swedish baritone 182, 184, 186, 202 Gun 186

Santini, Gabriel (1886–1964) Italian conductor 76, 77

Sari, Ada (1886–1968) Polish soprano 84, 114, 134

Schaaf, Myrtle (mezzo) 100

Schipa, Tito (1888–1965) Italian tenor 52, 56, 58, 59

Schöene, Lotte (1894–) soprano 85

Schultz-Lindberg, Maj (Swedish soprano) 28

Schwartz, Valentine (soprano) 15

Sciarretti, Alberto (Italian accompanist) 112, 128, 139, 140, 141, 142, 145, 146, 165

Scotney, Evelyn (1896–1967) Australian soprano 114, 136

Scots songs, character of 131

Scott, Cyril (1879–1970) English composer 142, 198

Scott, Michael (writer on opera) 205

Scotti, Antonio (1866–1936) Italian baritone 7, 57, 58, 63, 87, 99, 100, 102, 103, 104, 112

Scotto, Ottavio (Italian impresario) 72, 73, 75

Seacombe, Dorothy (actress) 168 (photo)

Secombe, Sir Harry (1921–) Welsh tenor and comedian 115, 204

Seidl, Lea (Austrian soprano) 170, 172

Sembach, Johannes (1881–1944) German tenor 54, 59

Serafin, Tullio (1878–1968) Italian conductor 39, 40, 75

Sharpe, Cedric (1891–) cellist 120
Short, George (Scottish accompanist
  and arranger) 113, 114, 121, 123,
  133, 155
Shuard, Amy (1924–75) English
  soprano 192
Siloti, Alexander (1863–1945) Russian
  pianist 128
Simon, Herr (Berlin agent) 94
Sjöblom, Hans (friend of Hislop) 10,
  28
Skilondz, Andrejewa von (1882–1969)
  Russian soprano 30, 32, 184
Skogman, Magna (1874–1949)
  Swedish soprano 25
Slezák, Leo (1873–1946) Austrian
  tenor 122
Smirnoff, Dimitry (1882–1944)
  Russian tenor 72
Smith, William (Methuen Simpson
  Ltd, Edinburgh) 154
Smythe, Ronnie (English accompanist)
  195
Söderman
  Greta (1891–1969) Swedish soprano
    32, 68, 93, 178
  Ingalill (1902–) Swedish soprano 178
Solheim, Karsten (cantor) 156
Solti, Sir Georg (1912–) Hungarian/
  British conductor 192, 193
Sörvik, Birger (friend of Hislop) 202
Spani, Hina (1896–1969) Argentinian
  soprano 83
Stabile, Mariano (1888–1968) Italian
  baritone 86
Stangenberg, Mr (opera director) 186
Steane, John (English writer and
  broadcaster) 67, 205
Stedingk, Count Hans von (director,
  Swedish Royal Opera) 20, 22, 184
Stevens, Horace (1876–1954)
  Australian bass-baritone 118
Stiebel, Emile (1876–1950) Swedish
  bass 28, 121, 123
Stockman, David (1879–1951) Swed-
  ish tenor 30, 31, 32
Storchio, Rosina (1876–1945) Italian
  soprano 54, 56, 57
Stracciari, Riccardo (1875–1955)
  Italian baritone 64, 68, 83,
    101, 102, 104

Strandin, Ebon (1894–1977) Swedish
  dancer and soprano 39
Stuart, John (tenor) 156
Suneson, Ingeborg (1885–1984)
  Swedish soprano 31, 130
Sybille, Madeleine (French soprano)
  82
Szekely, Zoltan (1903–) Hungarian
  violinist 138

Tait, J. Nevin (tour manager) 148
Tauber, Richard (1892–1948)
  Austrian/British tenor 93, 107, 169,
    170, 205
Tetrazzini, Luisa (1871–1940) Italian
  soprano 54, 156
Teyte, Dame Maggie (1888–1976)
  English soprano 69, 70
Temianka, Henri (violinist) 120
Thibaud, Jacques (1880–1953) French
  violinist 127, 128
Thomas, John Charles (1891–1960)
  American baritone 114
Thompson, Ron (Scottish journalist
  and broadcaster) 202
Thomson, Marie (Scottish soprano)
  131
Thornton, Edna (English contralto)
  118
Tillius, Carl (1905–) Swedish pianist
  and professor 124, 152, 154, 156,
    159, 169
Toscanini, Arturo (1867–1957) Italian
  conductor 54, 62, 65, 78
Tovey, Prof. Donald (1875–1940)
  English composer 91
Travers, Ben (1886–1980) English
  dramatist and novelist 166
Trevelyan, R.C. (librettist and poet) 91
Trobeck (conductor) 21
Turner, Dame Eva (1892–1990)
  English soprano 44, 205

Ullmann, Maria (Latvian soprano) 106
Urbano, Umberto (1894–1969) Italian
  baritone 68

Valente, Alessandro (Italian tenor) 156
Vallin, Ninon (1886–1961) French
  soprano 76, 124
Vasa, Knight of (Sweden) 85

Vavpetich, Rudolph (American concert agent) 146

Vidas, Raoul (violinist) 113

Vince, Geoffrey (accompanist) 195

Vitaphone (sound recording system) 165

Vitulli, Thea (1900–) Argentinian soprano 77

Voghera, Tullio (1879–1943) Italian conductor and coach 25, 30, 31, 39, 68, 184

Votto, Antonino (1896–) Italian conductor 70

Wallace, Ian (1919–) Scottish buffo bass 192, 205, 206

Wallgren, Åke (1873–1939) Swedish bass-baritone 18, 19, 20, 25, 28, 178

Walls, Tom (English comic actor) 166

Walter, Bruno (1876–1962) German conductor 87

Warner Brothers (American film company) 145, 146, 165

Webster, Sir David (1903–70) opera house director 190, 191 (photo)

Wennberg, Vivan (accompanist) 125

Western Electric (sound reproduction system) 165

Widdop, Walter (1892–1949) English tenor 69

Wiklund, Adolf (1879–1950) conductor 25, 120, 121, 122

Wilcox, Sir Herbert (Irish film director) 166, 167 (photo), 168

Williams
Harold (1893–1976) Australian baritone 136
Col. (The Gramophone Company) 88

Williamson, J.C. (Australian agents) 105, 139, 148

Wood, Sir Henry (1869–1944) English conductor 118, 119, 134

Woodman, Flora (soprano) 118, 138

Wright, Peter (accompanist) 195

Yeomans, Walter (critic) 174

Young, Freddie OBE (director of film photography) 166

Ysaye
Eugène (1858–1931) violinist and concert agent 72, 120
Theo (1865–1918) his brother 71, 95, 155

Zachrisson
Bruno (Hislop friend) son of Waldemar 202
Waldemar (Gothenburg) 7, 8, 9, 10, 13, 202, 205

Zalits, J (critic) 106

Zamora, Michael (Scottish/Polish barber) 202

Zeppelin, Count von (1838–1917) dirigible balloon inventor 18

Ziegler, Edward (Metropolitan Opera assistant manager) 57, 58, 65, 68

Zonophone (Gramophone Company budget record label) 23, 27, 49